T0283538

The Shadows
of Socrates

The Shadows of Socrates

THE HERESY, WAR, AND TREACHERY BEHIND THE TRIAL OF SOCRATES

MATT GATTON

PEGASUS BOOKS
NEW YORK LONDON

THE SHADOWS OF SOCRATES

Pegasus Books, Ltd.
148 West 37th Street, 13th Floor
New York, NY 10018

First Pegasus Books cloth edition February 2024

Interior design by Maria Fernandez

Library of Congress Cataloging-in-Publication Data is available.

ISBN: 978-1-63936-582-1

10 9 8 7 6 5 4 3 2 1

Printed in the United States of America
Distributed by Simon & Schuster
www.pegasusbooks.com

στη Μέγκαν και τον Αουγκούστ

Contents

Dramatis Personae

PRINCIPAL

Socrates—Stonemason, philosopher
Alcibiades—Athenian general, statesman, student of Socrates
Callias—Priest of the Mysteries of Eleusis, "half" brother of Alcibiades

SECONDARY

Andocides—Aristocrat, philosopher
Glaucon—Brother of Plato, dialogue partner of Socrates
Hipparete—Wife of Alcibiades, sister of Callias
Kritias—Aristocrat, student of Socrates, oligarch
Nicias—Athenian general, statesman, acquaintance of Socrates
Plato—Philosopher, student of Socrates
Xanthippe—Wife of Socrates

MINOR

Athenians
Anytus—Pro-democracy hero, accuser of Socrates
Crito—Follower of Socrates

Hermogenes—Philosopher, brother of Callias and Hipparete
Hipponicus—Father of Callias and Hipparete
Lycon—Accuser of Socrates, friend of Callias
Meletus—Accuser of Socrates, operative of Callias
Peisander—Aristocrat, negotiator
Pericles—Athenian general, statesman, legal guardian of Alcibiades,
    Callias, and Hipparete
Phaedo—Follower of Socrates
Theramenes—Athenian statesman, oligarch
Thrasybulus—Athenian general, pro-democracy leader

Spartans
Agis—King of Sparta
Gylippus—Spartan general
Lysander—Spartan general
Timaea—Queen of Sparta

Persians
Pharnabazus—Persian governor
Tissaphernes—Persian governor

DEITIES

Apollo—God of the sun, light, truth, music, and poetry
Asclepius—God of healing and medicine, son of Apollo
Athena—Goddess of war and wisdom, patron goddess of Athens
Demeter—Goddess of the harvest, mother of Persephone
Hades—God of the underworld, husband of Persephone
Hermes—Herald of the gods, protector of messengers and travelers
Persephone—Goddess of spring, queen of the underworld
Zeus—God of the sky, chief god, father of Persephone, brother of Hades

Introduction

The influence of the ancient Greek philosopher Socrates has been profound. Even today, more than two thousand years after his death, he remains one of the most renowned humans to have ever lived, occupying a stratum with the likes of Buddha, Jesus, Muhammed, Confucius, and Moses. Think of it: modern-day followers of Jesus may know little of Buddha and vice versa, and similarly the readers of Confucius may know little of Muhammed or Moses, but the followers of all these important figures know Socrates. The ideas of Socrates form a bridge across cultures regardless of location, religion, or language. It may not be too much to say that Socrates is the single most recognizable name in the history of all humanity.

Socrates was a self-professed pest—annoying, ugly, crude—and a man of singular philosophical focus. He asked questions that people didn't want to answer, questions that upset them. He did so anyway. And yet, as much as he irked people, he managed to live a very long life in astonishingly turbulent times. He fought in wars, endured famine, outlasted contagion, and survived violent political upheavals. Then, in 399 B.C.E., at age seventy—yes, seventy—he was charged, tried, and put to death for impiety and corrupting the youth. The prosecution's case was not recorded, so the precise reasons for his death sentence have been the subject of significant speculation. From this vantage point, thousands of years later, the charges seem impossibly vague, the trial unjust, and the penalty exceedingly severe. The general consensus among scholars is there must have been some unspoken vendetta that probably had something to do with his former student Alcibiades. But what exactly? Hundreds of millions of people alive today have read about Socrates, as the *Allegory of the Cave* and the *Trial of Socrates* are fixtures in curricula the world over, and most readers have come away with a lingering sense that Socrates was set up. But how and why?

The death of Socrates is, in some ways, the most famous unsolved murder mystery in history. This book will solve that mystery, revealing for the first time how he was set up, who did it, and why. What follows is not a dry philosophical tract but something closer to a telenovela made all the more compelling because it's true. This is a real-life whodunit, a thriller without parallel, intertwined within a long-running war, rivalry, sex addiction, betrayal, sedition, starvation, epic bravery, and pure unadulterated intellectual clarity. Socrates was the most rational of men living in the most irrational of times.

I will not discuss the trial as an isolated occurrence but rather provide the historical context of Socrates's life. The people around him were fascinatingly complex and deeply flawed. You will get to know them, because they are the ones, after all, who killed him. And you might find yourself, even just a little, agreeing with their reasons. Impiety—lack of reverence for the gods—is a religious crime. From the perspective of the religious authorities of the time, the charge of impiety against Socrates was warranted, the trial just, and the penalty appropriate. To understand what happened and how it happened, we have to come to terms with the motives of the priests and, as important, Socrates's motives for provoking them. The priests did not tolerate scrutiny, even in the form of philosophical critique. Socrates knew the rules of the game. His trial is set in the first, but not last, great battle between philosophy and religion.

If faith systems rely on the concept of a Supernatural Realm—a "beyond" where spirits and deities hold sway over physical reality—then philosophical systems rely on the concept of an Abstract Plane—a domain beyond physical reality where ideas, not gods, rule. Philosophy involves a critical examination of how we know what we know, and how to apply what we know; inquiries into existence, belief, and practice. The concerns of philosophy are largely the same as those of faith systems—what is this world, how does it operate, how are people to act?—except philosophy comes at the questions from a different direction. The trial of Socrates is the story of intellectual light versus divine light, even if, paradoxically, it played out in shadow.

The powerful religious rituals at the heart of Athenian culture were the hallowed Mysteries of Eleusis.[1] The term "Mystery" comes from the Greek root *myein*, "to close," which is normally interpreted to mean to keep the mouth closed because the initiates were sworn to silence, but the root may also indicate that what the initiates learned at a Mystery could not be talked about.[2] The Mysteries could be shown, they could be witnessed or revealed, but they could not be explained.[3] The famed Mysteries of Eleusis were dedicated to the mother/daughter goddesses Demeter and Persephone and were held for the better part of two millennia, from at least 1500 B.C.E. to 392 C.E.[4] In their time, the Mysteries of Eleusis were considered a centerpiece of the civilized world. One ancient source offers, "Athens has given many excellent and divine things to humanity, but none is better than those Mysteries."[5] The author considered Eleusis even more important than all the other marvelous advances of Athenian culture—art, architecture, science, mathematics, medicine, drama, democracy, history, poetry, painting, and philosophy. He was not alone. Another ancient chronicler writes, "Eleusis is a shrine common to the whole earth, and of all the divine things that exist among men, it is both the most awesome and the most luminous."[6] To observers at the time, the Mysteries of Eleusis were the greatest spectacle that humankind had ever witnessed. Another ancient writer states, "It was the common belief in Athens that whoever had been taught the Mysteries would, when he died, be deemed worthy of divine glory."[7] One source explains, "Thrice happy are those mortals who depart for Hades having seen those rites, for them alone it is granted to have true life there; to the rest all is evil."[8] Another describes the Mysteries of Eleusis as "the holy rite which inspires in those who partake of it sweeter hopes regarding both the end of life and all eternity . . ."⁹ Eleusis offered initiates the promise of a blissful afterlife, and in so doing, it made the struggles of daily life more bearable.

The Mysteries of Eleusis were a massive spectacle with up to three thousand people being initiated in one night. When Athens came under Roman control, even Roman emperors would come to be initiated. And while Eleusis may have been the most important annual event in the ancient world for around two thousand years, its footprint in the body of ancient literature is rather paltry. This is because the penalty for talking about the rites was death. The ritual procession to the temple passed standing stones inscribed with the names of individuals who had spoken about or profaned the mysteries, with lists of all their possessions that were forfeited before they were killed. The point was clear: speak of Eleusis and the penalty will be swift and certain, carried out, it was said, by the hand of the goddess herself.

But the influence of Eleusis goes far beyond religious practice. Clement of Alexandria, a founding father of the Christian Church who seemed to have personal experience with Mystery religions, described the revelation at Eleusis: "It is no longer a matter of learning but contemplating and pondering nature and concrete realities."¹⁰ Pondering the nature of reality is the essence of ancient Greek philosophical thought. Athenian philosophers, just like other Athenians, had spent the night in the temple of Eleusis and had seen the "Great Vision."¹¹ But certain philosophers came away with a different understanding. The question is: When the goddess appeared as light at the climax of the rite, was it the Truth or a falsity? From the perspective of the religious leaders of the time, particularly the all-powerful priests of Eleusis, the manifestation of the goddess as pure light was the ultimate truth. But to some key Athenian philosophers the visions were just forms of representation, and therefore deceptive. Mere shadows. From the philosopher's view, people ought not put stock in the illusion of the physical world. "Real" reality lies elsewhere, in the realm of ideas. The light of the Eleusinian rite was the same for both priests and philosophers, but the interpretation was different. This had consequences. Ultimately, the light of the leading minds of Athens and the light of the deities of Olympus were set on a collision course. Trying to explain what happened to Socrates without talking about the Mysteries of Eleusis is like trying to explain what happened to Galileo without mentioning the Catholic Church.

The main impediment to understanding the trial of Socrates is that information has become compartmentalized over time. Ancient Athenian politics, with its pendulum swings between democracy and oligarchy, is its own field of study. The Peloponnesian War between Athens and Sparta, with all its battles, factions, and tactics, is its own scholarly domain. The study of the philosophical discourse of the time is its own field entirely. The religious practices of ancient Athens are, likewise, their own distinct area of study, as are Athenian arts and architecture. In general, the modern academic system of organization, categorization, and specialization of ever smaller and more distinct fields of study has produced advances in our understanding, but it has also served to obscure one of the greatest stories in human history. To know Socrates, we must come to understand all the forces that swirled around him at the time, including political, military, religious, intellectual, artistic, and personal elements that made up his mind's milieu. It wasn't a group of strangers that sentenced Socrates to death. It was people he knew, some very well.

Sex is another reason the story of Socrates gets very little treatment in popular media, movies, and television. They try to give you snippets of his mind in books while hiding his actual life. The romantic customs of ancient Athenians have long been considered outré by modern standards. In ancient Athens, men had sexual relations with women and also other men. Today, it would be called bisexuality, but in ancient Athens it was not described as such, because it was the norm. It is impossible to tell the true story of Socrates without discussing the relationships of the people around him. Socrates had a wife and children but also multiple male lovers, which was typical at the time. The philosophical, religious, military, and political figures discussed in this book have not only professional and familial entanglements but also romantic histories among one another. Without some understanding of these affiliations—the hard feelings from jilted lovers and the deep connections between others—the happenings in ancient Athens are difficult to decipher. The ancient Greek poet Sappho wrote poems to her many female lovers. Sappho lived on the island of Lesbos, whose denizens were called Lesbians, which is where we get our modern English term for women who have sex with other women. As we move through this book, there will be some puzzling actions that will raise questions. Love will sometimes be the answer to these questions, even if it's the sort of love that could never be discussed on an episode of *Ozzie and Harriet*.

The charge of corrupting the youth only makes sense if we consider the personal entanglements in Socrates's life. Who were the youth? And how exactly did they go astray? The problems all start when Pericles, the great Athenian general, and his two legitimate heirs perished during a plague that swept through Athens in 429 B.C.E. Two other young men who had been raised in the house of Pericles would vie for primacy in the post-Periclean landscape. One was Alcibiades, whose mother was a cousin of Pericles and had moved in with Pericles when her husband died in battle. The other was Callias, who was the son (from a prior relationship) of a woman who later married Pericles. These two young men were about the same age but opposites in terms of dispositions and attributes. Alcibiades was powerfully built, handsome, charismatic, and seductive. He was a presumed future military leader of Athens. Callias, on the other hand, was measured, brilliant, and, according to an ancient text, an "evil genius."[12] Callias would inherit the silver mine concession and become the richest man in Athens, and more importantly would assume a lifetime appointment as the second-highest-ranking priest, the Light-Bearer, at Mysteries of Eleusis. Alcibiades would wield the power of the sword, Callias the power of the goddess. If Alcibiades's life was characterized by decisive action and cunning split-second decisions, then Callias's was characterized by stealthy backroom maneuvers. The body of literature about Alcibiades is extensive, largely because he was such an outlandish character, while there is much less extant information on Callias, but, pay attention, the Mysteries of Eleusis played an enormous role in the events of the time, and as a ranking official of

Eleusis, Callias would have been involved in every action, charge, banishment, and death sentence issued by Eleusis. Whenever the ancient texts say that the Mysteries of Eleusis did something, understand that Callias was among those pulling the strings.

Socrates and Alcibiades became associated with each other during the Battle of Potidaea. Socrates, then in his late thirties, would save a teenage Alcibiades from certain death on the battlefield. Alcibiades would become devoted to Socrates, developing into his most dedicated student. Several years later, Alcibiades would return the favor of sorts and protect Socrates during a frantic retreat at the Battle of Delium. These two formed the sort of deep bond known only to soldiers who have fought side by side in war. Socrates saw in Alcibiades the opportunity to make a philosopher-king, a leader who ruled by reason. Alcibiades became steeped in the Abstract Plane, in the intellectual light of Socrates, while Callias assumed his station as an official of the Eleusinian Mysteries and a defender (and creator) of divine light of the Supernatural Realm. Socrates was never shy about criticizing or complimenting Alcibiades or Callias (or anyone else for that matter), and he became a pivotal player in the troubled relationship between Alcibiades and Callias. Callias would suffer at the hands of Alcibiades. Was his teacher, Socrates, to blame? Ultimately, there was a battle, fought on many fronts, between these two "half" brothers for control of Athens. The all-consuming desire to eliminate the other would contribute, in no small way, to the eventual fall of Athens. In between the treachery, villainy, and cruelty of these two warring brothers stood Socrates, steadfast in his virtue. It would cost him his life.

The story is structured as follows: first, we will explore the religious systems and orthodoxies of ancient Athens; second, we will survey the philosophical issues in play at the time; third, we will examine the intricate personal entanglements of Socrates and the momentous events that shaped Athenian life; and finally, I will use the compiled information to offer a new view of the trial of Socrates. The configuration of the personal relationships is rather like a triangle, with Socrates, Alcibiades, and Callias each occupying one vertex. The Socrates/Alcibiades side of the triangle will be explained first; then there will be several chapters on the Alcibiades/Callias side of the triangle; and finally, the Callias/Socrates side will be explained. We start with Socrates, and we end with Socrates. The story takes us all the way around the triangle. Alcibiades is the embodiment of the war, Callias the personification of the religion, and Socrates the representative of reason. The religion and the war are intertwined, and metaphorically speaking, they are tied around Socrates's neck.

The death sentence against Socrates was meant to silence him. His mouth forever closed. The Mysteries of Eleusis demanded silence. It was the law of the goddess. The details of the rite couldn't be discussed even in an official legal proceeding. Socrates's line of thinking was derivative, pro and con, of the great Mysteries, which had existed for more than a thousand years before the time of Socrates and would continue on for another eight centuries after his death. The trial of Socrates can, in some ways, be seen as a personal duel between Socrates and Callias, but in another way, the two men were merely proxies for the confrontation of the Supernatural Realm and the Abstract Plane. And the Supernatural Realm won, at least at first, but many readers will have never heard of Callias, or Alcibiades, or even the Mysteries of Eleusis, yet almost all will have heard of Socrates. In this way, Socrates won. They could kill the man, but not the ideas. The Supernatural Realm won initially, and the Abstract Plane won eventually. This is the true genius of Socrates.

> *The jailer enters the room, carrying the poison in a cup. He moves steadily, even solemnly; he is well-practiced. Socrates says, "Sir, you understand these things, how does this go?" The jailer replies, "Just drink it. Then walk around until your legs feel heavy. Then lay down. The poison will run its course." He hands the cup to Socrates . . .* [13]

1

Mysteries of Eleusis

The Mysteries of Eleusis were the eminent sect of a wide range of Mystery religions that dominated the religious landscape of a large swath of the ancient world, in Greece, Egypt, Anatolia, Syria, Persia, and Rome.[1] The term "Mystery" in this context can cause confusion, because the word, which is so recognizable, doesn't mean today exactly what it meant in the ancient world.

Back then, a "Mystery" was a religious ritual.

In fact, the term is used to mean "ritual" throughout the Greek Scriptures (New Testament) of the Christian Bible, whose writing documented an effort by the upstart religion to overcome the dominance of the Mystery religions. The use of the language and concepts of the Mysteries in the Bible helped to facilitate the conversion of adherents of Mystery religions to Christianity. It's always important to know the audience. Even if words can change meaning over time, as "mystery" clearly did, the lingering aspect of a "mystery" as something that is difficult to explain would certainly apply to the Mysteries of Eleusis.

As best we can tell, the Mysteries of Eleusis began some time before 1500 B.C.E.[2] Athens adopted the nearby Eleusinian Mysteries (Eleusis sits

22 kilometers, 14 miles, west of Athens) as part of its state religion around 600 B.C.E, and Eleusis was the premier spectacle of the ancient world during the lifetime of Socrates (470–399 B.C.E.). The temple of Eleusis was sacked in 170 C.E. by invading Sarmatian tribes and later rebuilt by the Roman emperor Marcus Aurelius. The rites began to fade with the rise of Christianity in Greece. Eleusis enjoyed a brief resurgence in the 360s C.E. under Julian the Apostate, the last Roman emperor to be initiated, but were doomed to oblivion when Theodosius the Great made Christianity the state religion of the Roman Empire and outlawed all Mystery religions at the end of the fourth century C.E. When the doors finally closed on Eleusis, the Mysteries had held sway for nearly two thousand years. The effectiveness of the Mysteries was due, in large part, to a convincing presentation of an otherworldly spectacle.[3]

The mythology invoked at Eleusis, as described in the Homeric hymn "To Demeter" (ca. 650 B.C.E.), is the story of the mother/daughter goddesses Demeter and Persephone. The beautiful Persephone is picking flowers in a field away from her mother, Demeter, the goddess of the harvest, when Hades, the god of the underworld, lures Persephone to a flower, abducts her, and takes her with him to his domain, the realm of the dead. Demeter searches endlessly for her lost daughter. She eventually learns that Zeus, the father of Persephone, had given her to Hades to be his wife. Demeter is consumed with anguish, hides among mortals, causes a drought, and even teaches the secret of agriculture to a mortal. Demeter eventually prevails upon Zeus to make Hades free Persephone. Persephone reunites with her mother, but in consequence of having eaten a pomegranate seed, she has to spend half of each year belowground. Thus, the agricultural cycle is tied to the movements of Persephone above and below the earth. Persephone is a liminal figure, a goddess of both the overworld and the underworld, the realms of the living and the dead.

The penalty for speaking about the Eleusinian Mysteries was death, so sensibly, people didn't talk about it. Almost all prominent Athenians had participated in the rites at least once in their lives, but they did not speak about them openly. We know that Socrates had been initiated only by inference. Which is typical. There are no attendance records, per se, outside of the names of those convicted of profaning the Mysteries. They were put to death and their names were recorded and publicly displayed in shame as a deterrent to others.

Despite the law of silence, ancient authors did let slip some tantalizing bits of information about the practices of various Mystery religions, which, when pieced together, allow scholars to get a good idea of what initiates experienced. One Roman author cautiously warns, "Behold, I relate to you things of which, though heard by you, you must necessarily remain ignorant. I therefore only relate that which may be expressed to the uninitiated without crime."[4] He then goes on to describe his initiation into a Greco–Roman Mystery cult of the Egyptian goddess Isis, an Egyptian cognate of the Greek goddess Demeter, who was celebrated at Eleusis.

> I approached the boundaries of death: and having trodden on the threshold of Persephone returned, having been carried through all the elements. In the depths of midnight, I saw the sun glittering with a splendid light, together with the gods of underworld and the overworld: and to these divinities who were near me, I paid the tribute of devout adoration.[5]

Clearly the author was trying to supply his readers with the general outline of the rites, while hedging against offering the sort of specifics that would trigger a charge of profanation. In each Mystery religion sect, temples were built for rituals to a particular divinity. Another ancient writing describes the general arc of Mystery rituals:

> . . . A rough and dreadful march through night and darkness. But now, when on the verge of death, which is prefigured by Initiation, everything wears a dreadful aspect; it is all trembling, horror and affright. But once passed, a marvellous and divine light discloses itself, revealing shining plains and flowery

meadows on all sides. Here the initiated are entertained with
hymns and dances, with the sublime doctrines of sacred knowledge, and with revered and holy visions.[6]

Notice that the author doesn't say exactly what the "sacred knowledge" or
"holy visions" were, but he does make clear the overall process. The rituals
were rehearsals of death and spiritual rebirth.[7] The gods were identified as
visions of light in Orphic, Eleusinian, Dionysian, Isisinian, and Apollonian
rites.[8] One ancient source adds, "In all the initiations and Mysteries, the
gods exhibit many forms of themselves, and appear in a variety of shapes:
and sometimes, indeed, a formless light of themselves is held forth to the
view; sometimes this light is according to a human form, and sometimes
it proceeds into a different shape."[9]

There was quite a bit of sharing or co-opting of methods between the
priestly classes of various temple cults.[10] For example, the Mysteries of
Serapis were founded with the consultation and advice of the priests
of Eleusis.[11] The Sanctuary of the Great Goddesses in the Arcadian
city of Megalopolis had ritual acts that were a copy of Eleusis's.[12] Rites held
in temples dedicated to Apollo (a god of sun, light, truth, healing, music,
and poetry) involved incubations in the dark, where visions of the gods
brought about healing transformations and sacred knowledge.[13] Apollo
was usually mediated through his son, Asclepius, the healer. The priests
of Asclepius temples were called Apollo Phôleutêrios, Apollo who hides in
the lair.[14] The worshippers were sequestered in dark spaces to have a direct
experience with divinities, which were said to ride in on a tube of light.[15]
Thus Apollo was a god of light who was worshipped and/or experienced
in complete darkness. A text dated to the second-century C.E. tells of the
events in an Egyptian version of an Asclepius temple where the mother of a
sufferer was visited by a god in shining raiment: "It was no dream or sleep,
for her eyes were open immovably, though not seeing clearly, for a divine
and terrifying vision came to her."[16] Darkness, light, and apparitions of
deities were the constants. The names in the myths changed, but the key
event remained the same.

But of all the many Mystery religions, Eleusis was the headliner, the main event, the ever and always champion of Mystery religions. Its rites were the most spectacular and the most profound. The actual performance of the Mysteries of Eleusis came in stages: before entering the temple, initiates ceremonially bathed to cleanse themselves spiritually and consumed a blessed elixir, which some scholars have proposed held a psycho-reactive substance, which would have intensified the coming experiences.[17]

Envision, if you will, the scene: the initiates slowly and solemnly file into the temple, a dim womb full of people huddled in fear and hope. Candlelight flickers across their faces as the lore is told and listened to. The candles are slowly extinguished one by one while the voices of the priests grow, extolling life and death, here and now and the ever after, the mythology and the meaning; retelling all that Persephone and Demeter endured and absorbing the wisdom of the goddesses. Suddenly the initiates are swallowed by darkness. The thunderous voice of Hades drives them on. Blindly they trudge forward, grasping, disoriented. Monstrous noises and clatters startle the soul. Fear and outright terror grip them, the sounds of weeping and wailing filling the thick air. There is physical pain in every step, but onward they march. They must. The initiates are taking a "horrifying"[18] journey to the underworld. Exultations and lamentations arise in the darkness, sobs and song, for here is what it means to die and learn what lays beyond the mortal vale.

And then there is nothingness.

Impenetrable, deathly still darkness.

Then a beam of light silently pours forth. The spectral form of the goddess Persephone manifests in the light. She is an epiphany (from the ancient Greek word *epiphaneia*, meaning "appearance"). Persephone utters a psalm of salvation, personally welcoming the initiate into her dominion of everlasting bliss. She connects to the sky above and the realm below, touching the eternal and indomitable. One ancient writer records that initiates "receive to their bosom in the purest manner the sacred light . . ."[19] Plato, albeit as an aside in the middle of a longer tract about something else, describes being permitted as initiates "to the sight of perfect, simple, calm and blissful apparitions, which we saw in the pure light . . ."[20] The Orphic hymn "To Melinoe" describes, albeit in poetic fashion, the appearance of spectral forms during the divine rite. One prominent figure even described the sacred vision: "I saw the *Kore*."[21] (*Kore* means "maiden" in ancient Greek, which in this context identifies Persephone and not her mother, Demeter.) Another ancient chronicler recorded that the sacred event was an apparition that floated off the ground.[22] Through Persephone's light, the initiates gain a piece of immortality and a peace for their own mortality. They have earned an afterlife. The shining image of the goddess brings the promise that when their health finally falters, the initiates will be reunited in the Elysium (heaven) with the others who have gone before. When the ceremony ends, the people leave exhausted and exhilarated, armed with the knowledge of the wheel of life and contentment with what lay on the other side.

Though the exact methods used to create the epiphany in light are as mysterious as the Mysteries themselves, their purpose is clear: light and dark, life and the afterlife; together, reciprocal; reconciled in a vision.

2

The Temple

The architectural configuration of the temple of Eleusis is itself an enigma. A large initiation hall (*telesterion*) held the initiates, and a smaller interior building (*anaktoron*) held the sacred focus of the rite. Only the priest (*hierophant*), "one who reveals the holy," could enter the *anaktoron*. To put this in modern-day terms, the situation of the *telesterion* and *anaktoron* is not unlike a basketball arena (*telesterion*) with a small house (*anaktoron*) being placed at center court. The chimney of the small house rose all the way out of the roof of the arena.[1]

The temple presents a formidable puzzle for researchers because it is so unlike the amphitheaters the ancient Greeks made, which had famously unobstructed sight lines and clear acoustics for stage performances. (You can still visit the ruins of the Odeon of Herodes Atticus in Athens to experience some semblance of the exquisite visual and acoustic perfection of Athenian design.) At the temple of Eleusis, the seating in the *telesterion* was much like that of an indoor sports arena today: there were increasingly raised levels of seating that merged into the external walls. The raised seating around the exterior seemed to indicate that the audience was to face the centrally located *anaktoron*, except a grid of columns would have blocked the view from many, if not most, angles.[2] There was really only one angle from which to see the *hierophant*, but his tall three-sided throne was placed perpendicular to the anaktoron and would have further shielded him from view and no one could have seen him once he entered the *anaktoron*. The seating, somewhat ironically, was not a place for viewing the purported spectacle. The ancient Greeks, who were so adept at functional architectural design, had made Eleusis as a sort of anti-theater, in which the lead performer was out of sight.

The situation is very confusing, and that's the point.[3]

The rites involved fruitless marches that left the initiates distraught and confused: they were herded through some sort of dark course before they came upon beatific visions. The columns did more than just hold up the roof; they also formed the framework of a dark maze, blocked views, and channeled initiates to the *anaktoron*.

While the *telesterion* was enlarged, step by step, over the centuries to accommodate larger audiences, the *anaktoron* held its general location and footprint. (Socrates lived during both the Cimonian version and the Periclean version of the temple, which was its grandest iteration.) Throughout the many reconfigurations of the hall, there was always a line of columns running parallel to the long, northeast side of the *anaktoron* at a distance of about eight meters (twenty-six feet). There is a definitive anchor point and gap aligned to the door of the *anaktoron*. The consistency of the *anaktoron* is the key to understanding the rite.[4]

According to one ancient source, a great light came from the *anaktoron*.[5] Another describes a fire.[6] Still another records the combatants in a pitched sea battle witnessing a brilliant light flashing out from Eleusis.[7] The light generated in the *anaktoron* was intense enough to shoot out of the roof and was visible at some distance out to sea. Based on these passages, the *anaktoron* held an absurdly bright light source. In addition, small female figurines, dating from the earliest phases forward, were recovered from the site.[8] So, back to the basketball arena analogy, the little building at center court contained some form of very bright fire and figurative female sculptures, while the surrounding arena could be held in pitch darkness.

There are testimonials from related temples that a veil or screen was hung closer to the *anaktoron*. One ancient source, writing of the rites of Isis (who was often conflated with Demeter), mentioned ceremonial curtains around the area that held the sculpture of the goddess.[9] Another writer explains how the curtains at the temple of Artemis at Ephesus were raised toward the ceiling, while the curtains at the temple of Olympus were lowered by ropes.[10] A fifth-century B.C.E. inventory of Eleusinian sanctuary included ropes, multiple pulleys, and a sizable quantity of Sicilian ox hides, as well as stone blocks and lumber sufficient to build temporary partitions.[11] Based on these ancient reports, contemporary scholars mentioned the possibility of the use of curtains or partitions in the Eleusinian initiation hall.[12] The presumption has always been that the curtains in these various mystery cults were opened to reveal a view of a physical sculpture in the holy of the holies, but this idea misses the point that the goddess manifested as an apparition of light. A group of officials at Eleusis, called the *neokoroi*, were in charge of decorating the sanctuary. The sorts of drapery, trimmings, and decorative banners they may have used in the hall are unknown, but if Eleusis was like the other temples, then there would have been curtains, which were convenient surfaces for light, closer to the *anaktoron*.

3

Vision of the Goddess

There are indications from two important ancient sources that the manifestation of the goddess as light at the climax of the rites of Eleusis was not quite what it seemed. One Roman source writes, "Such Mysteries when interpreted and rationalized are recognized as having more to do with nature than with gods."[1] The writer intimates that the sacred rites were a function of something other than divine forces. An early father of the Christian Church, Clement of Alexandria, writes: "And what if I go over the Mysteries? I will not divulge them in mockery, as they say Alcibiades did, but will expose right well by the word of truth the sorcery hidden in them . . ."[2] Clement equates Eleusis with stagecraft, labeling the charlatan magic of the Mysteries as a "stage machine."[3] These two writers suggest the rites of Eleusis were very much related to the natural sciences and stagecraft of ancient Greece.[4]

But what was this hypothetical stage machine? How did it operate? How were the priests able to manifest the apparition of the goddess? I led a series of experiments, which were published in *The Oxford Handbook of Light in Archaeology*, to assess a potential physical process for the manifestation of the light-borne apparition of the goddesses at Eleusis.[5] The field of optics (from the ancient Greek word *optikos*) is an important branch of physics that is concerned with the properties of light, including its genera-tion, propagation, and absorption. Light's role in antiquity is difficult to approach, because light does not last in an archaeologically durable form. One way to uncover the light of the past is to use extant information to construct a framework for a light-based research question.[6] This is possible because the laws of light are consistent, predictable, and reproducible.[7] Light behaves the same way today as it did in ancient Greece. The research question can be verified or disproved through physical experiments. This form of inquiry is called archeo-optics, which is a type of reconstruction archaeology, a subdiscipline of the larger field of sensory archeology, which seeks to understand human perceptions of the physical environment.

The situation of the temple elements—a very bright space (*anaktoron*) adjacent to a dark space (*telesterion*) where some form of light-borne spectre appeared—provided the structural framework of my inquiry. The question I would ask of the Mysteries of Eleusis had to do with an optical principle known as the camera obscura. Although the term "camera obscura" sounds like a piece of modern technology, it is, in fact, nothing more than a dark chamber with a hole in the side. Outside the chamber, light reflects off an object in all directions. Some of this light travels through the hole, pro-jecting an inverted, living image onto the interior surfaces of the chamber. The image appears like an upside-down movie. The effect, which seems magically manifested, is actually a matter of physics. A camera obscura, in the literal sense of the term, is not a human invention but simply the forces of optical physics acting in a predictable manner. The first pinhole eyes, lensless camera obscura eyes, evolved about 540 million years ago on a sea mollusk known as a nautilus during the Cambrian period. All the eyes in the world—on fish, insects, birds, reptiles, and mammals—testify to the primordial power of the camera obscura principle and how life on our planet has evolved to take advantage of it. The camera obscura principle is, however, not limited to eyes, or even lenses, but works with a small hole and a darkened space of any size or shape. In modern times, camera obscuras have been fashioned from shoeboxes, oatmeal boxes, soda cans, cookie containers, seashells, eggshells, refrigerators, tents, trucks, airplane hangars, and even hollowed-out cavities in piles of snow and dirt, to name but a few. A camera obscura can also be produced by a small hole in a roof, wall, or window shutter through which a view of the outside is projected onto the wall inside a darkened room.[8] Even Aristotle, a student of Plato, described the effects of the camera obscura.[9]

Readers who have personally experienced the inverted images inside a room-size camera obscura will find many of the ideas in this chapter almost self-evident, while those who have never been in a room-size camera obscura may find the ideas difficult to grasp. To the experienced, the effect is absurdly simple; to the unexperienced, it may sound simply absurd. The images can trigger different types of disbelief.

The camera obscura principle works irrespective of the scale of the dark and light areas. Most of the time a small dark room is surrounded by the bright sunlit world, which projects an image from the outside into the inside. But if the inside of a room is made very bright and the surrounding space is very dark, then the same hole will cast an image from the smaller space to the larger. The image always flows from light to dark.

> Research question: Could the *anaktoron*, the priest's holy fire-room, have acted as a box of light, illuminating the figurines and projecting their images out into the darkened *telesterion*?

For the experiments, I re-created the general situation of Eleusis: a large dark room next to a smaller room with a bright light source and a figurine. I used a racquetball court as a mock *telesterion* (large temple room) and the observation gallery as the *anaktoron*.[10] The dimensions of the racquetball court and gallery were roughly a three-quarter-scale version of the early, Solonian version of the initiation hall at Eleusis. The window between the gallery and the court was covered with opaque material. An aperture (small hole) was poked through the opaque material that separated the gallery and the court. Lights were set up in the gallery to emulate the fire in the *anaktoron*. (We have no idea what materials the ancient Greeks were burning to make the bright fire to which they attest.) A plaster figurine was mounted on a post (upside down—that is, on its head) and placed by the lights and in front of the aperture. The lights were turned on in the gallery, illuminating the figurine, and the court was kept completely dark. Light reflected off the figurine, through the aperture, and went into the darkened court. Slowly, as the observer's eyes adjusted to the darkness (which takes twenty to fifty minutes, depending upon the inherent ability, health, and age of the viewer), an image of the figurine emerged on the far wall of the court. The appearance of the image became far more dramatic if the aperture was covered, allowing no light into the court during the time the observer's eyes adjusted to the darkness, and then uncovered so that the image would appear instantly and seemingly out of nowhere.

The projected image exhibited five very interesting behaviors: dimensionality, mutability, evasiveness, vibration, and animation. First, the image read as a three-dimensional presence, even though it was a projection on a two-dimensional surface. The all-encompassing darkness was interpreted as empty space, and when the image appeared, the three-dimensional cues within the image asserted the illusion of dimensionality.

The observers didn't see the screen; they saw the thing.

Second, the image shifted from an amorphous blob of light to a more distinct image, depending on how far the object was from the aperture. The optical law of focal length affected the clarity of the image. When the figurine was moved closer to or farther from the aperture, it caused the image to fall into and out of focus, creating a mesmerizing effect. Remember the ancient description about the gods manifesting in "formless light" that could transmute into "human form"?[11]

Third, the image's appearance was tantalizingly evasive. When stared at directly, a portion of the image would almost disappear, but when the viewer's eyes glanced to another portion, the prior portion would snap back into existence. The viewer's eyes ended up dancing around the image in a cat-and-mouse game that oddly animated the image even when the figurine was not being moved. This effect was caused by the specialization of the two types of photoreceptors, rods and cones, in the eye. The cones, which register acuity and color, function well in bright light and are concentrated in the fovea centralis, but they become ineffective in low light, causing a centralized blind spot. In the darkness, the eyes had to rely on the rods, which dominate peripheral vision and function well in low light.[12] Remember the ancient testimonial that a viewer's "eyes were open" but did not see "clearly"?[13]

Fourth, the animation of the image was enhanced by visual vibration of the rods. The constant vibration of the rods made the arms, hands, and facial features of the image appear to move. The imagination took over and made the movements appear anatomically sensible.

Fifth, slight movements of the observer's head, which are usually imperceptible, read as movement by the image because of a lack of environmental cues caused by the darkness. The optical mechanics of light and the physiology of human vision conspired to make the image spring to life.

The effects were as peculiar as they were mystifying.

The ancient Greeks were known to have made good-quality lenses.[14] If a lens had been employed at Eleusis, it would have dramatically widened the aperture, brightened the cast image, and reduced the amount of light necessary to project a convincing image. A possible third factor, lens focal length, would have dictated a set image-throw distance, perhaps explaining the fixed spatial relationship between the *anaktoron* and a course of columns. But since no lenses were ever discovered in the excavations of Eleusis, these experiments were run without them. However, the possibility of their use is an open question.[15]

The results of the experiments show the optical feasibility of a simple projection booth, what I have dubbed the Eleusinian Projector.[16] The initiates were not directing their attention toward the priest or the *anaktoron* but were looking in the other direction at spectral images that they believed were gods, shining and moving about, viewing a kind of sacred movie.[17] In a time long before actual movies, this would have been a mind-blowing experience. The passage of millennia has made it possible to safely assay the methods of the *hierophant*. Time has created space for objectivity.

The appearance of the goddess as light can be explained mythologically as well as physically.[18] The Eleusinian Projector, a carefully controlled optical apparatus, had a value far greater than its material means. The priests served as intermediaries between the visible world and the hidden world of the gods, accessing a sacred (though physics-based) conduit of light. In its day, the rite was the source of imponderable mystery.

The goddess manifested in its light.[19]

Today, the rites of Eleusis seem like some obscure historical footnote, but elements of the ritual have found ways to live on in other forms. The ritual program at Eleusis, with its guided visit to the realm of the dead, Hades (underworld) and Elysium (heaven), provided a template for some of the western world's greatest works of literature. Ovid's *Metamorphosis*, Homer's *Odyssey*, Virgil's *Aeneid*, and Dante's *Divine Comedy* all partake, in one way or another, of the narrative arc of the rites of Eleusis. In fact, the term "Elysium" (heaven) is thought to derive from "Eleusis." Moreover, the widest-read book in the history of the western world, the Holy Bible, places great emphasis on making sure its followers do not worship figurines (idols). The book of Ezekiel repeats the warning against idol worship but delves into more detail, implicating the Mysteries (remembering that satellite cults were almost everywhere in the ancient world). Ezekiel is shown the abominations in the houses of worship of Judah: "Then he brought me to the entrance to the court. I looked, and I saw a hole in the wall" (Ezekiel 8:7, NIV). Ezekiel is instructed to dig through the wall, to, in effect, gouge out the hole, destroying the aperture that projected light-borne images. Ezekiel is asked, "Son of man, have you seen what the leaders of Israel are doing with their idols in dark rooms?" (Ezekiel 8:12, NLT). This critical passage in Ezekiel 8 is thought by some scholars to be an allusion to the Mystery religions in general, and the Mysteries of Eleusis specifically.[20] Rabbi Jonathan Sacks explains the importance of knowing the ancient religious landscape: "The more we understand what the Bible is arguing against, the deeper we understand the Bible."[21]

The Bible is arguing against the Mysteries.

The Judeo-Christian tradition is, in some very important ways, a reaction against the Mysteries, even if some factions did incorporate certain Mystery religion elements into their ritual practices. Living rituals like baptism (from the ancient Greek word for "immerse") and Eucharist (from the ancient Greek word for "giving thanks") are distant echoes of the rituals of Eleusis, which included ritual bathing and drinking of a sacred elixir. But even more than that, the concepts employed at Eleusis, which may owe something to even older traditions, are very much alive today: the sense of divine judgment in relation to the afterlife lives on, as does the sense of suffering to attain enlightenment. The Mysteries of Eleusis are very likely the most influential ancient religious rituals in the history of the western world, even if they are now largely forgotten by modern culture.

The replicative light experiments I performed were narrowly focused on the ritual mechanics used to create the appearance of the goddess as light at the Mysteries of Eleusis. The implications of the experiments, however, were entirely unexpected, as they bore a peculiar, and potentially troubling, relationship to key elements of Socrates's philosophical perspective, particularly the influential and enduring *Allegory of the Cave*.

4

Socratic Thought

S ocrates, a chronically underemployed stonemason, is considered the father of western philosophy.[1] His mind was as beautiful as his face was ugly. He looked like a frog, with bulging eyes and an equally bulging belly; except unlike a frog, he was covered in hair everywhere except the top of his bald pate. From this unsightly mug came some of the world's most important intellectual contributions. He spoke on a wide variety of topics over his long life, but I would like to narrow the focus to three key concepts—the Theory of Forms, the Divided Line, and, of course, the *Allegory of the Cave*. In this and the following chapter, we will look at these well-known ideas through the filter of the Eleusinian Mysteries. Socrates once told one of his dialogue partners to get initiated into the Mysteries so the man might better understand Socrates's philosophical perspective.[2] We will follow Socrates's advice.

Up front, you must know that the foremost issue in deciphering Socrates is that he wrote nothing down (just like Buddha, Jesus, and Muhammad). We know only what others wrote about Socrates, which adds a layer of bias. The primary source for stories about Socrates is in the writings of his student, Plato. It is somewhat difficult to discern the true voice of Socrates in the words of Plato. How much of these writings are Plato's interjections of his own ideas, and how much is what Socrates really said? Did Plato merely use his deceased teacher as the basis for his own literary creation? Judging by the generally consistent character of Socrates as reported by a number of ancient authors, we are operating under the assumption that Plato's descriptions of Socrates have some substantive basis in Socrates's actual words and deeds, even if we cannot be sure of each specific line. Plato's seminal work, *Republic*, which features Socrates, was produced over two decades after the death of Socrates. It's beyond my abilities to assess how precisely, at that point, Plato remembered his teacher's words. It's also easy to envision a young Plato following Socrates around and keeping notes on everything he said and compiling the work later. Ultimately, Plato's portrayal of Socrates may fall short of being a verbatim record, but it is not a literary creation from whole cloth either. Socrates was real. And his impact profound.

Another important issue that must be embraced from the outset is the vagaries of the path by which the works of ancient authors have come down to us. Yes, we have some fragments of the writings of Plato from near his lifetime, over two thousand years ago, but the oldest existing complete version of Plato's *Republic* dates to more than a thousand years after his life. In those intervening centuries, his works were copied and dispersed, translated and transliterated into other languages. At this point, there is no way to tell how much modification, purposeful or accidental, occurred over those many centuries. Another complicating factor is that languages change over time and the Greek that Plato spoke is not the same as the Greek spoken today, in much the same way that the English spoken today is very different than the English of two thousand years ago. (This is, of course, a trick statement—the English language had not yet even developed two thousand years ago.) The point is, I would like you to keep in the back of your mind the notion that we are dealing with some semblance of the writings of the ancients, but we cannot be absolutely sure that what we read today is a perfect match for what was written over two thousand years ago. Time always fuzzies the picture.

Even with these caveats, we can safely say that Socrates employed a dialectic approach, known as the Socratic method, which is a form of inquiry that involved questions and answers. Socrates did not simply state his position on the matter at hand but questioned his students and led them to the right answers, helping them find the truth within themselves. Socrates's questions about terms, meanings, ideas, definitions, and even questions about the questions exposed suppositions and errors in his students' arguments. In this sense, the Socratic method involved leading a person to truth by first exposing them to their own ignorance. So often it is the unspoken and therefore unchallenged assumptions that are the source of mistakes. Wisdom then involves divorcing oneself from one's own mental constructs, unlearning, so as to let the information, and only the information, guide one to some greater eternal truth. Socrates's emphasis in many of the dialogues is ethics, the moral principles that govern behavior, including discussions on virtue and an abiding interest in distinguishing between the "just" and the "unjust." To Socrates, there is an obligation, a duty, to consider one's own actions as a way of leading a purposeful and meaningful existence: "The unexamined life is not worth living."[3]

Socrates presents two related frameworks for examining one's existence and the reality in which it's enmeshed, the Theory of Forms and the Divided Line, which are portrayed, at least in part, in Plato's magnum opus, the *Republic*. This famous work opens with Socrates and Glaucon, Plato's brother, taking in the inaugural Athenian festival of a Thracian goddess held at the port (Piraeus). It's a fine day to witness a new addition to the Athenian religious calendar. After watching a procession of Thracian and Athenian officials, Socrates and Glaucon go over to a friend's house with a few others to while away the hours until nightfall, when a torchlight horseback relay race will occur. This is a new spectacle and Socrates is intrigued by it. At their friend's house the elderly patriarch of the family, Cephalus, sits on a couch with cushions and bids the arrivals to sit down in a circle of seats. He urges his guests to converse, because "the more the pleasures of the body fade away with age, the more pleasure I take in good conversation."[4] Socrates enthusiastically takes up his request, saying, "There is nothing I would like better, Cephalus, than conversing with you; for I regard the aged as travelers who have gone on a journey which I too must go, and from whom I ought to inquire." Thus begins an hours-long conversation that covers a wide range of topics and constitutes the source material of Plato's ten-volume *Republic*. During the course of the conversation, people filter in and out, as is natural, but the great bulk of the dialogue consists of Socrates asking questions of Glaucon, for the amusement and edification of the others.

THEORY OF FORMS

We pick up the winding dialogue part of the way through, as Socrates moves to the conceptual structure of physical reality.[5]

SOCRATES: Well then, shall we begin the inquiry in our usual manner: Whenever a number of individual objects have a common name, we assume them to have also a corresponding idea or form. Do you understand me?

GLAUCON: I do.

SOCRATES: Let us take any common instance; there are beds and tables in the world—plenty of them, are there not?

GLAUCON: Yes.

SOCRATES: But there are only two ideas or forms of them— one the idea of a bed, the other of a table.

GLAUCON: True.

SOCRATES: And the maker of either of them makes a bed or he makes a table for our use, in accordance with the idea—that is our way of speaking in this and similar instances—but no artificer makes the ideas themselves: how could he?

GLAUCON: Impossible . . .

SOCRATES: . . . Well then, here are three beds: one existing as an idea, which is made by God, as I think that we may say—for no one else can be the creator?

GLAUCON: No.

SOCRATES: There is another which is the work of the carpenter?

GLAUCON: Yes.

SOCRATES: And a representation of a bed by a painter is a third?

GLAUCON: Yes.

SOCRATES: Beds, then, are of three kinds, and there are three artists who superintend them: God, the carpenter, and the painter?

GLAUCON: Yes, there are three of them . . .

SOCRATES: . . . Shall we, then, speak of God as the natural author or creator of the bed?

GLAUCON: Yes . . . inasmuch as by the natural process of creation He is the author of this and of all other things.

SOCRATES: And what shall we say of the carpenter—is not he also the maker of the bed?

GLAUCON: Yes.

SOCRATES: But would you call the painter a creator and maker?

GLAUCON: Certainly not.

SOCRATES: Yet if he is not the maker, what is he in relation to the bed?

GLAUCON: I think . . . that we may fairly designate him as the imitator of that which the others make.

SOCRATES: Good . . .

The Theory of Forms is a potent example of the intellectual power of the Abstract Plane. The Theory of Forms holds that ultimate truth resides in abstract objects, conceptual entities that are imperceptible but intelligible (sensible by thought). The Theory of Forms emphasizes thought over perception. All physical objects are copies of an ideal form. The core metaphysical question—what is real?—is problematic because perceptions can be deceiving and the physical world is ever-changing. Socrates's answer is that reality lies in the realm of eternal, unchangeable forms, pure ideas. There are ultimate truths waiting to be understood by those willing to pursue them. Socrates holds that the many thousands of beds that inhabit the world are mere copies of the original idea and that the depictions of beds in artworks are further removed from the source form. In this view, people shouldn't put stock in an illusion. "Real" reality lies elsewhere.

The Mysteries of Eleusis have a peculiar relationship to the Theory of Forms. But this relationship is discernible only if the operations of the Eleusinian Projector are well understood, which, as we have seen, was

extremely privileged information. Only the priests of Eleusis were authorized to possess it.

To see the connection, let's first remove the bed from Socrates's explanation of the Theory of Forms and replace it with another object—a
sculpture of the goddess. The sculpture is already an artwork, an appearance, and the representation of the sculpture as a light-borne image is an
imitation of an imitation. Socrates sees the image as extremely deceptive, but the religious orthodoxy of the time saw it as the ultimate truth.
Socrates flips the established order, providing a hierarchy that values
intellectual forms over objects and appearances. For an appearance-based,
epiphany driven, religion, which was typical at the time, the appearance
of the deity was of the greatest value, with domain over real objects and
even ideas. Socrates's focus on the limited value of sense perception can
be understood, at least in part, as a reaction to the Mysteries. To Socrates,
seeing is not believing, thinking is true reality, and physical reality is
but an illusion. With this, the foundational ritual concept behind the
effectiveness of the Eleusinian rite and all the other Mystery religion
rites—seeing is believing—is subverted.

DIVIDED LINE

In the middle of this long-running conversation at Cephalus's house,
Socrates offers the Divided Line as a means to illustrate grades of reality,
distinguishing between the visible world and the intelligible world (sensible
by thought).[6] The Divided Line is simply the Theory of Forms presented
as a diagram. It's one long horizontal line crossed with just three vertical
lines. Think of it as a four-inch ruler, with each inch corresponding to one
of his categories of reality. Socrates continues questioning Glaucon as they
await the upcoming nighttime festivities.[7]

> SOCRATES: Now take a line which has been cut into two
> unequal parts, and divide each of them again in the same

proportion, and suppose the two main divisions are one visible and the other intelligible, and then compare the subdivisions in respect of their clearness and lack of clearness, and you will find that the first section in the quadrant of the "visible" consists of images, which are representations of things . . . Do you understand?

GLAUCON: Yes, I understand.

SOCRATES: Imagine, now, that the other section of the "visible" includes actual objects and beings, like animals, plants, and made items.

GLAUCON: Very good.

SOCRATES: Would you not admit that both the sections of this "visible" division have different degrees of truth, and that the copy is to the original as the sphere of opinion is to the sphere of knowledge?

GLAUCON: Most undoubtedly.

SOCRATES: Next proceed to consider the manner in which the "intelligible" [or intellectual] section is to be divided.

GLAUCON: In what manner? . . .

Socrates goes on to give the example of mathematics as the first category of the "intelligible." And while mathematics makes use of drawings, figures, and diagrams, they are not themselves the matter but are illustrations of reasoning at work. Then, Socrates describes the next and most elevated section of the intelligible quadrant, the realm of forms, where ideas lead through ideas to other ideas.

SOCRATES: . . . And when I speak of the other division of the intelligible, you will understand me to speak of that other sort of knowledge which reason attains alone . . . and now, corresponding to these four divisions, let there be four faculties in the soul—reason answering to the highest, understanding to the second, faith to the third, and perception of shadows to the last. And let there be a scale of them, and let us suppose that the several faculties have clearness in the same degree that their objects have truth.

Again, the Divided Line is just the Theory of Forms presented as a simple diagram. Socrates sees images as consigned to the realm of opinion, steps removed from ultimate truth, whereas mathematics and conceptual forms belong to the intelligible world, the place of real truth, which is the philosopher's preferred realm. Notions that flow upward from images to physical objects are often misleading, whereas notions that begin in pure thought are the most cogent and pure forms of inquiry. The categories of information and their attendant thought flow patterns are critical components of Socrates's viewpoint.

Now, let's look at the Divided Line from the perspective of the Mysteries of Eleusis. The image of the goddess fits neatly into Socrates's Divided Line paradigm, but at the least desirable, or least truthful, end of the line. The great danger is that an illusion leads to belief without ever moving into the intelligible realm, where it would be scrutinized. The type of knowledge derived from the experience of an illusion is specious at best and, according to Socrates, not worth considering. In the Divided Line, Socrates elevates the idea of forms, the ideal concepts of the Abstract Plane, to the highest and most desirable position and consigns the illusions and beliefs of the most important religious ritual of his time to utter worthlessness.[8] But make no mistake, it's the same conceptual structure, just viewed from the opposite end.

And remember, the professed reason Plato was hypothetically able to get all this dialogue down was because Socrates was waiting around to watch a torchlight horseback relay race. It's delightful to consider that one of the most influential philosophical books ever written exists, at least in part, because of a horse race. From sport comes philosophy? Who knows, maybe there's a handful of buddies killing time between horse races somewhere today, shooting the breeze and tossing around notions of novel forms of thought? There are plenty of would-be Socrateses at any given racetrack. (In reality, Socrates's conversations likely occurred at different times and in different places and were compiled into one longer narrative—that is, the *Republic*—at a much later date.)

Socrates's Divided Line is a construct that extends from his Theory of Forms and leads directly to the *Allegory of the Cave*, which is the subject of the next chapter.

5

Allegory of the Cave

The most widely read and influential philosophical writing in the western world occurs in book seven of Plato's *Republic*, a section commonly referred to as the *Allegory of the Cave*, in which Socrates describes to Plato's brother, Glaucon, a cave where prisoners spend their whole lives chained to a wall.[1]

> SOCRATES: And now . . . let me show in a figure how far our nature is enlightened or unenlightened. Behold, human beings living in an underground den . . . here they have been since childhood, and have their legs and necks chained so that they cannot move, and can only see in front of them . . . Above and behind them a fire is blazing at a distance, and between the fire and the prisoners there is a raised way; and you will see, if you look, a low wall built along the way, like the screen which marionette players have in front of them, over which they show the puppets.

> GLAUCON: I see.

SOCRATES: And do you see . . . men passing along the wall carrying all sorts of vessels, and statues and figures of animals made of wood and stone and various materials, which appear over the wall? Some of them are talking, others silent.

GLAUCON: You have shown me a strange image, and they are strange prisoners.

SOCRATES: Like ourselves . . . and they see only the shadows, which the fire throws on the opposite wall of the cave?

GLAUCON: True . . . how could they see anything but the shadows if they were never allowed to move their heads?

SOCRATES: And of the objects which are being carried in like manner they would only see the shadows?

GLAUCON: Yes . . .

SOCRATES: And if they were able to converse with one another, would they not suppose that they were naming what was actually before them?

GLAUCON: Very true.

SOCRATES: And suppose further that the prison had an echo which came from the other side, would they not be sure to fancy when one of the passers-by spoke that the voice which they heard came from the passing shadow?

GLAUCON: No question . . .

SOCRATES: To them . . . the truth would be literally nothing but the shadows of images.

GLAUCON: That is certain . . .

SOCRATES: . . . And now look again, and see what will naturally follow if one of the prisoners is released and shown his error. At first, when he is liberated and compelled suddenly to stand up and turn his neck round and walk and look towards the light, he will suffer sharp pains; the glare will distress him, and he will be unable to see the realities of which in his former state he had seen the shadows; and then conceive someone saying to him, that what he saw before was an illusion, but that now, when he is approaching nearer to being and his eye is turned towards more real existence, he has a clearer vision—what will be his reply? And you may further imagine that his instructor is pointing to the objects as they pass and requiring him to name them—will he not be perplexed? Will he not fancy that the shadows which he formerly saw are truer than the objects which are now shown to him?

GLAUCON: Far truer.

SOCRATES: And if he is compelled to look straight at the light, will he not have a pain in his eyes which will make him turn away to take refuge in the objects of vision which he can see, and which he will conceive to be in reality clearer than the things which are now being shown to him?

GLAUCON: True . . .

SOCRATES: And suppose once more, that he is reluctantly dragged up a steep and rugged ascent, and held fast until he is forced into the presence of the sun itself, is he not likely to be pained and irritated? When he approaches the light his eyes will be dazzled, and he will not be able to see anything at all of what are now called realities.

GLAUCON: Not all in a moment . . .

SOCRATES: He will require to grow accustomed to the sight of the upper world . . .

GLAUCON: Certainly.

SOCRATES: Last of all he will be able to see the sun . . . he will see it in its own proper place, and . . . he will contemplate it as it is.

GLAUCON: Certainly . . .

SOCRATES: . . . And when he remembered his old habitation, and the wisdom of the den and his fellow-prisoners, do you not suppose that he would . . . pity them?

GLAUCON: Certainly, he would.

SOCRATES: And if the prisoners were in the habit of conferring honors among themselves on those who were quickest to observe the passing shadows and to remark which of them went before, and which followed after, and which were together; and who were therefore best able to draw conclusions as to the future, do you think that he would care for such honors and glories, or envy the possessors of them? . . . and to endure anything, rather than think as they do and live after their manner?

GLAUCON: Yes . . . I think that he would rather suffer anything than entertain these false notions and live in this miserable manner.

SOCRATES: Imagine once more . . . the released prisoner then coming suddenly out of the sun to be placed back in his old situation in the cave; would he not be certain to have his eyes full of darkness?

GLAUCON: To be sure . . .

SOCRATES: And if there were a contest, and he had to compete in measuring the shadows with the prisoners who had never moved out of the den, while his sight was still weak, and before his eyes had become steady (and the time which would be needed to acquire this new habit of sight might be very considerable), would he not be ridiculous? Men would say of him that up he went and down he came without his eyes; and that it was better not even to think of ascending; and if any one tried to free another and lead him up to the light, let them only catch the offender, and they would put him to death.

The last line is very important, because it says that anyone who tries to free people from the illusions of shadows and bring them up to the true light should be caught and killed. This was written more than two decades after the death of Socrates, and this line succinctly described what happened to Socrates, which is made more poignant because Socrates is the speaker.

SOCRATES: The prison-house is the world of sight, the light of the fire is the sun, and you will not misapprehend me if you interpret the journey upwards to be the ascent of the soul into the intellectual world . . . my opinion is that in the world of knowledge the idea of good appears last of all, and is seen only with an effort; and, when seen, is also inferred to be the universal author of all things beautiful and right, parent of light and of the lord of light in this visible world, and the immediate source of reason and truth in the intellectual; and that this is the power upon which he who would act rationally either in public or private life must have his eye fixed.

GLAUCON: I agree . . . as far as I am able to understand you . . .

SOCRATES: . . . Moreover . . . you must not wonder that those who attain to this beatific vision are unwilling to descend to human affairs; for their souls are ever hastening into the upper world where they desire to dwell; which desire of theirs is very natural, if our allegory may be trusted.

GLAUCON: Yes, very natural.

SOCRATES: And is there anything surprising in one who passes from divine contemplations to the evil state of man, misbehaving himself in a ridiculous manner; if, while his eyes are blinking and before he has become accustomed to the surrounding darkness, he is compelled to fight in courts of law, or in other places, about the images or the shadows of images of justice, and is endeavoring to meet the conceptions of those who have never yet seen absolute justice?

Here Socrates is arguing about the absurdity of having to fight in the court of law about "the images or shadows of images . . ." which is exactly what the trial of Socrates will be about, if the newly revealed optical operations of the Eleusinian Mysteries are to be taken into account. Next, Socrates turns the discussion toward the role of education in the development of young minds and the administration of the state. Socrates is ever concerned with the idea of the "just" and how it applies to good governance. He then returns to the case of the released prisoner, as an example of the best minds ascending until they arrive at the good, but for the sake of the state being compelled to return to the cave.

SOCRATES: They must be made to descend again among the prisoners in the den, and partake of their labors and honors, whether they are worth having or not.

To Socrates, those who attain the true intellectual light must be made to return to the depths and guide the general populace whether it is appreciated or not. In this sense, Socrates is describing the rationale of his own mission in life, but also Plato is outlining the process by which Socrates will meet his end.

The *Allegory of the Cave* is a wonderful literary image that has had profound metaphorical resonance down through the centuries. It has been recast many times. Pedro Calderón de la Barca's 1636 stage play *La vida es sueño* (Life Is a Dream) is structured on the *Allegory*. Karl Marx adapted the cave allegory as, interestingly enough, a camera obscura in the nineteenth century.[2] In more recent times, the *Matrix* movies, a sci-fi action series, use the *Allegory* as the basis for a postapocalyptic false reality; the movie *The Truman Show* offers a domed film set as a quasi-cave of limited reality; and the movie *Inception* has constructed realities from levels of dreams. The *Allegory*, regardless of its source, has been and remains a potent trope across time.

Scholars have often wondered where Plato got such an extraordinary construct. One researcher, John Henry Wright, surmised, "It is hardly possible that this picture originated in pure imagination . . ."[3] So Wright went on a search of Greek caves, looking for one that exactly matched the description in the *Allegory*.[4] None did.[5] I offer that the *Allegory of the Cave* was formed from an understanding of the inner workings of the Mysteries of Eleusis, discussed in an earlier chapter, where a bright fire was used to project the image of a sculpture of the goddess via the camera obscura principle, as part of an all-important ritual to confer a harmonious afterlife upon the initiates. The prisoners in the cave believe in "shadows of images cast through a light," just as initiates into the Mysteries believe in the projected images of sculptures cast by a light.[6] In the *Allegory*, men carry sculptures in front of a fire, just as the *hierophant* carries a sculpture of the goddess in front of a great fire. The *Allegory* substitutes a darkened cave for the darkened temple. The initiates become poor souls chained to a wall. Pitiable creatures. Believers of illusions.

During the writing of the Republic, in which the *Allegory* appears, Plato lived under the same societal rules that Socrates had lived under, including the law of silence about the Mysteries, so Plato would have needed to change key elements to shroud the source. An allegory, in general, offers a safer means of discussion, particularly if important details are obscured or misdirected. Still, with the *Allegory*, Socrates and/or Plato turn Athenian order on its head. The deceptiveness of the staged Eleusinian light show spurred Socrates to consider an alternate type of truth and supplied him with the template for the *Allegory of the Cave*. The *hierophant* and the philosopher had markedly different understandings of the meaning of the Eleusinian rites, but make no mistake, the physical light was the same.

If Socrates had presented the *Allegory* openly in the agora, the public marketplace where he normally held his discussions with his followers, he would have invited the wrath of the state religion, particularly if his delivery was at all more overt than the version we read in Plato. A priest from the Eleusinian Mysteries would have interpreted the *Allegory* as a description of the secret rite. Socrates's prisoners in the dark who believe in cast shadows would have instantly been understood as, and equated with, the initiates and vision of the goddess. This would have desperately alarmed the priests. They would have believed he was talking directly about them, shockingly unveiling their secret. To the Eleusinian mind, the most egregious aspect of the *Allegory* was the way Socrates portrayed the shadows—that is to say the goddess Persephone—as empty falsehood, the lowest of the low, with even concrete reality holding more truth. He took the ultimate experience for many people, Eleusis, and rendered it useless. The Socratic notions of the Theory of Forms and the Divided Line may point to intellectual interpretations of the Mysteries.

But the *Allegory* went well beyond mere philosophical musings.

The *Allegory*, in the context of its day, was heresy.

A capital offense.

6

Bonds of War

Even if my interpretation of the *Allegory* as a critique of the Eleusinian Mysteries is correct, it covers only one half of the charges against Socrates. Remember, he will be charged with the religious crime of impiety (lack of reverence for the gods) and leading the youth astray. To understand the second half of the charges, we'll need to delve into Socrates's impact on the youth and one youth in particular, a stunningly beautiful young man named Alcibiades.

The story of the unlikely association of Socrates and Alcibiades largely begins on the battlefield of Potidaea in 432 B.C.E. The colony of Potidaea is situated on a peninsula in northern Greece and pays tribute to Athens as a member of the Delian League. Athens fears Potidaea will come under the influence of the Macedonians, and so it issues harsh demands on Potidaea that have the adverse effect of causing Potidaea to revolt. Athens sends a fleet to put down the rebellion. Among the Athenian soldiers are Socrates, then in his late thirties, and a teenaged Alcibiades.

Envision the scene: The Athenian forces disembark, gather in formation, and advance on the Potidaean position. Once in range, a volley of arrows arcs into the sky. Shields up. The formation of tightly bunched Athenian soldiers crouch under their shields like some giant, thousand-legged tortoise. The arrows hiss with evil intent just as they reach their target but bounce off the shields, sounding not unlike a hailstorm on a roof. The Athenians proceed, spears trained on the enemy. The two armies clash in violent combat. Grunts, yells, and shrieks fill the air, along with the bang of sword on shield, the clank of sword on sword, and the sick thud of sword on bone. It is all blood, dirt, sweat, adrenaline, and the stench of severed bowels. The Athenians struggle to maintain their lines. Alcibiades ferociously attacks the enemy, but out of either the rashness of youth or a pure passion for hand-to-hand combat, he goes well beyond the Athenian line, where he is cut down. He lays injured and exposed, unable to move or defend himself. He is, at this point, all but dead. Socrates, even while engaged in combat himself, notices Alcibiades's bravery or stupidity and, risking his own life, fights his way over to where Alcibiades lays bleeding, straddles him, and fends off attackers, parrying thrusts, blocking blows, while never moving his feet from either side of Alcibiades. Socrates takes advantage of a momentary pause in the action and hoists Alcibiades onto his shoulder and carries him back to the Athenian line, where his injuries could be treated and the bleeding stanched. Alcibiades describes what happened at Potidaea from his perspective.[1]

> ALCIBIADES: . . . I was wounded and Socrates would not leave me, but he rescued me and my arms; and he ought to have received the prize of valor . . . but he was more eager . . . that I should have the prize and not he.[2]

Socrates saves Alcibiades's life during the battle and even presses for Alcibiades to receive a prize of valor. Socrates's act of bravery and self-lessness leaves a deep impression on Alcibiades, who becomes emotionally indebted to Socrates. Alcibiades and Socrates become tentmates, and Socrates nurses Alcibiades back to health. The Battle of Potidaea is considered a catalyst for the larger Peloponnesian War, which will be a protracted affair that pits Athens and Sparta against each other for roughly a quarter century (431–405 B.C.E.). The Peloponnesian War will come to dominate the lives of all Athenians—Socrates, Alcibiades, and Callias included.

In addition to battlefield courage, Socrates also exhibits an extraordinary ability to withstand hardships, which leaves a deep impression on young Alcibiades. Sometimes the troops are cut off from supplies, as is often the case in war. Alcibiades explains, "We are compelled to go without food," which has an adverse effect on the soldiers but appears to have no effect whatsoever on Socrates, because "his endurance is simply amazing."[3] He carries on as normal even as the other soldiers wilt. Socrates is also impervious to extreme temperatures. During one severe winter frost, which forces the soldiers to pile on an amazing quantity of clothes and swath their feet in felt and fleece, Socrates in his ordinary clothing "marches better with his bare feet on the ice than the rest of us did in our shoes."[4]

One peculiar occurrence in the camp goes a long way in illustrating Socrates's powers of concentration, which it would seem were the source of his considerable physical stamina. Mind over matter.

> ALCIBIADES: One morning Socrates is thinking about something which he could not resolve; he would not give it up, but continues thinking from early dawn until noon—there he stands fixed in thought; and at noon attention is drawn to him, and the rumor runs through the wondering crowd that Socrates has been standing and thinking about something ever since the break of day. At last, in the evening after supper, some of the soldiers purely out of curiosity (I should explain that this was not in winter but in summer), bring out their mats and sleep in the open air so that they might watch him and see whether he would stand all night. There he stands until the following morning; and with the return of light he offers up a prayer to the sun, and goes his way.[5]

Socrates stands in place unmoving for twenty-four hours as he ponders some unknown question, which becomes almost a spectator sport for members of the ranks and makes him even more of a legend to his fellow soldiers. Alcibiades is clearly in awe of Socrates.

A few years later, at the Battle of Delium, Alcibiades is on horseback and has a better vantage point to witness Socrates's bravery as a foot soldier. As the battle progresses, the Athenians are forced to retreat.[6] Alcibiades uses his horse to shield Socrates from the enemy during the retreat, and although this is not the extreme act of bravery that Socrates performed for Alcibiades at Potidaea, it does show Alcibiades trying to repay his debt by going out of his way to protect Socrates. A connection strengthened. These two men, Socrates and Alcibiades, formed a bond known only to people who have fought in war together. Their affection, familiarity, and concern for each other would blossom into a mentor/mentee relationship, as it was understood and practiced then in ancient Greece.

7

Examination of Alcibiades

S ocrates routinely holds court in Athens at the agora, which was something like a town square surrounded by impressive buildings with long colonnades. Much of the time, the agora functions as an open-air market. Picture the scene: the sky is an intense Mediterranean blue, a gentle breeze blows in from the sea, and the faint scent of olive oil wafts by. Socrates, with his large paunch stretching his threadbare tunic, enjoys the shade of a little copse of trees. Alcibiades, with his chiseled good looks and powerful physique, is perfectly coifed and resplendent in glorious robes as he confidently strides across the agora. These two are ever and always such opposites. Alcibiades has decided that he's now old enough and experienced enough to stand before the Assembly and assume his place in the political hierarchy. This is his birthright after all, and in his mind, he is ready to assume the mantle. He joins Socrates under the trees and tells him his plan.[1]

> SOCRATES: You do, then, mean . . . to come forward in a little while as an adviser of the Athenians? And suppose that when you are ascending the dais, I pull you by the sleeve and say, Alcibiades, you are getting up to advise the Athenians—do

you know the matter about which they are going to deliberate, better than they? How would you answer?

ALCIBIADES: I should reply, that I was going to advise them about a matter which I do know better than they.

SOCRATES: Then you are a good adviser about the things which you know?

ALCIBIADES: Certainly.

SOCRATES: And do you know anything but what you have learned from others, or found out yourself?

ALCIBIADES: That is all . . .

SOCRATES: . . . I think that I know tolerably well the extent of your schooling; and you must tell me if I forget any of them: according to my recollection, you learned the arts of writing, of playing the lyre, and of wrestling; the flute you never would learn; this is the sum of your accomplishments, unless there were some which you acquired in secret; and I think that secrecy was hardly possible, as you could not have come out of your door, either by day or night, without my seeing you.

ALCIBIADES: Yes, that was the whole of my schooling.

SOCRATES: And are you going to get up in the Athenian Assembly, and give them advice about writing?

ALCIBIADES: No, indeed.

SOCRATES: Or about playing the lyre?

ALCIBIADES: Certainly not . . .

SOCRATES: . . . Then what are the deliberations in which you propose to advise them? Surely not about building?

ALCIBIADES: No.

SOCRATES: For the builder will advise better than you will about that?

ALCIBIADES: He will . . .

SOCRATES: . . . Whether he be little or great, good or ill-looking, noble or ignoble—makes no difference.

ALCIBIADES: Certainly not.

SOCRATES: A man is a good adviser about anything, not because he has riches, but because he has knowledge?

ALCIBIADES: Assuredly . . .

SOCRATES: . . . Then about what concerns of theirs will you advise them?

ALCIBIADES: About war, Socrates, or about peace, or about any other concerns of the state.

SOCRATES: You mean, when they deliberate with whom they ought to make peace, and with whom they ought to go to war, and in what manner?

ALCIBIADES: Yes . . .

The topics of war and peace spur Socrates toward universal ideas, or forms, that serve as the conceptual basis of political and military action.

> SOCRATES: . . . But you surely know the charges which we bring against one another, when we arrive at the point of making war, and what name we give them?

> ALCIBIADES: Yes, certainly. We say that deceit or violence has been employed, or that we have been defrauded.

> SOCRATES: And how does this happen? Will you tell me how? For there may be a difference in the manner.

> ALCIBIADES: Do you mean by "how," Socrates, whether we suffered these things justly or unjustly?

> SOCRATES: Exactly.

> ALCIBIADES: There can be no greater difference than between just and unjust . . .

> SOCRATES: . . . Have you been to the schoolmaster without my knowledge, and has he taught you to discern the just from the unjust? Who is he? I wish you would tell me, that I may go and learn of him—you shall introduce me.

> ALCIBIADES: You are mocking, Socrates.

> SOCRATES: No, indeed. I most solemnly declare to you by Zeus, who is the God of our common friendship, and whom I never will foreswear, that I am not. Tell me, then, who this instructor is, if he exists.

ALCIBIADES: But, perhaps, he does not exist; may I not have acquired the knowledge of just and unjust in some other way?

SOCRATES: Yes, if you have discovered them.

Socrates presses Alcibiades about where he learned the difference between "just" and "unjust."

ALCIBIADES: I suppose . . . I learned them in the same way that other people learn.

SOCRATES: I must again ask, from whom? Do tell me.

ALCIBIADES: From "the many."

Alcibiades offers that he learned of the "just" and "unjust" in a natural way from the society around him—from "the many." Socrates, however, has a dim view of "the many" and sets out to question Alcibiades on this point, but Alcibiades has a clever retort.

ALCIBIADES: Why, for example, I learned to speak Greek from "the many," and I cannot say who was my teacher, or to whom I am to attribute my knowledge of Greek, if not to those good-for-nothing teachers, as you call them.

SOCRATES: Why, yes, my friend; and "the many" are good enough teachers of Greek, and some of their instructions in that line may be justly praised.

ALCIBIADES: Why is that?

SOCRATES: Why, because they have the qualities which good teachers ought to have.

ALCIBIADES: What qualities?

SOCRATES: Knowledge. Why, you know that knowledge is the first qualification of any teacher?

ALCIBIADES: Certainly . . .

Socrates acknowledges that "the many" are indeed qualified to teach spoken Greek, because it's a subject in which they have expertise. But this is only possible because there's general agreement as to the meaning of the words. If there was significant disagreement, then the language itself would not function and "the many" would be unable to teach it. Socrates makes clear that on subjects where there is accordance, "the many" are apt instructors, but what happens with topics on which "the many" have no agreement?

SOCRATES: Well, but are "the many" agreed with themselves, or with one another, about the justice or injustice of men and things?

ALCIBIADES: Assuredly not, Socrates.

SOCRATES: There is no subject about which they are more at variance?

ALCIBIADES: None . . .

SOCRATES: . . . But of the quarrels about justice and injustice, even if you have never seen them, you have certainly heard from many people, including Homer; for you have heard of the *Iliad* and *Odyssey*?

ALCIBIADES: To be sure, Socrates.

SOCRATES: A difference of just and unjust is the argument of those poems?

ALCIBIADES: True.

SOCRATES: This difference caused all the wars and deaths of Trojans and Achaeans, and the deaths of the suitors of Penelope in their quarrel with Odysseus.

ALCIBIADES: Very true.

SOCRATES: And when the Athenians and Spartans and Boeotians fell at Tanagra, and afterward in the battle of Coronea, at which your father met his end, the question was one of justice—this was the sole cause of the battles, and of their deaths.

ALCIBIADES: Very true.

SOCRATES: But can they be said to understand that about which they are quarrelling to the death?

ALCIBIADES: Clearly not.

SOCRATES: And yet those whom you thus allow to be ignorant are the teachers to whom you are appealing.

ALCIBIADES: Very true.

This section of the examination of Alcibiades draws to a close with a funny and yet poignant illustration of the brilliance of the Socratic method.

SOCRATES: Now let us put the case generally: Whenever there is a question and answer, who is the speaker—the questioner or the answerer?

ALCIBIADES: I should say, Socrates, that the answerer was the speaker.

SOCRATES: And have I not been the questioner all through?

ALCIBIADES: Yes.

SOCRATES: And you the answerer?

ALCIBIADES: Just so.

SOCRATES: Which of us, then, was the speaker?

ALCIBIADES: The inference is, Socrates, that I was the speaker.

SOCRATES: Did not someone say that Alcibiades not understanding about just and unjust, but thinking that he did understand, was going to the Assembly to advise the Athenians about what he did not know? Was not that said?

ALCIBIADES: Very true.

SOCRATES: Then, Alcibiades, the result may be expressed in the language of the tragedies. I think that you have heard all this "from yourself, and not from me."

Socrates ribs Alcibiades not because he's a cruel taskmaster but rather because he has deep affection for Alcibiades and sees in him the opportunity to cultivate a proper philosopher-king. Socrates is trying to get Alcibiades to develop his mind, but to do this Socrates must first expose the inadequacies of Alcibiades's thought process, which, quite understandably, causes Alcibiades some discomfort. Alcibiades's acknowledgment of his ignorance is the first step in the long intellectual journey toward philosophical enlightenment. At this point, Socrates has penetrated Alcibiades's shield of arrogance, and the real learning can begin.

> SOCRATES: . . . Ask yourself: Are you in any perplexity about things of which you know you do not know? You know, for example, that you know nothing about the preparation of food.

> ALCIBIADES: Very true.

> SOCRATES: And do you think and perplex yourself about the preparation of food, or do you leave that to someone who understands how to prepare food?

> ALCIBIADES: The latter.

> SOCRATES: Or if you were on a voyage, would you bewilder yourself by considering whether the rudder is to be drawn inward or outward, or do you leave that to the pilot, and do nothing?

> ALCIBIADES: That would be the concern of the pilot.

> SOCRATES: Then you are not perplexed about what you do not know, so long as you know that you do not know it?

> ALCIBIADES: I imagine not . . .

SOCRATES: . . . And so there is a category of persons who do not make mistakes in life, because they trust others about things of which they know they do not know?

ALCIBIADES: True.

SOCRATES: Who, then, are the people who make mistakes? They cannot, of course, be "those who know"?

ALCIBIADES: Certainly not.

SOCRATES: But if neither "those who know" nor those who "know that they don't know" make mistakes, then there remains only the category of people who "don't know that they don't know" to make most of the mistakes in the world.

ALCIBIADES: Yes, only those . . .

The discussion about the three categories of humanity—"those that know," "those that know they don't know," and those that "don't know they don't know"—is quintessential Socrates. People who "know" are less likely to make mistakes because they have experience in their field. People who "know they don't know" will logically leave things to those who know. But it's the people who "don't know that they don't know," who are burdened with the conceit of knowledge without actually having the knowledge, who are prone to significant error. This is not to say that experts don't sometimes make mistakes, just that they are much rarer. This illustration is as accurate today as it was in the ancient Greek world, which is part of the reason that Socrates is still so widely studied to this very day. In fact, in 2002, during a military intelligence briefing, then US secretary of defense Donald Rumsfeld recast Socrates's knowledge categories as "known knowns," "known unknowns," and "unknown unknowns"; that is, there is information the government knows it knows, information it knows it doesn't know, and information it doesn't know it doesn't know. What Socrates might have made of Rumsfeld's exposition of his idea is an interesting, if futile, rabbit hole to go down.

Socrates drives home the point that, when it comes to the idea of the "just," Alcibiades falls into the category of those who "don't know they don't know." Alcibiades, who was so confident at the beginning of the conversation, has been humbled by the end. He pledges to think about justice and says, "I will be the disciple, and you shall be my master." To which Socrates replies, "Like the stork I shall be cherished by the bird whom I have hatched." But Socrates issues a warning: "And I hope that you will persist; although I have fears, not because I doubt you; but I see the power of the state, which may be too much for both of us." As we shall see in subsequent chapters, Socrates has cause for concern.

Socrates's verbal examination of Alcibiades offers insights into the mentor/mentee relationship between the two and is also a prime example of the Socratic method in action, yielding a greater truth that has been applicable to humans across time. This dialogue helps to explain Alcibiades's intense fascination with Socrates, a man so different from himself. Socrates is completely unconcerned with the trappings of power and wealth that Alcibiades had been born into and so identified with.

They are opposites, united by a love of the mind.

8

The Seduction

The romantic relationship between Alcibiades and Socrates is a topic covered by various ancient authors who have different perspectives as to who pursued whom and why. Some say it was Socrates who seduced Alcibiades, and some say it was the other way around. Among the best accounts is in Plato's *Symposium*, which describes a dinner party where Socrates and others discuss the meaning and value of love. The heady and earnest discussion is occasionally and comedically interrupted by the playwright Aristophanes (more on him later), who suffers from a bout of hiccups. A drunk Alcibiades joins the party late and chimes in on the topic of love, speaking about his feelings for Socrates in vino veritas (in wine comes truth).[1]

> ALCIBIADES: I saw in him [Socrates] divine and golden images of such fascinating beauty that I was ready to do in a moment whatever Socrates commanded ... Now I fancied that he was seriously enamored of my beauty, and I thought that I should therefore have a grand opportunity of hearing him tell what he knew, for I had a wonderful opinion of the attractions of my youth.

Alcibiades is enraptured by Socrates, despite Socrates being much older, famously ugly, foul-smelling, and occasionally obnoxious. But Alcibiades is smitten with Socrates's mind. Alcibiades tells the group the story of his attempt to seduce Socrates, even with Socrates among the audience. Alcibiades is nothing if not audacious.

> ALCIBIADES: When I next went to him, I sent away the attendant who usually accompanied me (I will confess the whole truth, and beg you to listen; and if I speak falsely, Socrates will expose any falsehood). Well, he and I were alone together, and I thought that when there was nobody with us, I should hear him speak the language which lovers use to their loves when they are by themselves, and I was delighted. Nothing of the sort: he conversed as usual, and spent the day with me and then went away. Afterward I challenged him to wrestle; and we wrestled when there was no one present; I fancied that I might succeed in this manner. Not a bit; I made no way with him. Lastly, as I had failed up to this point, I thought that I must take stronger measures and attack him boldly, and, as I had begun, not give him up, but see how matters stood between him and me. So, I invited him to have dinner with me, just as if he were a fair youth, and I a designing lover. He was not easily persuaded to come; he did, however, after a while accept the invitation, and when he came the first time, he went away at once as soon as supper was over, and I had not the face to detain him.

Alcibiades schemes to get Socrates alone but fails to arouse any interest. Alcibiades, however, will not be deterred.

> ALCIBIADES: The second time, still in pursuance of my design, after we had eaten dinner, I went on conversing far into the night, and when he wanted to go away, I pretended that the hour was late and that he had better stay. So he lay down on

the couch next to me . . . and there was no one but ourselves
there. All this may be told without shame to anyone. But what
follows I could hardly tell you if I were sober . . . Moreover, I
have felt the serpent's sting; and he who has suffered, as they
say, is willing to tell his fellow sufferers only, as they alone will
be likely to understand him, and will not be extreme in judgment of the sayings or doings which have been wrung from
his agony. For I had been bitten by more than a viper's tooth; I
have known in my soul, or in my heart, or in some other part,
that worst of pangs, more violent in ingenuous youth than any
serpent's tooth, the pang of philosophy . . .

The description of the "serpent's tooth of philosophy" is poetic gold.
Once the lamps are extinguished and the servants leave them alone, Alcibiades makes his move.

ALCIBIADES: . . . I thought that I must be plain with him
and have no more ambiguity. So, I gave him a shake, and I
said: "Socrates, are you asleep?" "No," he said. "Do you know
what I am thinking?" "What are you thinking?" he said. "I
think," I replied, "that of all the lovers whom I have ever had
you are the only one who is worthy of me, and you appear to be
too modest to speak. Now I feel that I should be a fool to
refuse you this or any other favor, and therefore I come
to lay at your feet all that I have and all that my friends have,
in the hope that you will assist me in the way of virtue, which I
desire above all things, and in which I believe that you can help
me better than anyone else. And I should certainly have more
reason to be ashamed of what wise men would say if I were to
refuse a favor to such as you, than of what the world, who are
mostly fools, would say of me if I granted it." To these words
he replied in the ironical manner which is so characteristic of
him: "Alcibiades, my friend, you have indeed an elevated aim

if what you say is true, and if there really is in me any power by which you may become better; truly you must see in me some rare beauty of a kind infinitely higher than any which I see in you. And therefore, if you mean to share with me and to exchange beauty for beauty, you will have greatly the advantage of me; you will gain true beauty in return for appearance—like gold in exchange for brass. But look again, my friend, and see whether you are not deceived in me. The mind begins to grow critical when the bodily eye fails, and it will be a long time before you get old."

Alcibiades offers sexual pleasure to Socrates in exchange for philosophical wisdom. Socrates sees the offer as being equivalent to exchanging brass for gold, making clear that one is far more valuable than the other.

ALCIBIADES: Hearing this, I said: "I have told you my purpose, which is quite serious, and do you consider what you think best for you and me." "That is good," he said, "at some other time then we will consider and act as seems best about this and about other matters." Whereupon, I fancied that he was smitten, and that the words which I had uttered like arrows had wounded him, and so without waiting to hear more I got up, and throwing my coat about him crept under his threadbare cloak, as the time of year was winter, and there I lay during the whole night having this wonderful monster in my arms. This again, Socrates will not deny. And yet, notwithstanding all, he was so superior to my solicitations, so contemptuous and derisive and disdainful of my beauty—which really, as I fancied, had some attractions—hear, O judges; for judges you shall be of the haughty virtue of Socrates—nothing more happened, but in the morning when I awoke (let all the gods and goddesses be my witnesses) I arose as from the couch of a father or an elder brother.

Alcibiades has Socrates in his arms, but nothing, absolutely nothing, happens.

> ALCIBIADES: What do you suppose must have been my feelings, after this rejection, at the thought of my own dishonor? And yet I could not help wondering at his natural temperance and self-restraint and manliness. I never imagined that I could have met with a man such as he is in wisdom and endurance. And therefore, I could not be angry with him or renounce his company, any more than I could hope to win him . . . and my only chance of captivating him by my personal attractions had failed. So, I was at my wit's end; no one was ever more hopelessly enslaved by another.

Even after Socrates's rejection of Alcibiades's advances, Alcibiades is still hopelessly obsessed with Socrates. When Alcibiades finishes speaking, there is laughter at his outspokenness, "for he seemed to be still in love with Socrates." Socrates's response is fairly terse.

> SOCRATES: Alcibiades, you are not drunk; in fact, you are quite sober . . .

Socrates clearly doesn't buy Alcibiades's explanation that it was wine that caused him to speak so freely. Socrates sees something more calculated in it. Other ancient writers paint a different picture of the relationship between the two, with Socrates seducing Alcibiades. Either way, by the time of the *Symposium*, Socrates has already lost whatever romantic interest he might have had in Alcibiades, if he ever had any in the first place. Alcibiades seems genuinely hurt by the rejection.

One way to look at the relationship between Alcibiades and Socrates is to consider the deeper needs of both individuals. It can be argued that Alcibiades, who lost his father early in life, was seeking a father figure, whether he was aware of it or not. One time, after his father had died and he had been living in the house of Pericles, Alcibiades ran away, which may be an indication that he did not see Pericles as a worthy replacement for his own father. In Socrates, Alcibiades found a man old enough to be his father, who was strong, valiant, and brilliant. Socrates's interests in protecting Alcibiades from physical harm and, most importantly, of developing his mind were almost paternal. Alcibiades's attempt to use his physical beauty to "keep" Socrates seems to speak to his own self-worth. Conversely, Socrates did not yet have children of his own during the time of his association with Alcibiades, so Socrates may have been fulfilling a paternal need of his own to mold the mind of a promising young would-be philosopher-king. (Socrates did eventually have three sons, but their births were much later in life. In fact, two of his sons were said to still have been children at the time of his death at age seventy.) The bond that Socrates and Alcibiades formed was born of shared experiences: fighting together in military battles and in earnest dialogues about greater philosophical truths. There is little doubt that these two loved each other, whether sexually or nonsexually, for they found in each other what they each so desperately needed.

Together they might have saved Athens.

9

Alcibiades and Callias
(The Early Years)

Alcibiades and Callias were raised in the house of the great Athenian statesman Pericles, despite Pericles not being the biological father of either. Alcibiades's father was killed at the Battle of Coroneia in 447 B.C.E., when Alcibiades was a small child.[1] Alcibiades's mother then moved in with Pericles, who was her cousin. Callias was the son of Hipponicus, then the wealthiest man in Athens, but Callias's mother later left Hipponicus and married Pericles. In this way, young Alcibiades and young Callias, scions of separate aristocratic lineages (each perhaps feeling superior to the other) came to live under the same roof.

Pericles was a larger-than-life figure. He played a significant role in the development of Athenian democracy, oversaw the monumental building program that included the Acropolis and its Parthenon, extended Athenian dominion over the Delian League, and is largely responsible for making Athens the political and cultural heart of ancient Greece. His political and military accomplishments owe rather a lot to his estimable communication skills. Pericles's funeral oration for Athens's war dead is considered one of the greatest speeches ever given: the testaments to Pericles's brave soldiers were "engraved not on stone but in the hearts of men . . ."[2] (Some scholars consider Pericles's funeral oration to be the basis for US president Abraham Lincoln's famed Gettysburg Address. Sometimes it pays to study the classics.)[3] Pericles largely authored Athens's famed Golden Age, which is also rightly referred to as the Age of Pericles. But as able as he was as a statesman, he may not have been the most effective parent, at least according to Socrates, who addresses the point during a discussion with an adult Callias, Alcibiades, and the biological sons of Pericles (as well as another student of Socrates, named Kritias, who will play a significant role in later events). Socrates manages to criticize not only Pericles's parenting skills but also impugns the character of his sons, who just so happen to be sitting right beside him.[4] Socrates can be needlessly harsh, but he makes his point nonetheless.

> SOCRATES: . . . Pericles, the father of these young men, who gave them excellent instruction in all that could be learned from masters, in his own department of politics neither taught them, nor gave them teachers; but they were allowed to wander at their own free will in a sort of hope that they would pick up virtue of their own accord. Or take another example: there was the younger brother of our friend Alcibiades here, of whom this very same Pericles was the guardian; and Pericles was concerned that he would be corrupted by Alcibiades, and took him away, and placed him in the house of another man to be educated; but before six months had passed, the man sent him back, not knowing what to do with him.

Clearly, Socrates has a rather low opinion of Pericles's guidance of the young men under his care. And this is not the only time Socrates says so, as he makes similar statements about "magnificent" Pericles and the (mis) education of his sons in another dialogue.[5] Socrates argues about the teachability of virtue with, among others, Anytus, who will become an accuser at Socrates's trial (which we will discuss in detail later). Pericles, though, was probably doing the best he could under the circumstances, what with managing the affairs of Athens and leading troops in war, and I think he deserves some credit for being attentive enough to recognize that "corrupt" Alcibiades was a problem in the household. Moreover, Pericles probably paid greater attention to his own biological sons and rightful heirs than the boys who came under his roof for other reasons, not that Pericles had much time to spend with his offspring or his wards. But even among the wards there is a difference in the household pecking order between a wife's child (Callias) and a cousin's child (Alcibiades).

All told, there were significant advantages and disadvantages to being raised in the house of Pericles. Doubtless, the boys enjoyed a level of aristocratic ease and comfort. They likely never wanted for food, clothing, or other material possessions. But more importantly, they had inside access to the chambers of power, witnessing momentous decisions and strategic conversations that steered the ship of state. The boys would have seen the way Pericles carried himself and modeled a leader's demeanor. They might even have imagined they would do things better when they grew up. But of course, they would be wrong. Athens would never see the likes of a Pericles again.

The disadvantages of being raised in the house of Pericles are several: the pressures that Pericles was under may have sometimes cast a shadow on homelife; there was the weight of expectations to expand the empire and to attain in adult life something equal to or better than Pericles; and there was competition between real siblings and quasi-siblings for attention and favor. Household dynamics were likely quite complicated, as merged families can have their difficulties. The passage of a small boy who has lost his own father into the house of a truly dominant male figure and a raft of siblings would not have been without its fair share of tears, fears, and discomforts. We don't know the order in which Alcibiades and Callias were integrated into the household, who established a presence in the house first, or how long one was there before the other arrived. Regardless, whoever came first had to find a way to fit in with Pericles's biological children, and then when the next one arrived, it would have opened up the prospect of a reshuffling of the established pecking order. Alcibiades and Callias, both at very fragile ages and having endured family trauma, may have been perceived as threats to each other from the moment the other one arrived at the house of Pericles. Of course, shared experiences can help to form bonds between small children, but that would not be the case between these two.

Stories about the formative years of Alcibiades and Callias are, like everything else, heavily weighted toward Alcibiades. There is really only one description of Callias as a child, whereas there are pages and pages of anecdotes about young Alcibiades. However, the one comment about Callias is quite telling. An ancient writer claims that it was widely known around Athens that when Callias was young he was an "evil genius."[6] Callias had somehow upset or altered the financial tables of his father, Hipponicus.[7] Now, what he did specifically to the account has been lost to the mists of time, but it must have been something quite extraordinary and quite devious to earn such a description, especially at such a young age. And as we shall see, the "evil genius" label will apply to certain key episodes in Callias's adult life, too. Sometimes, children carry distinct personality traits with them throughout life.

Likewise, Alcibiades is a lion from the get-go. A young Alcibiades is wrestling with another boy, and just as the other boy has Alcibiades in his clutches and is about to win, Alcibiades bites him ferociously. The other boy lets out a cry and insults Alcibiades—"You bite, just like a girl"—and Alcibiades responds, "No, like a lion."[8] A fierce determination not to be defeated, and a penchant for working outside the rules of the contest, any contest, will be hallmarks of Alcibiades. While playing a game called knucklebones, which is something like jacks, with other boys in the street, Alcibiades is just about to take his turn to throw when a heavily loaded wagon comes barreling down the street. Alcibiades doesn't want the wagon to run over the game pieces and screams at the driver to stop, but the driver pays no heed. All the other boys scatter as the wagon bears down on them, but Alcibiades throws himself on the ground directly in the path of the wagon. The terrified driver pulls up his team sharply, and adult bystanders run out to help Alcibiades.[9] This anecdote shows that

Alcibiades's split-second impulse to jump bravely into harm's way was there from childhood. Alcibiades will use whatever power he has at his disposal, in this instance only the protective instinct of nearby adults, to achieve his ends. The game pieces are not disturbed, and Alcibiades has his turn.

At school, Alcibiades refuses to play the flute, arguing that unlike other musical instruments, the flute robs the player of his voice and speech: "Flutes then are for the sons of Thebes, because they don't know how to converse; but we Athenians, as our fathers say, have Athena for our founder and Apollo for our patron, one of whom cast the flute away in disgust and the other flayed a presumptuous flute player."[10] In this way, Alcibiades frees himself and the rest of the students from having to play the flute, and eventually the flute program is dropped from liberal education altogether.[11] Such is the early influence of Alcibiades. Once, Alcibiades asks the school teacher for a work by Homer, but when the teacher says he doesn't have it, Alcibiades punches him.[12] This violence is needless, but at this point people just chalk it up to the high spirit of youth.

On another occasion, Alcibiades runs away from home. Pericles's brother advises Pericles to have the town crier announce Alcibiades as missing. But Pericles says, "If he is dead, we will know it only one day sooner because of the announcement; whereas, if he's alive, he will be as good as dead for the rest of his life."[13] Clearly, Pericles is tired of Alcibiades's antics. At a different time, Alcibiades wants to speak with Pericles, but he is sent away because Pericles is working on how to render his account to the Athenians, that is, to demonstrate that he's conducting activities according to the rules. Alcibiades goes away, remarking as snidely as possible, "Wouldn't it be better for him to work on how *not* to render his accounts to the Athenians?"[14] This is Alcibiades. One ancient chronicler recounts an especially interesting conversation between Alcibiades and Pericles.[15]

ALCIBIADES: Please, Pericles, can you teach me what a law is?

PERICLES: To be sure I can.

ALCIBIADES: I should be so much obliged if you would do so. One so often hears the epithet "law-abiding" applied in a complimentary sense; yet, it strikes me, one hardly deserves the compliment, if one does not know what a law is.

PERICLES: Fortunately, there is a ready answer to your difficulty. You wish to know what a law is? Well, those are laws which the majority, being met together in Assembly, approve and enact as to what it is right to do, and what it is right to abstain from doing.

ALCIBIADES: Enact on the hypothesis that it is right to do what is good? Or to do what is bad?

PERICLES: What is good, to be sure, young sir, not what is bad.

ALCIBIADES: Supposing it is not the majority, but, as in the case of an oligarchy, the minority, who meet and enact the rules of conduct, what are these?

PERICLES: Whatever the ruling power of the state after deliberation enacts as our duty to do, goes by the name of laws.

ALCIBIADES: Then if a tyrant, holding the chief power in the state, enacts rules of conduct for the citizens, are these enactments law?

PERICLES: Yes, anything which a tyrant as head of the state enacts, also goes by the name of law.

ALCIBIADES: But, Pericles, violence and lawlessness—how do we define them? Is it not when a stronger man forces a weaker to do what seems right to him—not by persuasion but by compulsion?

PERICLES: I should say so.

ALCIBIADES: It would seem to follow that if a tyrant, without persuading the citizens, drives them by enactment to do certain things—that is lawlessness?

PERICLES: You are right; and I retract the statement that measures passed by a tyrant without persuasion of the citizens are law.

ALCIBIADES: And what of measures passed by a minority, not by persuasion of the majority, but in the exercise of its power only? Are we, or are we not, to apply the term violence to these?

PERICLES: I think that anything which anyone forces another to do without persuasion, whether by enactment or not, is violence rather than law.

ALCIBIADES: It would seem that everything which the majority, in the exercise of its power over the possessors of wealth, and without persuading them, chooses to enact, is of the nature of violence rather than of law?

PERICLES: To be sure. At your age we were clever hands at such quibbles ourselves. It was just such subtleties which we used to practice our wits upon as you do now, if I'm not mistaken.

ALCIBIADES: Ah, Pericles, I do wish we could have met in those days when you were at your best . . .

I'm not sure how Pericles had the restraint not to crush Alcibiades on the spot. Perhaps things would have turned out better for Athens if he had.

At still another time, Alcibiades punches Hipponicus, the father of Callias, for no apparent reason.[16] He just walks up and bops him one. Word of the senseless deed spreads throughout the city, and the people are aghast. The next morning, Alcibiades goes to Hipponicus's house and takes off his cloak, exposing his bare back to him, and beseeches Hipponicus to whip and punish him as he sees fit. Hipponicus instead forgives Alcibiades.[17]

The world always seems to forgive Alcibiades in hopes that he will eventually straighten up.

10

A Marriage and an Assassination Plot

Pericles, regardless of his parenting skills, dies during a plague that sweeps through Athens in 429 B.C.E., along with his two legitimate heirs. At the time of Pericles's death, Alcibiades and Callias are both around twenty years old and just starting their rise to prominence. The deaths of Pericles's biological sons open up greater opportunities for Alcibiades and Callias. Two separate paths to power materialize, because of their distinct lineages. Callias comes into his silver mine fortune around 424 B.C.E. and he is a member of the aristocratic Kerykes clan, which traditionally supplies officials to the Eleusinian Mysteries. Callias assumes a lifetime appointment as a *dadouchos*, a torchbearer, whose job at the Mysteries is to provide the lighting, which, as we have seen, is very important to the climax of the rites. A *dadouchos* is the second-highest-ranking position at the Mysteries behind the chief priest, the *hierophant*. Alcibiades's aristocratic line comes from the powerful Alcmaeonidae family, which included great leaders like Megacles and Pericles himself, and affords Alcibiades a fast track to high-ranking political and military positions.

Callias hosts a dinner party that gives an important insight into his mindset as he comes into his own as an adult. As the richest person in

Athens, he spares no expense to entertain his guests. The evening begins with oil rubdowns and baths followed by a banquet of delicacies no normal person could afford. Servants buzz around the feasting guests. Once the meal is over, the table is removed, libations poured, and a hymn sung. Performers of many types follow in succession: a jester, then a flute player, a dancer, a singer, and an acrobat who does somersaults over upright swords. A fresh spritz of perfume is offered to each guest. This lighthearted gathering has several people in attendance, including Socrates, who is in high spirits, and Lycon (who will be one of the three accusers of Socrates at his trial decades later). After the merriment has concluded, the group settles into philosophical matters.[1]

SOCRATES: Nothing would please me better than to have Callias keep his promise. He told us, you recollect, if we would dine with him, he would give us an exhibition of his wisdom.

CALLIAS: Yes, that I will readily do, if the rest of you, one and all, will declare some virtue of which you claim to have knowledge.

SOCRATES: At any rate, no one will object to declaring what particular knowledge he feels is most valuable.

CALLIAS: For my part, I proclaim at once, that I am proudest of my ability to make people better.

OTHER GUEST: Make people better! How? by teaching them a craft? or teaching them nobility of soul?

CALLIAS: The latter, if justice is synonymous with nobility of virtue.

OTHER GUEST: Of course, it is the most indisputable . . .

CALLIAS: Well then, as soon as everyone has stated his specific virtue, I will tell you of the art by which I achieve my noble end. So now, each person tell us on what knowledge you most take pride in.

One guest offers that he is proud that he can recite the *Iliad* and the *Odyssey* by heart. Another guest is proud of his friends, another of his beauty, one of his wealth, and still another of his ability to make people laugh.

SOCRATES: And you, Charmides, on what do you pride yourself?

CHARMIDES: Oh, I, for my part, pride myself on poverty.

SOCRATES: Upon my word, a charming business! Poverty! Of all things the least liable to envy; seldom, if ever, an object of contention; you never have to guard it, yet it's always safe; the more you starve it, the stronger it grows.

CALLIAS: And you, Socrates, yourself, what is it you pride yourself upon?

SOCRATES: On pandering.

All laugh.

SOCRATES: Laugh to your hearts' content, my friends; but I am certain I could make a fortune at it. . . .

ANOTHER GUEST: And now you, Lycon, tell us, won't you, what you take the greatest pride in?

LYCON: You already know, it is my son here.

The group then asks Lycon's son, who is called Autolycus, in what he prides himself.

AUTOLYCUS: On my father . . .

CALLIAS: Do you know you are the richest man in the whole world, Lycon?

LYCON: Really, I was not aware of that before.

CALLIAS: Why then, has it escaped you that you would refuse the whole of Persia's wealth, in exchange for your own son.

LYCON: Most true, I plead guilty; here and now I am convicted of being the wealthiest man in all the world!

Remember this moment, as Lycon's deep affection for his son will have some bearing on the trial of Socrates decades later.[2]

SOCRATES: Now we must prove in turn that what we each have professed is actually valuable.

CALLIAS: I will go first. My case is this, that while the rest of you go on debating what justice and uprightness are, I spend my time actually making people more just and upright.

SOCRATES: And how do you do that, good sir?

CALLIAS: By giving money, to be sure.

OTHER GUEST: Do you think that human beings harbor justice in their souls or in their purses, Callias?

CALLIAS: In their souls.

OTHER GUEST: And do you pretend to make their souls more righteous by putting money in their pockets?

CALLIAS: Undoubtedly.

OTHER GUEST: How?

CALLIAS: In this way: When they know that they are furnished with the means, that is to say, my money, to buy necessities, they would rather not incur the risk of committing crimes, and why should they?

OTHER GUEST: And do they repay you these same moneys?

CALLIAS: I cannot say they do.

OTHER GUEST: Well then, do they requite your gifts of gold with gratitude?

CALLIAS: No, not so much as a single "thank you." In fact, some of them are even worse disposed toward me when they have got my money than before.

OTHER GUEST: Now, this is remarkable! You can render people just to all the world, but not toward yourself?

CALLIAS: Oh, there's nothing remarkable about it. Do you not see scores of carpenters and housebuilders who spend their time building houses for others; but cannot build houses for themselves, and are forced to rent lodgings? And so admit it, my friend, you are beaten.

> SOCRATES: Upon my soul, we had best accept the result. Why, after all, fortune-tellers that see the future for others, cannot foresee their own futures.

There is something noble, vain, and slightly sad about Callias's professed means of making people better. Even Socrates thinks Callias's argument wins the day. In this story, Callias comes across as intelligent, earnest, and well-liked. There is warmth in the conversation, which is evidence of the camaraderie among the assembled group. Callias is assured of himself and is well on his way to becoming a person of prominence. At the end of the get-together, Callias asks Socrates if he will help him seek political office, and Socrates agrees as long as Callias keeps his eye on virtue. Part of what makes this dialogue so remarkable is that it shows that Socrates was once on favorable terms, even close, with Callias and Lycon, which will make the way things turn out all the more excruciating. It also shows that Callias and Lycon had been in league with each other for decades before charges were brought against Socrates. The question is: How did Callias go from the earnest and appealing young adult portrayed in this dialogue to the evil puppet master he would later become? Callias will endure some truly awful experiences in his young adult years that will harden his heart, that would harden anyone's heart, and many of these traumatic experiences will have Alcibiades as the root cause.

Meanwhile, Alcibiades's youthful indiscretions take a sinister turn as he passes into adulthood. Alcibiades owns a beautiful and expensive dog. He has its tail cut off. Friends and foes alike are furious at the abusive treatment of this beautiful and clearly beloved pet. Alcibiades bursts out laughing, "That's just what I want! I want Athens to talk about this, so they won't say anything worse about me."[3] Another time, Alcibiades declines an invitation to a friend's dinner party, but then he goes over to the host's house and orders his own attendants to take half of the gold and silver drinking cups that are on the table and carry them back to his house (more on this later).[4] Alcibiades's actions are difficult to understand, particularly this brazen theft from a friend, and he doesn't just steal; he does it in front of people. He wants an audience to witness his reckless power, and maybe that's the point. Alcibiades has a penchant for ambitious displays and self-aggrandizement.

He enters seven chariot racing teams in the Olympic games, something that no one, not king nor commoner, had ever done before.[5] Alcibiades's teams sweep the event.[6] A hymn of victory is sung in Alcibiades's honor:

> *Thee will I sing, Oh child of Cleinias;*
> *A fair thing is victory, but fairest is what no other Greek has achieved,*
> *To run first, and second, and third in the contest of racing-chariots,*
> *And to come off unwearied, and, wreathed with the olive of Zeus,*
> *To furnish theme for herald's proclamation.*[7]

Oh, did Alcibiades ever relish fame and glory, for its own sake, of course, but it also enables the cruel things he does in private. It's as though the public displays earn him enough credit with the populace to allow him to engage in ever more brutal and twisted behaviors. An ancient source explains:

> . . . his voluntary contributions of money, his support of public exhibitions, his unsurpassed munificence toward the city, the glory of his ancestry, the power of his eloquence, the beauty and vigor of his person, together with his experience and prowess in war, made Athenians lenient and tolerant toward everything else. They were forever giving the mildest of names to his transgressions, calling them the product of youthful spirits and ambitions.[8]

As an example, Alcibiades persuades the famous painter Agatharcus to accompany him home, because he wants to talk to him about doing a painting. Agatharcus is interested in the job but says he can't do it immediately because he has other commissions lined up. Alcibiades doesn't like this answer and threatens to imprison Agatharcus if he doesn't start painting right away. Agatharcus thinks this absurd. Alcibiades has his attendants lock Agatharcus in a room. And then as the days turn into weeks, they let out Agatharcus only to paint, while under guard. After three months of false imprisonment and forced labor, Agatharcus escapes. Alcibiades then has the gall to claim that Agatharcus has done him wrong because he left the paintings unfinished.[9] This is pure Alcibiades: the abuser blaming the victim of the abuse.

Hipponicus, the wealthiest man in Athens and the man Alcibiades punched for no reason, has a lovely daughter named Hipparete. She is the full sister of Callias. Alcibiades marries her. Alcibiades receives an extravagant dowry from Hipponicus of ten talents (a talent is roughly equivalent to twenty-six kilograms, or fifty-seven pounds, of pure silver), a sum greater than anyone has ever seen or imagined. When Hipparete gives birth to their first child, Alcibiades demands that Callias, who is now in control of the family fortune, pay him another ten talents. A payment for fathering children is unheard of, but gives a rather clear indication of what Alcibiades is truly after.

One ancient source alleges that Alcibiades's plan is to gain sole possession of the estate of Hipponicus by assassinating Callias, because with Callias dead, the money would then pass to Hipparete's husband, which, of course, is Alcibiades.[10] Such are the laws of the time. Callias is so frightened of Alcibiades that he goes to the Assembly and makes a public proclamation that if he were to die without heirs of his own, then all his holdings would go to the state and not Alcibiades.[11] Callias thwarts Alcibiades's plot. Perhaps just. Alcibiades does not see Callias's declaration coming: Who could imagine a man of Callias's wealth offering to give it all away? Callias is clever, staying a half-step ahead of his "half" brother. In response, Alcibiades directs his energies elsewhere.

Alcibiades and Hipparete now view each other with suspicion and no longer talk or even share the same bed. Hipparete's focus is on the baby (or babies—one account says that she had two children by Alcibiades). Alcibiades now completely ignores Hipparete, acts as if she isn't even there, and brings many lovers—Athenians, foreigners, free persons, slaves, men and women—into the marital house. He walks them right past her.

Even in these sexually uninhibited times, this is too much. Hipparete is by all accounts a good and decent human being, nurturing by nature but dealing with a wild man for a husband. It is easy to imagine that one day, he walks in with a woman she knows, maybe even considers a friend, and the emotional dam breaks, and Hipparete lets him have it, releasing her rage with verbal force. Alcibiades barely glances her way and leads the woman into the bedchamber. Hipparete, tears running down her face, scoops up the baby and rushes out of the house. The baby's soft skin pressed against hers gives her resolve. She goes to Callias, who's sympathetic to her situation, and he allows her to move in with him. Alcibiades doesn't mind this at all and continues his wanton ways.[12] Even from the safety of Callias's house, she feels continually humiliated as word of Alcibiades's ongoing debauchery filters in. When Hipparete can take no more, she goes to the magistrate to file for divorce, but before she can enter her action, Alcibiades appears, grabs her, picks her up, and carries her off, through the marketplace and back to their marital house.[13] Hipparete dies shortly thereafter.[14]

Did Alcibiades murder her?

We do not know. The ancient sources are ambiguous on this point.

He is said to be out of town when she dies, at least according to one source, but that doesn't mean that he didn't have someone else or some other way to kill her. Alcibiades was using Hipparete to get at Callias's money. When that plot fell through, Alcibiades had no further use for Hipparete. Maybe she died of natural causes, but it is likelier that she was dispatched either directly or indirectly by Alcibiades. Given the assassination plot against Callias and the treatment and death of his sister Hipparete, it's easy to see why Callias will view his "half" brother Alcibiades as a mortal enemy. Callias will use the power of the Mysteries of Eleusis to seek revenge against Alcibiades, and in so doing, he will learn a method for eliminating anyone else he sees as an enemy. Alcibiades will counter in ever more bizarre and sometimes effective tactics. In the following chapters, the battle for Athens begins, but first I'd like to step back and analyze the developmental aspects of the personalities of these two "half" brothers. We will need to understand this part to make sense of what happens next.

Classics professor Norman Sandridge explains that Alcibiades "shares many character traits with the contemporary construct of the psycho-path . . ."[15] Alcibiades has no empathy for others, uses people for per-sonal gain, has a charming but manipulative personality, lacks fear, has no guilt, engages in risk-taking behaviors, uses instrumental and even sadistic aggression, doesn't form lasting relationships, and is, yes, a sex addict. Alcibiades wants what he wants, and he doesn't care who he hurts, imprisons, steals from, lies about, or kills to get it. The signs of psychopathy (or, more properly, antisocial personality disorder, ASPD) typically first appear in childhood with violence toward others, animal cruelty, lying, and stealing—all of which Alcibiades did. Currently, it's not entirely understood how much of psychopathy is nature and how much is nurture. There is believed to be a genetic predisposition to psychopathy, a dysfunc-tion in the areas of the brain that control emotions, that can be triggered or exacerbated by traumatic life experiences such as abuse or neglect in early childhood. In this sense, people are born with psychopathy, but the neurobiological factors that make psychopathy exist are typically influenced by social environmental factors. Regardless, Alcibiades may have been the result of a perfect storm of factors, as his depravity and licentiousness will know no bounds as he becomes older and more powerful. Callias grew up with a psychopath for a brother, which must have been very difficult; it left scars, lifelong scars.

The assassination plot against Callias and the death of Hipparete mark turning points in the fraught relationship between Alcibiades and Callias.

11

Breaking the Peace

T he battle lines between Alcibiades and Callias are fairly well set as they each assert their adult authority over their respective domains: Alcibiades with the military and Callias with the Mysteries. Here I need to add one more hereditary position to Callias's score. He serves as a proxenus, or form of Athenian consul, to Sparta. In practical terms, that means he hosts Sparta's ambassadors at his house whenever they come to Athens to negotiate, which is often. His wining and dining with the Spartan envoys will, over the coming years, give Callias a special connection and backdoor channel to inside information regarding certain aspects of Spartan operations. Callias will use these to his advantage.

Just as Alcibiades is ready to take a leadership role in the Athenian military, his lust for power is blunted by the most unlikely of occurrences: Sparta agrees to peace with Athens. A pact known as the Peace of Nicias is negotiated in 421 B.C.E. and forges an alliance that is designed to endure for generations. It is named for the Athenian general Nicias, who brokered the deal, making him beloved by Athenians and Spartans alike. The treaty ensures free access to temples, the return of prisoners of war, the return of some conquered lands, and clearly defines which territories are under Athenian control and which are under Spartan control.[1] In addition, they also signed a mutual defense pact that binds Athens and Sparta to come to the aid of the other for fifty years. This is, all in all, a very sensible solution to the conflict.

Most people are elated at the prospect of lasting peace, but not Alcibiades. The armistice, which is so hopeful for the people of Athens and Sparta, presents a significant problem for Alcibiades's ambitions. How can he become a general without a war to win? And how can he become the leader of Athens with the older Nicias already established as the favorite of Athens? Alcibiades is deeply jealous of Nicias.[2] If there is going to be peace, then Alcibiades wants to be the one to negotiate it. Alcibiades wants the accolades—all of them. Again, Alcibiades doesn't care who he hurts or how many people have to die for him to get what he wants. Alcibiades needs to gin up a war and use it to eclipse or eliminate the much-admired Nicias. This won't be easy. Athens is tired of war, and Nicias is a steady and well-respected pragmatist. (Unfortunately, the art of fomenting needless war is still practiced today and continues to ruin countless lives just as it did in antiquity.)

General Nicias is a man of character, intellect, and demeanor. Plato records a dialogue with Socrates, Nicias, and fellow general Laches (and a couple of others) about the definition of courage.[3] These three are older, experienced men who have fought in battles together (in fact, Socrates was retreating with Laches at the Battle of Delium when Alcibiades came to their aid), and so have tremendous respect for one another, which allows for some forthright and even comical exchanges between the three. The discussion starts off about the merits of training soldiers to fight with or without armor, but Socrates then turns the conversation to the larger concept of courage. Nicias offers a definition of courage that is indicative of his personality.[4]

> NICIAS: . . . courage is the knowledge of what to avoid and what to risk in war, or in anything.

To Nicias, courage involves a fair dose of wisdom. It will be his guiding principle in future battles and we will return to this notion as events unfold. Ultimately, Socrates, Nicias, and Laches reach no conclusion on a definition of courage and mutually decide that it's time to go and they bid one another fond farewells and plan to take up the topic again at a later date. Interestingly, this is one of the few Socratic dialogues that doesn't end with a resolution. The matter of courage is left up in the air. This dialogue shows Nicias as a considered and considerable man. He is willing to stand toe to toe with Socrates and argue to a draw. Moreover, Nicias does so without vindictive statements or pejoratives; he allows his verbal combatants to leave the discussion with dignity intact, with warmth and respect for one another. This ability is what makes him both a great leader of men but also a great negotiator of peace. Nicias is a statesman.

Alcibiades can't stand it. He is distressed beyond measure and, in his envy, plans a violation of the solemn treaty.[5] Alcibiades knows that the people of Argos hate and fear the Spartans, having warred with them before, and do not like their position as "neutral" under the treaty, so he meets with their leaders in secret and encourages them to align with Athens, which would break the treaty.[6] Sparta, for its part, returns the fortress of Panactum to Athens, as agreed upon in the treaty, but it had already been destroyed by another group. The destruction of Panactum infuriates Athens. Alcibiades sees an opportunity to inveigh against Nicias and the treaty at the Athenian Assembly.[7] Hearing of Athens's discontent, Sparta sends ambassadors to Athens to reassure them of their intentions to honor the treaty. They come with full powers to negotiate a resolution to the matter. Alcibiades, fearing a peaceful outcome, manages to secure a private conference with the Spartan envoys in advance.[8] Once he has them alone, he initiates a nefarious plan.[9]

ALCIBIADES: What is the matter with you, men of Sparta? Why are you blind to the fact that the council is always moderate and courteous toward those who have dealings with it, while the people's Assembly is haughty and has great ambitions? If you say to them that you have come with unlimited powers, they will lay their commands and compulsions upon you without any feeling. Come now, put away such simplicity as this, and if you wish to get moderate terms from the Athenians, and to suffer no compulsion at their hands which you cannot yourselves approve, then discuss with them what would be a just settlement of your case, assuring them that you do *not* have full powers to act. I will cooperate with you, out of my regard for Sparta.

Alcibiades gives them his oath. The following day, the Athenian Assembly convenes at its large outdoor space with a formal raised speaking platform on a hill beside the Acropolis and overlooking the agora. When all are assembled, Alcibiades courteously asks the Spartan ambassadors under what powers they have come.[10] As per Alcibiades's guidance, they reply that they have not come with full and independent powers.[11] At once, Alcibiades assails them with angry shouts, as though he's the injured party, calling them faithless and fickle men who have not come in good faith.[12] The Assembly is indignant and the Spartan envoys confused. We can only imagine what the Spartan envoys had to say about Alcibiades when they arrive back at Callias's house. After this fiasco, the Assembly appoints Alcibiades to the rank of general. He immediately brings the Argives, Mantineans, and Eleans into alliance with Athens, which has great effect, dividing all of Greece.[13] Skirmishes break out between various factions across Greece.

Alcibiades breaks the Peace of Nicias. It takes a year and a half of maneuvering to accomplish the task.

12

The Golden Horse
Takes the Cake

While Alcibiades plunges Athens back into conflict and actively works his way up the military ranks, Socrates enters into a conflict of his own: he marries a woman named Xanthippe. Her name means "golden horse." At the time of their union, probably around 417 B.C.E., she is in her early twenties while he is in his fifties. Despite this age difference, they share some interesting character traits. She is as brilliant as he, as argumentative, and as unattractive. They are equally matched in many ways. One time, a friend asks him why he married such a difficult woman, and Socrates offers an explanation that relates to the meaning of her name.

SOCRATES: Because I see that the man who aims at skill in horsemanship does not care to own a soft-mouthed, docile animal, but prefers a horse with spirit, in the belief, no doubt, if he can manage a feisty creature, it will be easy enough for him to deal with every other horse besides. And that is just my case. I wish to deal with human beings, to associate with people in

general; hence my choice of wife. I know full well, if I can deal
with her spirit, then I can deal with any other person with ease.[1]

There is no doubt that Socrates's greatest love in life is dialogue, spar-
ring with words about ideas. He chooses a partner who can give and take
as well as he. In Xanthippe he has found that rare person as opinionated
and outspoken as himself.

In reality, people tend to pair up with their intellectual equals. A couple
needs to be able to "get" each other. The greater the difference in cognitive abilities between the two, the more difficult the communication and the less likely
a bond forms. People who are exceptionally brilliant—extreme outliers, as they
are called today—are at a numerical disadvantage when finding a partner.
For example, a person of average intelligence will find approximately
sixty-seven intellectual equals out of every one hundred potential mates, a
veritable smorgasbord of amor, while a person who is one-in-a-thousand
smart, like Socrates and Xanthippe, will have to sift through 999 potential
mates to find just one person who is their equal. In the ancient world, a
person might not even meet that many potential mates in a lifetime. There
was probably a level of desperation and exhaustion on the parts of Socrates
and Xanthippe in finding mates, including the temptation to settle for an
ill-suited partner or just resignation to be alone.

Women at the time usually married in their teens, so Xanthippe, who
is in her twenties, was already considered an an old maid, and her family,
probably despairing to find her a match, was willing to entertain the idea
of a much older man. Socrates, for his part, was probably weary of being
a stonemason, which is physically demanding work for a man his age, and
the attraction of her dowry, which was ample (she was of higher social
standing), would allow him to quit cutting stones and pursue his passion
for philosophy full-time. The wedding of Socrates and Xanthippe makes
sense on several levels.

In celebration, Alcibiades sends a beautiful cake in a basket to Socrates's
house. Socrates receives the gift, but Xanthippe, ever aware of Alcibiades's
history with Socrates, grabs the basket, dumps the cake on the floor, and

stomps on it.[2] Xanthippe sees Alcibiades as he is, a conniving and wicked man. He is a threat to her new marriage, and she doesn't want Socrates to associate with him.

Socrates gets the message.

In time, Xanthippe becomes pregnant. Impending parenthood tends to reframe a person's priorities and worldview, but particularly for a person as advanced in age as Socrates. In ancient Athens, most people in their fifties were already grandparents. Socrates is facing the humbling awareness of his own mortality, just as the miracle of birth and the circle of life take priority in his life. Xanthippe and Socrates welcome a son, Lamprocles, named after her father, in 416 B.C.E. Around the same time, Alcibiades's military and procreative rampage enters a new phase.

Alcibiades leads a fleet of Athenian ships to blockade the unaffiliated island city of Melos in the Aegean Sea. The Athenians enter into a protracted and still famous negotiation with the Melians for their surrender.[3] (This Melian Dialogue, as it is called, is still used as a case study in negotiation and conflict management courses in universities to this day. It pays to know the classics.) The Melians refuse to capitulate. When reinforcements arrive from Athens, the Athenians lay siege. Melos falls quickly. Alcibiades then rounds up all the people of Melos and has every grown man executed on the spot and sells all the women and children into slavery. And because he is Alcibiades, he impregnates one of the Melian women.[4] Melos is repopulated by Athenians.

In this way, and within nine months of each other, Socrates becomes a doting father, flush with the joys of new parenthood, while Alcibiades spreads his seed brutally and indiscriminately. Alcibiades is a reproductive machine, but he is no parent.

13

Run-up to War

An envoy from Egesta, an Athenian-affiliated city in Sicily, comes to Athens to ask the Assembly for help in defending themselves from Selinus and Syracuse, the largest, most powerful city-state in Sicily.[1] The Egestaeans even offer to pay an exorbitant sum for Athens's help. Alcibiades likes the prospect of gaining a foothold in Sicily with an aim of taking control of the entire wealthy island. Athenian envoys are dispatched to Sicily.[2] In time, the envoys return to Athens with a contingent of Egestaeans bearing sixty talents of silver, which is enough to afford sixty ships. The Athenian Assembly hears the testimony of the envoys and votes to send sixty ships to Sicily, appointing Generals Nicias, Alcibiades, and Lamachus as commanders. Five days later the Assembly is called back into session to vote on additional equipment and materials the generals might require.[3] Nicias thinks the conquest of Sicily is a very bad idea, on diplomatic and practical grounds, so he steps to the dais to dissuade the Assembly from such an undertaking.[4]

NICIAS: Although this Assembly was convened to consider the preparations for sailing to Sicily, I think, notwithstanding,

that we still have this question to examine, whether it is better
to send out the ships at all, and that we ought not to give so
little consideration to a matter of such grave importance, or let
ourselves be persuaded by foreigners into undertaking a war with
which we have nothing to do . . . I will, therefore, content myself
with showing you that your passion for war is out of place, and
that your ambition will be exceedingly difficult to accomplish.

The Assembly is unprepared for this argument at this point. All eyes
are on the highly respected Nicias.

> NICIAS: . . . Some of our nearby enemies are at open war with
> us . . . and it is only too probable that if they found our power
> divided, as we are hurrying to divide it now, they would attack
> us vigorously . . . A man ought, therefore, to consider this point,
> and not to think of running unnecessary risks with our country
> placed so critically, or of grasping at another empire before we
> have secured the one we have already . . . The Sicilians, even if
> conquered, are too far off and too numerous to be ruled without
> difficulty. Now it is folly to go against men who could not be kept
> under control even if conquered, while failure would leave us in
> a very different position from that which we occupied before the
> enterprise . . . Our struggle, therefore, if we are wise, will not be
> for the Egestaeans in Sicily, but how to defend ourselves most
> effectually against the oligarchical machinations of Sparta . . .
> . . . We should also remember that we are but now enjoying
> some respite from a great pestilence and from war, which is no
> small benefit to our estates and persons, and that it is right to
> employ these at home on our own behalf, instead of using them
> on behalf of these Egestaeans [from Sicily] . . .

Nicias then assails the motives and character of Alcibiades, while
demeaning him even further by not saying his name.

NICIAS: And if there is a man here, overjoyed at being chosen to command, who urges you to make the expedition, merely for ends of his own—especially if he is still too young to command—who seeks to be admired for his stud of horses, but on account of its heavy expenses hopes for some profit from his appointment, do not allow such a person to maintain his private splendor at his country's risk, but remember that such a person will injure the public fortune while he squanders his own. This proposed expedition is a matter of importance, and not for a young man to decide or hastily to take in hand. When I see people sitting here at the side of this individual, it alarms me.

Nicias then implores the Assembly to focus on their duty to do what is best for Athens.

NICIAS: I, in my turn, summon the older men that may have such a person sitting next to them not to let themselves be shamed down, for fear of being thought a coward if he doesn't vote for war, but remembering how rarely success is achieved by wishing . . . and drop this mad dream of conquest. As a true lover of his country, now threatened by the greatest danger in its history, each hold up his hand against the expedition . . . if you think it your duty to care for our commonwealth, and if you wish to show yourself a good citizen, put the question to the vote, and take a second time the opinions of the Athenians. If you are afraid to move the question again, consider that a violation of the law cannot carry any prejudice with so many here, that you are the caretakers of our misguided city, and that the virtue of men in office is to do their country as much good as they can, or in any case no harm that they can avoid.

The cogent arguments of Nicias are able to persuade some members of the Assembly to change their minds and turn against the expedition.

Alcibiades, sensing this and concerned that his opportunity for military glory is about to be lost, steps up to address the Assembly.

> ALCIBIADES: Athenians, I have a better right to command than others—I must begin with this as Nicias has attacked me—and at the same time I believe myself to be worthy of it. The things for which I am abused, brings fame to my ancestors and to myself, and to the country profit besides. The Greeks, after expecting to see our city ruined by the war, concluded it to be even greater than it really is, by reason of the magnificence with which I represented it at the Olympic games, when I sent into the lists seven chariots, a number never before entered by any private person, and won the first prize, and was second and third, and took care to have everything else in a style worthy of my victory.

Yes, Alcibiades begins his explanation of the rationale for the Sicilian Expedition by bragging about his horses. This is quintessential Alcibiades.

> ALCIBIADES: Custom regards such displays as honorable, and they cannot be made without leaving behind an impression of power. Again, any splendor that I may have exhibited at home in providing choruses or otherwise, is naturally envied by my fellow citizens, but in the eyes of foreigners has an air of strength. And this is no useless folly, when a man at his own private cost benefits not himself only, but his city . . .

Alcibiades claims that he paid for these displays for the glory of Athens. The art of self-aggrandizement is to convince others that you did it, whatever it is, for them. Ultimately, Alcibiades wants to be seen as a hero to his countrymen.

> ALCIBIADES: . . . Such are my aspirations, and however I am slandered for them in private, the question is whether anyone

manages public affairs better than I do . . . Thus did my youth and so-called monstrous folly find fitting arguments to deal with the power of the foreigners, and by its ardor win their confidence and prevail. And do not be afraid of my youth now, but while I am still in its flower, and Nicias appears fortunate, avail yourselves to the utmost of the services of us both. Neither rescind your resolution to sail to Sicily, on the grounds that you would be going to attack a great power. The cities in Sicily are peopled by motley rabbles, and easily change their institutions and adopt new ones in their stead; and consequently the inhabitants, being without any feeling of patriotism, are not provided with arms . . .

After downplaying the Sicilian defenses, Alcibiades moves to what he sees as the larger issue.

ALCIBIADES: . . . Men do not rest content with parrying the attacks of a superior, but often strike the first blow to prevent the attack being made. And we cannot fix the exact point at which our empire shall stop; we have reached a position in which we must not be content with retaining but must find a way to extend it, for, if we cease to rule others, we are in danger of being ruled ourselves . . . And do not let the do-nothing policy which Nicias advocates, or his setting of the young against the old, turn you from your purpose, but in the good old fashion by which our fathers, old and young together, by their united counsels brought our affairs to their present height. Do you endeavor still to advance them? Understand that neither youth nor old age can do anything the one without the other, but that levity, sobriety, and deliberate judgment are strongest when united, and that, by sinking into inaction, the city, like everything else, will wear itself out, and its skill in everything decay; while each fresh struggle will give it fresh experience, and make it stronger at

defending itself not in word but in deed. In short, my conviction
is that a city not inactive by nature could not choose a quicker
way to ruin itself than by suddenly adopting a policy of inaction, and that the safest rule of life is to take one's character and
institutions for better and for worse, and to live up to them . . .

With this sweeping oratory, Alcibiades is able to appeal to the Assembly's sense of glory and duty and sway them to increase their passion for
the expedition. Nicias perceives that it has become useless to try to stop the
expedition by his first line of argument. He changes course.

NICIAS: I see, Athenians, that you are thoroughly bent upon
going to war. I accept the decision, and hope it will turn out
as you wish. Let me proceed to give you my advice. From all
that I hear we are going against cities that are great and not
subject to one another, or in need of change, so as to be glad to
pass from slavery to an easier condition, or in the least likely
to accept our rule . . .

Against a power of this kind, it will not do to have merely a
weak naval armament, but we shall want also a large land army
to sail with us, if we are to do anything worthy of our ambition, and are not to be shut out from the country by a numerous
cavalry; especially if the cities should take alarm and combine,
and we should be left without friends (except the Egestaeans)
to furnish us with horses to defend ourselves with. It would be
disgraceful to have to retire under compulsion, or to send back
for reinforcements, owing to want of reflection at first: we must
therefore start from home with a competent force, seeing that
we are going to sail far from our country, and upon an expedition not like any which we have undertaken before. Usually,
we can get additional supplies easily from close-by friendly territories; but in Sicily we will be too far away, cutting ourselves
off entirely . . .

. . . I think, therefore, that we ought to take great numbers of heavy infantry, both from Athens and from our allies, and not merely from our subjects, but also any we may be able to get for love or for money from our territories, and great numbers also of archers and slingers, to make head against the Sicilian horse. Meanwhile we must have an overwhelming superiority at sea, to enable us the more easily to carry in what we want; and we must take our own food stores in merchant vessels . . .

Indeed, even if we leave Athens with a force not only equal to that of the enemy except in the number of heavy infantry in the field, but even at all points superior to him, we shall still find it difficult to conquer Sicily or save ourselves . . . We shall need good counsel and more good fortune—a hard matter for mortal man to aspire to—I wish as far as may be to make myself independent of fortune before sailing, and when I do sail, to be as safe as a strong force can make me. This I believe to be surest for the country at large, and safest for us who are going on the expedition. If anyone thinks differently, I resign my command to him.

Nicias is hopeful that the Athenians will balk at the sheer magnitude and staggering cost of the expedition.[5] Unfortunately for him, his speech has the opposite effect. The Assembly becomes even more eager for the expedition, seeing in Nicias's wise counsel a way to make a force so overwhelming that it will be the safest expedition ever.[6] With this enthusiasm of the majority, the few who do not like it are afraid to appear unpatriotic and so keep quiet.[7] Next the Assembly asks Nicias for specific numbers. Nicias says that they need at least one hundred galleys and no fewer than five thousand heavy infantrymen, with a corresponding number of archers and slingers.[8] The Assembly then votes to give the generals—Nicias, Alcibiades, and Lamachus—full powers to assemble the expedition.[9]

Preparations begin at once.

Athens is in high spirits.

But Socrates, a veteran of three military campaigns, chooses to sit this one out. He's at home playing with his now one-year-old son. Socrates holds out no hope that any good will come from Alcibiades's Sicilian Expedition.[10]

SOCRATES: It will be the ruin of Athens.[11]

14

Desecration of the Mysteries of Eleusis

In 415 B.C.E., just a few days before the expedition is set to leave for Sicily, a peculiar and troubling set of events occurs in Athens, which casts a pall over the mission. People awake one morning to discover the stone sculptures of the god Hermes, which stand outside temples and private homes alike, have been vandalized. Hermes is the herald of the gods and the protector of travelers, so it is common to keep a sculpture of him posted outside for protection as one leaves the house. The stone sculptures of Hermes in ancient Athens have a peculiar style, which consists of a rectangular pillar with a square base. On top of the pillar is placed the head and neck of Hermes. About halfway down the front side of the rectangular pillar is an erect penis and a pair of testicles. There are no shoulders, arms, torso, legs, feet, or other anatomical features. To repeat, because I know this sounds odd, these Hermes sculptures are just rectangular pillars with a human head on top and male genitalia on the front. That's it. The vandals hacked off the faces and penises of the sculptures. Which, I'll admit, sounds pretty funny, except that in ancient Athens the vandalism was considered an affront to the gods and a blasphemous act that could anger the gods and cause them to rain down their wrath upon the city. People are frightened, for themselves but also for the thousands of souls who are about to set sail and travel a great distance to wage war in Sicily. This is not the day to wrong the divine protector of travelers: this is an ill omen.

As the day progresses, rumors swirl, conflicting stories come to light, and various people and groups are implicated. An inquiry is launched and witnesses are offered immunity if they testify. Some flee town. The Council and Assembly meet many times over the next few days and scrutinize every suspicious piece of evidence and possible circumstance.[1] At this point, a well-respected leader brings forth witnesses to describe what happened.[2] A witness rises before the people and gives testimony:[3]

> FIRST WITNESS: Athenians, you are about to dispatch a large force upon a dangerous enterprise. Yet your general, Alcibiades and others, have profaned the sacred Eleusinian Mysteries in a private house. If you will grant immunity to the persons I indicate, I shall produce a slave belonging to someone present, and although he is not an initiate, he will be able to tell you what happened. You may deal with me as you please, if my statements prove false.

The first slave is brought in, and after he is granted immunity, he tells how Alcibiades and several of his friends performed the Mysteries.[4] Other witnesses are brought forth, including a flute player and another slave.[5] The witnesses describe Alcibiades hosting a party that turns into a drunken revel, where he and his guests make a parody of the Mysteries of Eleusis, with Alcibiades acting as the chief priest, one guest playing the part of the torchbearer (this is Callias's official role), and another being the herald.[6] The rest of the attendees act as initiates. After the mockery of the Mysteries, some of them go out into the streets, impiety coursing through their veins, gather other people, and deface (and de-penis) the Hermes sculptures. In this way the profanation of the Mysteries and the mutilation of the Hermes sculptures are tied together as parts of a single crime. A foreign man is brought in to corroborate this version of events.

Which portions of the Eleusinian rite the accused reenacted or how they performed them was left unrecorded. Did they somehow manage to re-create the epiphany in light? And if so, by what channel would Alcibiades have gotten that information? The most obvious source would have been his "half" brother Callias, the Eleusinian priest. Whether Alcibiades had overheard something when they were younger and possibly on better terms, even if only temporarily, or Alcibiades coerced information out of Callias is another question entirely. Another possibility is through Hipparete, who was also of the lineage. Alcibiades, malicious as he is, may have seduced, cajoled, or by use of force extracted the information from her, if she had it in the first place. Then, of course, there is Socrates, who at a later date reveals his knowledge of the inner workings of Eleusis.

What would Alcibiades's motivation have been in performing the Mysteries? To mock Callias? To undermine the religion? Was Alcibiades just so consumed with the superiority of being a military general that he no longer felt obliged to respect the norms of Athenian society? In reality, there may not have been much motivation to it at all, just a drunken braggart's display and nothing more, but many felt it was an attack on hallowed Athenian institutions, including democracy itself. Whatever the reason, Alcibiades is, as we have seen, a wanton man, and outlandish behavior is a trademark.

But there is another way to look at the incident. It may not have happened. There is a lingering sense in the versions of the events as recorded by ancient sources that someone had somehow induced false witnesses. "Sundry vague suspicions and calumnies" were leveled against Alcibiades by "foreigners and slaves."[7] The implication is that the witnesses were working with other unnamed enemies of Alcibiades to slander and eliminate him. If this was the case, the prime suspect would most likely be Callias, using his authority as a priest of Eleusis and his puppet master skills to orchestrate a false charge of profaning the Eleusinian Mysteries against Alcibiades. Callias had plenty of reasons to want Alcibiades dead. Either way, whether Alcibiades actually did profane the Mysteries or Callias set him up, charges are prepared against the profaners and Alcibiades is brought before the Assembly.[8]

> ALCIBIADES: Athenians, I demand the opportunity to clear myself of these charges, and since all is now ready for us to set sail, I wish to be tried immediately. If I am found guilty (which I am not) then I should be punished, but if I am acquitted then I can retain my command. If I am across the sea leading Athens in battle, I will have no way to refute the false charges which might be propagated against me in my absence. Countrymen, would it not be wiser to not send a general who has so serious an accusation hanging over him on so important a command? Let's have the case now, so that we can put the matter to rest, one way or the other. The expedition cannot wait.

Alcibiades knows that he has an army assembled outside, including over one thousand soldiers from allied states, who will fight only for him and may in fact go home and not join the expedition to Sicily if he's convicted.[9] Alcibiades has leverage in this moment. Even if he were to be convicted, he would likely get off with a light sentence so the expedition could proceed. Athens is too invested in its success. The unnamed but well-coordinated enemies of Alcibiades in the Assembly are aware of this and use his argument against him.[10]

> MEMBER OF THE ASSEMBLY: It is absurd that when a general has been appointed with full powers over such a vast force, and when his armament and allies are all assembled, to destroy this beckoning opportunity by casting lots for jurors and measuring out time for the case. Nay, let him sail now, and may the gods be with him! But when the war is over, then let

him come and make his defense. The laws will be the same then as now.

Their arguments prevail and Alcibiades is ordered to set sail. Alcibiades knows that his prosecution has only been delayed. He needs to return triumphant to stave off future charges.

Victory is his only option.

15

The Expedition to Sicily

Alcibiades joins his fellow generals Nicias and Lamachus in final preparation to lead a substantial naval armada of about 140 ships. These wooden ships are called triremes, because they have three banks of oars, which total around 170 oars per boat. Each ship is equipped with a sail and a metal-clad battering ram on the front that looks not unlike the maw of some giant sea monster. Eyes are sometimes painted on the sides of the ships to enhance the effect. These triremes are fast, maneuverable, and powerful. They are the source of Athenian naval superiority. The fleet will be powered by more than 20,000 oarsmen and will carry 5,000 combat-ready soldiers and 1,300 archers and slingers.

The Athenian forces muster at the dock early in the morning, with almost the entire population of Athens accompanying them.[1] Circles of families and friends bid heartfelt farewells to their brave soldiers. The people are full of hope and full of tears: hope of conquering Sicily and tears because they're afraid they will never see their loved ones again, but their spirits are buoyed at the sight of the immensity of the fleet and of the abundance of its provisions.[2] Never had a greater expedition been sent to a foreign land; never was there an enterprise in which the hope of future success seemed better justified.[3] When the ships are finally manned and loaded, the sound of a trumpet proclaims silence. A hush ensues. In one voice, all the soldiers on all the ships and all the civilians looking on from land solemnly recite the customary prayers.[4] Then cups of wine are distributed on every deck to officers and marines alike. The crews drink their libations, praise the gods, and put to sea.[5] The crowd erupts in great fanfare.

And so, under a cloud of suspicion and bad omen, the expedition to Sicily begins.

The ships row to Corcyra, where they meet with ships from other provinces. The sight of the assembled fleet is impressive to behold, and news of the armada makes its way to Sicily. An assembly is called in Syracuse, Sicily's largest and most powerful city-state and the prize that Athens seeks. An assemblyman issues a warning.[6]

SYRACUSAN ASSEMBLYMAN: I daresay that, like others, I shall not be believed when I tell you that the Athenian expedition is really coming. I am well aware that others who have reported this news have failed to convince you. Yet, when the city is in danger, fear shall not stop my mouth; for I am convinced in my own mind that I have better information than anybody. The Athenians, wonder as you may, are coming against us with a great fleet and army; they profess to be assisting their Egestaean allies, but the truth is that they covet Sicily, and especially our city. They think that, if they can conquer us, they will easily conquer the rest. They will soon be here, and you must consider how with our present resources we can make the best defense. You should not let them take you by surprise because you despise them, or neglect the whole matter because you will not believe that they are coming at all . . . The very greatness of their armament may be an advantage to us; the other Sicilian cities will be alarmed and in their terror will be the more ready to assist us.

The leader of Syracuse is a doubter of the reports. He thinks that the Athenians are far too wise and experienced to be so foolish as to go out of their way to pick a fight with another great power like Syracuse when they're already involved in conflicts with Sparta.[7]

> SYRACUSAN LEADER: Even if the rumor of their coming should turn out to be true, I am sure that Sicily is better positioned than the Greeks to maintain a great war. Our whole island is better supplied in every way, and our own city is herself far more than a match for the army which is said to be threatening us.

A Syracusan general speaks next.[8]

> SYRACUSAN GENERAL: In view of the reported danger, let's see how the whole city and every man in it may take measures for resisting the invaders. Why should not the city be richly furnished with arms, horses, and all the pride and pomp of war; where is the harm even if they should not be needed? We, who are generals, will take in hand all these matters and examine into them ourselves; and we will send messengers to the neighboring cities in order to obtain information, and for any other purpose which may be necessary. Some precautions we have taken already, and whatever comes to our notice we will communicate to you.

With this, the Syracusans fortify their defenses and send out envoys to the rest of Sicily and Italy to build a coalition to stand against the coming Athenians.

Nicias, Alcibiades, and Lamachus review the ships and divide them into three divisions each under the command of one general.[9] The Athenian fleet goes onward and reunites at Rhegium, which is located at the extreme tip of Italy, the best place from which to launch an attack on Sicily. Here

Nicias, Alcibiades, and Lamachus strategize their plan of attack.[10] Nicias wants to attack only a place called Silenus, then go to Egesta and squeeze the Egestaeans for payment (the Athenians are there at their request, after all), then sail around the island to impress and awe the other cities and then head back to Athens as quickly as possible.[11] Nicias's chief concern is that Athens is under-defended against a possible attack by Sparta. He wants to get the job done and get back. Nicias's approach is indicative of his philosophical approach to war—real courage is knowing what to avoid and what to venture in war—which he explained during an earlier dialogue with Socrates. However, Socrates did not completely buy Nicias's argument and peppered him with questions, but Nicias held his own and defended his position admirably. Lamachus is more interested in the whole of Sicily and wants to sail directly to Syracuse and attack it from the sea before they have time to prepare. (He doesn't yet know that Syracuse is already reenforcing its defenses.) Alcibiades, likewise, wants to take all of Sicily, but he thinks it best to start the campaign on a part of the island far away from Syracuse and then win the support and resources of various local cities and tribes as they march overland toward Syracuse as an ever-expanding and overwhelming force.[12] He wants to make it a land battle, and he wants to pile up small victories to bolster public support back in Athens. He needs the goodwill of Athenians more than the other generals. The three put it to a vote, and Lamachus sides with Alcibiades, and the Alcibiades plan is adopted.

Alcibiades may be a tactical genius, but Socrates's issue with him is that his motives are never pure; he's not driven by a sense of duty or any other higher concept (form), but purely by self-interest. Even as Alcibiades is negotiating and strategizing about the manner of attack on Sicily, he has another urgent matter on his mind: the malice of the postponement of his profanation trial has not escaped him.[13] Alcibiades suspects that once the army is preoccupied with battle in Sicily, charges will be brought against him back in Athens. He knows Callias, and he also knows that once he's taken back to Athens to stand trial, he will be at Callias's mercy. There would be no army to save him this time. This is, however, not an admission of guilt about having profaned the Mysteries but a clear-sighted acknowledgment that Callias has him where he wants him. Callias is going to use the powers of his station as an Eleusinian priest to execute Alcibiades, whether Alcibiades profaned the Mysteries or not. Callias has revenge for his beloved sister in mind, and maybe also revenge for himself. There are many scores to settle. As Alcibiades is busy planning the attack of Sicily with his fellow generals, he is also searching, in the back of his mind, for an escape plan.

The goddess is coming for him.

The first order of business for Alcibiades is to head to shore and convince the people of Messenè to join with the Athenians and march on Syracuse.[14] He is rebuffed. Perhaps the Syracusan emissaries have already gotten to them, or perhaps the idea of joining the faraway Athenians on a conquest of a powerful neighbor seems unwise, given that the Athenians would eventually go back to Athens but Syracuse would still be right there. This presents a serious problem for Alcibiades: not only does he need local support for his plan to attack Syracuse, but more importantly, he also needs local support to avoid being hauled back to Athens to face trial. He wants to be far inland, hard to reach, and difficult to find when Callias's functionaries, the officers from the Athenian Assembly, come for him. Alcibiades wants to be surrounded by non-Athenian troops who would be loyal to him and far less likely to acquiesce to the demands of Athenian civil authorities. If he is on a boat when the officers get there, he will be a sitting duck.

The clock is ticking.

16

Prosecution, Prison, Torture, and Death

Back in Athens, the investigation into the profanation of the Eleusinian Mysteries and mutilation of the Hermes sculptures builds momentum and gains prosecutorial teeth. All those who are implicated are apprehended and thrown into prison.[1] Athens has a law that citizens cannot be tortured, but the council has the power to suspend that law in cases of extreme crisis. The reason the profanation and mutilation are considered so grave is that they, in the religious understanding of the time, could turn three patron gods—Persephone, Demeter, and Hermes—against Athens. These gods, who the people of Athens depend on for their very survival, would have been deeply offended by the profanation and could, if they so choose, destroy Athens. People are genuinely scared. The gods have been wronged, and a divine reckoning looms. To make amends to the gods, the city's leaders need to avenge them and quickly. The council votes unanimously to suspend the law against torture.[2] Forty-two people are ordered to the rack.[3] Their ankles are tied to one end of the contraption and their wrists to the other. A crank slowly pulls the two sides apart, stretching the victim's tendons and ligaments. Their joints pop and crack. The victims either answer the questions to the torturer's satisfaction or their limbs are ripped off. Other suspects are whipped into submission. Not surprisingly, confessions and executions soon follow. This is the handiwork of Callias.

One of the accused, Andocides, is thrown into jail with all the male members of his extended family. Andocides is a young aristocrat and philosopher in his own right. Ancient texts do not mention him as being a student (follower) of Socrates, but they likely would have known of each other. Andocides certainly knows Callias. The prosecutorial strategy of throwing Andocides and his family in jail is meant to force him to turn state's witness or see his male line extinguished. Andocides explains the situation:[4]

> ANDOCIDES: We are all thrown into prison. When night comes and the jail is closed, there comes outside the walls to one prisoner his mother, to another his sister, and to another his wife and children, and there arises a piteous sound of weeping and lamentation for the present troubles.

A cousin who's the same age as Andocides and had grown up with him comes over to discuss their predicament.[5]

> COUSIN: Andocides, you see how serious our present situation is. So, although I have never said anything to trouble you, I now feel forced by our present misfortunes to speak. All your friends, with the exception of your actual family members, have either been put to death on the same charges which now threaten us, or else have admitted guilt by going into exile. So come now, if you have heard anything about this affair, please speak out and save, in the first place, yourself, save your father, whom you naturally love dearly, save your brother-in-law, the husband of your only sister. Save, too, your other kinsmen and me also.

The other members of the family follow, and one by one they encourage Andocides to save them. He thinks to himself:[6]

> ANDOCIDES: Oh, what a miserable and unfortunate wretch am I! Shall I see my kinsfolk put to death unjustly, their property confiscated and their names engraved upon the public tablets as though they had sinned against the gods, although they are wholly innocent of crime? And shall I see three hundred Athenians wrongfully put to death? Our city is involved in the most serious of calamities as the citizens hold each other in suspicion. Or shall I tell the Athenians what I heard from the real culprit?

Then another thought strikes him:[7]

> ANDOCIDES: Of those who had committed the offenses, some had already been put to death in consequence of the information of an informant, while others had fled into exile and had been sentenced to death in absentia, but there are still four of the criminals left, against whom the informant had not informed. The destruction of my family is imminent, unless Athens learns what really happened. Therefore, I decide it is better to deprive four men of their country . . . than allow my kinsmen to be put to death unjustly.

Andocides cuts a deal and receives immunity from punishment. He bears witness against the four, plus a number of his own household servants, which he throws in to make his story more believable. All are put to death, except those who flee.[8] Interestingly, one of the people who is acquitted based on Andocides's testimony is another of Socrates's former students, an aristocrat name Kritias, who will play a prominent role in later events. Andocides was in a very difficult position, and he did what he had to do to save his family. To be clear, Andocides saves his family by repeating something he says he heard from someone else. Interestingly enough, the two chief accusers, the slave and the foreigner, who got this whole mess started, receive payment of ten thousand drachmae and one thousand drachmae, respectively, for their testimony.[9] Officially this money comes from the state. But Callias, the richest man in Athens, is very good at spending money to get what he wants.

At the end of all these trials—with torture, banishments, and executions—Athens thinks it has a very clear understanding of what happened with the profanation of the Eleusinian Mysteries and the mutilation of the Hermes sculptures, and, most importantly, who was responsible for this conspiracy—Alcibiades. The enemies of Alcibiades, who had attacked him before he sailed, continued their machinations and stirred the people against him.[10] The ancient source doesn't say who the enemies of Alcibiades are, but we can understand that they are Callias and his subordinates.

Profanation is his purview.

17

Trouble in Sicily

Meanwhile, the Sicilian Expedition continues to have difficulty securing allies. After being turned away at Messenè, Alcibiades next sails to Naxos, where he is at least received into the city to make his case, which is an improvement, but Naxos's officials are unwilling to join the Athenian cause. He then sails to Catana, but they refuse him admission. Unbeknownst to Alcibiades, the Syracusans are already within Catana's walls.[1] Gaining allies who hold strategic points in Sicily is becoming a mounting difficulty. Alcibiades's plan is not working. The Athenians force their way onto land and set up camp outside the walls of Catana. A detachment of ten ships is sent to scope out the Syracusan defenses, and they return to report that the Syracusans do not have a navy in defensive position.

The entire Athenian fleet rows toward Syracuse. The armada is an incredibly intimidating sight, like none anyone had ever seen. We can only imagine what the Syracusans thought upon seeing the Athenians come into view, but they must have felt some level of shock, even though they had heard of its coming, and maybe even despair as they frantically rush soldiers to defensive positions.

The onslaught has come.

The Syracusans mobilize in a swift, preplanned frenzy.

Lay low, stay quiet.

Lure the Athenians into a trap.

The massive Athenian fleet slowly crosses the face of Syracuse's harbor.

The Syracusans wait for the Athenians to turn and enter the harbor, but the Athenian fleet never slows down or redirects. It just keeps moving, slowly disappearing from view around the bend. What are the Athenians up to? The Syracusans are both relieved that Athens has not launched a full-frontal assault but also deeply suspicious of what the Athenians are doing. The Athenians are famous for their feints and misdirection ploys. Syracuse must remain vigilant: the Athenians will come at them at some point. But how, from where, and when?

The Athenians land at nearby Camarina and try to persuade the Camarinaeans to join them in their conquest of Syracuse. They turn the Athenians away, just like so many others. Alcibiades's plan of attack is clearly not operationally feasible and needs to be abandoned; the generals must devise another approach. The problem is the three Athenian generals have different ideas and objectives. General Lamachus has always preferred the idea of a direct assault. The Athenian fleet makes landfall on the outskirts of Syracuse, perhaps so their leadership can devise a clear strategy or possibly to attack. As the first wave of Athenians disembark, the Syracusan cavalry sweeps in and kills a number of Athenian sailors on the beach, forcing the Athenians back onto their ships.[2] The mighty Athenian fleet is hamstrung by a lack of a well-defined and coordinated plan. They just keep sailing around, knocking on doors, like bad door-to-door salesmen, and are turned away as often. The deflated fleet rows back to Catana to regroup. This day has not gone their way.

The generals will need to meet as soon as they get back to camp at Catana. Along the way each general—Nicias, Alcibiades, and Lamachus—turns over in his mind what he will say to his counterparts, mentally going over arguments and counterarguments for how best to proceed. Alcibiades's mind is spinning the fastest. He is the youngest and least experienced general. Nicias had publicly said that Alcibiades wasn't ready to take command, and the failure of his plan has proven Nicias's point. This stings. Alcibiades needs to come up with a way to save face.

The fleet arrives back at Catana, with the generals focused on the coming task of negotiating a way forward. An official Athenian vessel is waiting for them. Perhaps there is news from Athens. The three generals meet the Athenian officials on shore. They read an order from the Athenian Assembly: Alcibiades's command is revoked. He is under arrest on the charge of profaning the Eleusinian Mysteries and is to be brought back to Athens to stand trial.

This is a tense moment.

It has to be handled with finesse, because the authorities in Athens are afraid of mutiny and do not want the troops upset or demoralized. Nor could Alcibiades turn his soldiers against the arresting officers because Nicias and Lamachus are both present and now officially in command of the entire army. Alcibiades is outnumbered and trapped. To avoid a disruptive scene, Alcibiades is not taken into custody per se, but rather ordered to have his boat follow the arresting officers' boat back to Athens. They depart Catana with Alcibiades's boat dutifully trailing behind.

Nicias couldn't be any happier to see Alcibiades go. From here on out, it will be his show.

The stopping-over point on the long voyage back to Athens is a port town called Thurii, and Alcibiades surmises that when they land at Thurii, he will be transferred to the officers' boat, where he will be kept under lock and key. Once on that boat, his fate will be sealed. Alcibiades has to act fast if he wants to escape the wrath of goddesses, or better stated, the vengeance of his "half" brother Callias. The ancient sources provide only an incomplete explanation of what happens next.[3] We might envision that when the two boats draw near to Thurii, the officers' ship docks first and the arresting officers jump ashore and position themselves to seize Alcibiades when he disembarks. On deck, Alcibiades quickly surrounds himself with his crew as his boat slides in next to the officers' ship. Alcibiades doffs his aristocratic robes and, slinking down, orders his crew to disembark en

masse. The officers wade into the group to seize Alcibiades, but in the confusion, Alcibiades deftly slips off. The ancient source text offers only that
Alcibiades "disappeared" into the bustling dock.[4] The arresting officers
scramble to find him.[5] They will be in tremendous trouble if they return
to Athens empty-handed.

The hunt for Alcibiades is on.

Back in Sicily, Generals Nicias and Lamachus realign the forces,
with each taking control of one half of the fleet. With Alcibiades no
longer present, Nicias becomes the de facto leader of the expedition. He
is relieved to be rid of the rash Alcibiades. The fleet sets off to follow
Nicias's original course of action: subdue Silenus and secure payment
from Egesta.[6] Along the way they try to dock at a place called Himera,
because the populace is of Greek origin, but are turned away, so they
move on to Hyccara and sack it, capturing the population and eventually
selling them into slavery for 120 talents. The Athenians give Hyccara
over to the Egestaeans.[7] Next, Nicias sails to Egesta proper and forces
them to pay him thirty talents of silver to cover some of the cost of the
expedition, which was originally taken on their behalf.[8] Nicias takes
the entire Athenian force back to Catana and, for reasons that seem difficult to fathom, has them sit there doing nothing. Nicias's original plan
was to get the money from Egesta and head back to Athens with the fleet
intact, ready to defend Athens from Sparta, but with Alcibiades out of the
way, he now sees an opportunity to earn the glory of victory for himself
alone. (Lamachus is rather a sidenote at this point.) If Nicias wins, he
won't have to share the honors with Alcibiades, who would surely have
painted himself the hero. But as Nicias turns over in his mind whether
to go back to Athens or press on with the attack of Syracuse, which as
you will remember he was against from the outset, his inaction causes
dissension among his soldiers. They came to fight, after all. Even the
Syracusans, who were once terrified at the prospect of an Athenian assault
on their city, begin to ride by the Athenian camp on horseback and goad
the listless Athenians: "Are you just going to settle down here near your
good friends, we Syracusans?"[9] The Athenian infantrymen are incensed.

As the Sicilian Expedition nears a pivotal point, the arresting officers in Thurii call off their fruitless search for Alcibiades. He is nowhere to be found. They return to Athens and give a report to the council. His trial proceeds without him. His official charges are on record:[10]

> Alcibiades is impeached for committing crimes against the goddesses of Eleusis, Demeter and Persephone, by mimicking the Mysteries and showing them forth to his companions in his own house, wearing a robe such as the High Priest wears when he shows forth the sacred secrets to the initiates, and calling himself High Priest . . . and hailing the rest of his companions as initiates, contrary to the laws and institutions of the Heralds and Priests of Eleusis.

Callias is not mentioned by name, of course, only by his title, Priest of Eleusis. It's the laws of the holy rites that he enforces. Under the rules of Athenian legal procedure, fleeing from trial is considered an admission of guilt. Alcibiades is summarily sentenced to death in absentia. His case goes by default, his property is confiscated, and it is decreed that his name be publicly cursed by all priests and priestesses.[11] Callias takes great pleasure in issuing a curse against Alcibiades.

Alcibiades is in trouble, and in time, that trouble will reflect onto Socrates as his former teacher, even though Alcibiades's actions are in complete opposition to Socrates's teachings. A teacher is often given credit for the accomplishments of good students—for Socrates, that's Plato—but also gets blamed for the bad ones. This applies across time, even to teachers teaching today.

Alcibiades, who's in hiding, receives news of his death sentence back in Athens.

ALCIBIADES: (*sneering*) I will make them feel that I am alive.[12]

18

Ruse in Syracuse

N icias, sitting with his army at Catana and his fleet at anchor, finally decides, perhaps at too great a length, to stay in Sicily and attack the walled city of Syracuse. But to do this, he needs to find a way to seize an advantageous topographical position from which to launch an assault. He has his eye on the grounds near the temple of Olympian Zeus, which lies just outside the walls of Syracuse proper.[1] The area around the temple is protected by walls, structures, trees, and a marsh on one side and by a line of cliffs on the other.[2] This site neutralizes Syracuse's cavalry advantage—horses can't climb walls or cliffs—while allowing the Athenians an ideal position for launching a siege of the city. The Athenians have the superior navy and numbers but do not have sufficient horses, and the Syracusans have a superior cavalry and homefield advantage. The problem for Nicias is how to get to the grounds of the temple of Olympian Zeus. If the Athenian fleet sails directly to Syracuse and disembarks on the beach, the Syracusan cavalry will cut Nicias's men down before they can reach the defensible land around the temple.[3] If he marches his army overland from Catana to Syracuse, they will be exposed on land and the Syracusan cavalry will, likewise, slaughter his troops.[4] With no obvious way to take the grounds of the temple of Olympian Zeus by force, Nicias devises a deception.[5]

Nicias selects a man from Catana whom he has reason to trust, but is also someone the Syracusans trust.[6] Nicias sends the man to Syracuse to present a plan to eliminate the Athenians. He tells the Syracusans that the Athenians sleep within the city of Catana every night but leave their weapons and a few soldiers outside at their camp. He proposes that if the Syracusans come with their whole force at dawn and attack the troops left in the camp, their partisans in Catana would shut the Athenians up in the town and burn all their ships. Syracuse could then attack the weaponless and boatless Athenians trapped inside Catana.[7] The Syracusan leaders are already looking for a way to attack the Athenians' camp and had already envisioned marching on Catana. They quickly fix a date to attack and send the man back to Catana to coordinate the attack with his supposed comrades.[8]

As the appointed day draws near, the Syracusans make the long march to Catana. The night before the planned dawn attack, the Syracusans camp near Catana but out of sight, by the river. The Athenians are, of course, aware of the Syracusans coming, and just before nightfall, they load their entire force onto their fleet and sail to Syracuse.[9] At dawn, at just about the same moment the Syracusan horsemen arrive in Catana to find the Athenians absent, the Athenians are disembarking in Syracuse opposite the temple of Olympian Zeus.[10] The Athenians easily seize the undefended temple grounds and quickly fall in constructing fortifications of earth, stone, and timber, as well as palisades to protect their ships.[11] Back at Catana, the Syracusan generals realize they've been tricked and order the entire Syracuse army, infantry and cavalry alike, to make a mad dash back to Syracuse in hopes of protecting their city.[12] By the time the Syracusan army arrives back at Syracuse, they are completely exhausted. The Athenian camp is already well fortified and preparing their attack. Nicias addresses the Athenians.[13]

> NICIAS: Soldiers, is there any need for a long exhortation when we are all united in the same cause? The mere sight of this great

army is more likely to put courage into you than an eloquent speech . . . The presence of so many brave comrades must inspire every one of us with a good hope of victory, especially when we reflect that our opponents are not like ourselves, not selected soldiers like us, but a group of mostly civilians thrown together to meet us? They are Sicilians, who, although they may despise us, will not stand their ground against us; for their skill is not equal to their courage. Consider again that we are far from home, and that there is no friendly land nearby except what you can win with your swords. The generals of the enemy, as I know well, are appealing to very different motives. They say to them, "You are fighting for your own country," but I say to you that you are fighting in a country which is not your own, and from which, if you do not conquer, retreat will be impossible, for swarms of cavalry will follow at your heels. Remember your own reputation, and charge valiantly, deeming the difficulties and necessities of your position to be more formidable than the enemy.

Nicias's point is that his army has no choice but to succeed. They are far away from home, and in some ways, they are more desperate than even the Syracusans and should therefore make battle with as much, if not more, spirit than the Syracusans. Nicias has an army of professionals, better trained, better armed, and overwhelming in number. He knows he will win this battle. His methodical approach to war, only engaging the enemy when he knows he has the best chance to prevail, references back to his discussion with Socrates earlier about the definition of courage. To Nicias, courage involves a fair dose of wisdom: courage is the knowledge of what to avoid and what to venture in war.

The trumpets blare, and Nicias leads the charge.

The weary Syracusans are in disarray and unprepared for the onslaught of the Athenians.[14] The Athenians advance in lockstep, as the Syracusans come running from every direction to join their formations. Teams of archers, slingers, and stone throwers launch projectiles. The two armies meet in a violent clash. The Syracusans fight for their country—every man for life now, and liberty hereafter—while the Athenians aim to gain a new country and to save the old from the disaster of defeat; on either side the only chance of life is victory.[15] The Syracusans put up a stubborn and determined resistance. Then comes lightning, thunder, and a deluge of rain, and the discipline of the Athenians is to their gain.[16] The Athenians first push back the inexperienced Syracusan left wing and then the right, collapsing the center and forcing them to take flight. When the fleeing Syracusans reach level ground, their cavalry sweeps in, a thunder of hooves striking the muddy ground, and holds off the Athenians long enough for the frantic Syracusan soldiers to make it back within the safety of the walls of Syracuse.[17] The Athenians return to their camp by the temple of Olympian Zeus and celebrate their victory while Syracusans try to come to terms with their defeat. They must confront their now untenable situation.

The enemy is at the gates.

19

Turning Traitor

Just as Nicias is using his tactical brilliance to put the Athenian army in a position to subdue Syracuse (taking the land around the temple of Olympian Zeus is something like mate in chess), Alcibiades is in his hideout, searching for options to his seemingly insurmountable problems. There is no way for him to return to Athens with the Eleusinian death sentence hanging over him, and neither can he rejoin the Athenian army in Syracuse, as they will know of his conviction and will likely execute him on the spot. He also can't stay put for too long; Callias's network will eventually find him and drag him back to Athens. Alcibiades has to make a move, and it needs to be beyond the reach of Callias.

Alcibiades sends a message to Sparta, Athens's dread enemy, asking them to take him in. He offers to make amends for all the harm he has done to Sparta in the past.[1] Sparta likely knows about Alcibiades's conviction on the charges of profaning the Eleusinian Mysteries and senses an opportunity to use his bitterness toward his homeland to flip him. Alcibiades, after all, has information Sparta can use.

Sparta responds with a message granting him safe passage.

Alcibiades defects to Sparta.[2]

The Spartans welcome Alcibiades. He swiftly conforms to Spartan ways, which are far more austere than the luxurious lifestyle he had once enjoyed in Athens. Like the Spartans, he takes cold baths and lets his beard and hair grow out.[3] He adopts the Spartan zeal for physical training and embraces their simplicity of life and severity of countenance.[4] He even eats their infamous black soup, which is a distasteful concoction of boiled meat, blood, salt, and vinegar. Legend has it that when one non-Spartan tasted black soup for the first time he said, "Now I know why Spartans aren't afraid to die." Black soup is that ghastly. The Spartans are amazed at Alcibiades's transformation and admire him for it: he becomes more Spartan than most Spartans. Alcibiades has one power that transcends all others, a useful tool for influencing people, the ability to assimilate and adapt himself to the pursuits and lives of others, thereby assuming more quick changes than a chameleon.[5] In this way, Alcibiades is able to win over the Spartans and become a respected and influential person.[6]

The very idea that a person would turn against his own people is the antithesis of Socrates's teachings on ethics and duty, but Alcibiades had long since broken away from Socrates. Alcibiades's ethic, if it can be called that at all, is one of utter ruthlessness. No deceit or treachery is beyond Alcibiades, not even joining Sparta, the sworn enemy of Athens. You see, as much as Socrates had once taught Alcibiades, Alcibiades taught Socrates an important lesson: virtue cannot be taught. Despite Socrates's best efforts, Alcibiades is entirely amoral.

This is one lesson the student teaches the master.

20

Boa Constrictor

Back in Syracuse, the Athenians collect the dead from the battlefield. They build a pyre for their own dead and return the Syracusan dead under a flag of truce. The Syracusans have lost about 260 men and the Athenians fewer than 50 men.[1] Nicias, ever the preparer, sends his ships out to collect supplies from other parts of Sicily and money and horses from Athens.[2] Even though he was victorious, he doesn't like Syracuse's calvary advantage and wants to acquire enough horses to at least match them, if not overwhelm them. Recall his discussion with Socrates, where he defined courage as knowing what to avoid and what to risk in war. His modus operandi is to make sure he's going to win before stepping foot on the battlefield. The Syracusans, for their part, call an assembly and resolve to reorganize their military structure and intensify drills and training.[3] They plan to be better prepared when the next assault comes.

Both the Athenians and the Syracusans send out envoys to other cities in Sicily in an attempt to gather support and forge alliances for the next phase of the war. As it so happens, both sets of envoys are at the city of Camarina at the same time and make their cases one after the other:[4]

SYRACUSAN ENVOY: We are here, Camarinaeans, not because we suppose the presence of the Athenian army is frightening, but because we are more afraid of their as-yet-unspoken words, which you may too readily believe if you hear them without first hearing us. You know the stated pretext on which they have come to Sicily, but we can only guess at their real intentions. If I am not mistaken, they want, not to just restore the Leontines to their city, but to drive us out of ours . . . We know the Athenians have reduced many peoples to slavery because those people would not stand together . . . Are we waiting until our cities are taken one by one, when we know that this is the only way in which we can be conquered? . . . If anyone thinks that not he, but the Syracusan, is the enemy of the Athenian, and asks indignantly, "Why should I risk myself for you?" let him consider that in fighting for my country he will be at the same time fighting in mine for his own. And he will fight with less danger, because I shall still be at his side . . . For though in name you may be saving me, in reality you will be saving yourselves. And you especially, Camarinaeans, who are our neighbor, and on whom the danger will fall next, should have anticipated all this, and not be so careless in your alliances . . . You must make a stand against them. And do not be afraid of their armament. There is no danger if we hold together—the danger is in disunion . . . If the Athenians subdue us, your decision will have helped them win the day; but the honor will be all their own, and you, the contributors to their victory, will be the prize of their next victory . . .

The Syracusan envoy speaks compelling words about Athenian intentions and their long history of dividing and conquering other territories. How will the Athenians respond to such seemingly persuasive arguments?[5]

ATHENIAN ENVOY: We have come to renew our former alliance with Camarina, but the verbal attack made against us by the Syracusan envoy makes it necessary for us to vindicate ourselves first . . . Our presence here is for your benefit as well as for ours. This we will prove to you; and our proofs shall be drawn from the slanders of the Syracusans . . . For we desire by the help of our friends to secure our position in Sicily. And we have not come to enslave you, but to save you from being enslaved. Let no one imagine that your welfare is no business of ours, for if you are preserved, and are strong enough to hold out against the Syracusans, they will be less likely to aid our enemies back home and injure us . . . And now they have the impudence to stir you up against those who resist them, and have thus far saved Sicily from coming under their yoke. As if you had no eyes! Far more real than the security offered by them is that to which we invite you, a security which we and you gain from one another, and we beseech you not to throw away. Reflect: the Syracusans are so numerous that with or without allies they can always find their way to you, but you will not often have the chance of defending yourself with the aid of an army such as ours . . . Do not reject the common salvation which is offered to you at this moment, as well as to all who seek it, but following the example of your fellow Sicilians and join with us, and instead of having always to watch the Syracusans, assert your equality and threaten them as they have long been threatening you.

The Camarinaeans have a dilemma. They need to cast their lot with the side that is most likely to win, but from their perspective the final outcome of a battle between these two great armies is far from clear. They might naturally side with the Syracusans, but Athens's recent victory gives them some hesitation.[6] The Camarinaeans decide that since the two are at war with each other, the best way to keep their oaths to each is to assist neither.[7] Camarinaean support would have helped either side significantly, whereas

Camarinaean neutrality helps Athens more. The greater number of other cities in Sicily that won't come to the aid of Syracuse, the easier it will be for Athens to defeat Syracuse.

From here, there ensues a steady drumbeat of more negotiations, backdoor communications, skullduggery, outright lies, troop movements, and occasional skirmishes. Ultimately, Nicias seizes even more land around Syracuse. He has his troops build a protective wall of their own.[8] But oddly the building crews go beyond their actual position and keep extending the wall around Syracuse. Nicias's Athenian army slowly wraps itself around Syracuse, not unlike a giant boa constrictor around its prey. Once the Syracusans realize they are being walled in, trapped for a final siege, they furiously try to build an intercepting wall of their own to block the progress of the Athenian wall.[9] Envision two enemy construction crews in a desperate race against each other. There are constant skirmishes as each side tries to slow down the other's wall-building crews.

The Athenians are well positioned for final victory, but they have not escaped the ill omens of the gods and goddesses. Nicias, the ever-able leader of the Athenian army, is suddenly struck with a debilitating case of kidney stones.[10] The excruciating pain draws his attention inward and away from the coming battle. He remains in his tent, lying on his mat, flush and perspiring. General Lamachus is then in charge of the construction crews and the soldiers. Lamachus is imprudently out beyond the wall by himself, inspecting the progress, when he is set upon by a detail of Syracusans.[11] Lamachus and a Syracusan soldier end up landing mortal blows on each other simultaneously.[12] They fall beside each other, and the other Syracusans scoop up Lamachus's body and armor and take it back with them to Syracuse as a trophy[13] This leaves a debilitated Nicias as the Athenian army's sole remaining general.

Even though Nicias is in unbearable physical pain from the kidney stones and feeling the loss of Lamachus, he has reason to be almost buoyant about the prospects of victory.[14] He has Syracuse in his grasp, and some other Sicilian cities, seeing that Athens is about to defeat Syracuse, are coming to his side. He also has large shipments of supplies coming in from every quarter.[15] Even more, the Syracusans are sending secret messages to him with treaty proposals.[16] He has his own staff receive the messages and deliver them to him, as he cannot let the Syracusans see how very ill he is. He must, as a leader, project power, so he hides from view, which, in a way, makes him even more ominous to the Syracusans. Nicias has every reason to believe that the Syracusans, who are afraid of certain defeat and enslavement in the coming siege, will surrender within days, if not hours, and he will soon be able to sail back to Athens triumphant.

If only he could just pee.

21

Treachery

Meanwhile, back in Sparta, Alcibiades is set to address King Agis, his generals, and the entire Spartan command. A wall of grave, bearded faces stare at him. The austerity of the scene seems to befit the gravity of the matter at hand. This is the moment for which Alcibiades was granted admittance into Sparta.[1]

> ALCIBIADES: I must endeavor first of all to remove any prejudice you may have against me, because you may be suspicious of me, and might turn a deaf ear to considerations of public interest . . . When you were making peace with Athens you negotiated through my enemy [Nicias], thereby conferring power on him, and bringing dishonor upon me. And if I then turned to the Mantineans and Argives and opposed you in that or in any other way, you were rightly served, and anyone who while the wound was recent may have been unduly exasperated against me should now take another and a truer view . . .
>
> There were manipulators, as there always have been, who led the people into evil ways, and it was they [Callias] who drove me out . . .

And now I will speak to you of the matter which you have in hand, and about which I, insofar as I have better information, am bound to instruct you. We Athenians sailed to Sicily hoping in the first place to conquer the Sicilian cities; then to proceed against Italy; and lastly, to make an attempt on the Carthaginian dominions, and on Carthage itself. If all or most of these enterprises succeeded, we meant finally to attack Sparta, bringing with us the whole Athenian power which we had gained abroad . . . We meant to build numerous additional triremes, with the timber which Italy supplies in such abundance, and with those boats blockade Sparta. At the same time making inroads by land with our infantry, we should have stormed some of your cities. Thus, we hoped to crush you easily, and to rule over the Greek world. For the better accomplishment of our various aims our newly acquired territory would supply money and provisions enough, apart from the revenue which we receive in Greece. You have heard the objects of our expedition from the one who knows them best. The Athenian generals who remain will persevere and carry them out if they can. And now let me prove to you that if you do not come to the rescue Sicily will be lost . . . . The Syracusans alone, whose whole forces have been already defeated, and who cannot move freely at sea, will be unable to withstand the power which the Athenians already have on the spot. And Syracuse once taken, the whole of Sicily is in Athens's hands; the subjugation of Italy will follow; and the danger which, as I was saying, threatens you from that quarter, will speedily overwhelm you. And therefore remember, every one of you that the safety, not of Sicily alone, but of Sparta, is at stake. No time should be lost. You must send to Sicily a force of soldiers who will themselves handle the oars and will take the field immediately on landing.

Alcibiades specifically suggests that Gylippus be named commander and that he go to Syracuse immediately and crush Nicias's Athenian army before it's too late.[2] It is difficult to determine how much of Alcibiades's advice is motivated by overall military strategy and how much by his jealousy of Nicias, or his bruised ego, as in "if I can't be the hero of Athens, then I'll make sure that no one is," or his rage at being sentenced to death by Athens, and specifically Callias. But suffice it to say, these emotions serve as undercurrents to Alcibiades's professed intentions.

Next, Alcibiades explains his rationale for helping Sparta:[3]

ALCIBIADES: How far these plans are executed, and with how much speed and energy, Sparta, depends on you; for I am confident that they are practicable, and I am not likely to be mistaken. In fairness, you shouldn't think the worse of me because, having once been a distinguished lover of my country, I now cast my lot with her worst foe and attack her with all my might; or suspect that I speak only with the eagerness of an exile. I am an exile indeed, but I have lost an ungrateful country, but I have not lost the power of doing you service, if you will listen to me. The true enemies of my country are not those who, like you, have injured her in open war, but those who have compelled her friends to become her enemies. I love Athens, not insofar as I am wronged by her, but insofar as I once enjoyed the privileges of a citizen. The country which I am attacking is no longer mine, but a lost country which I am seeking to regain. He is the true patriot, not who, when unjustly exiled, abstains from attacking his country, but who in the warmth of his affection seeks to recover her without regard to the means. I desire therefore that you, Spartans, will use me without scruple in any service however difficult or dangerous, remembering that, according to the familiar saying, "the more harm I did you as an enemy, the more good can I do you as a friend." For I know the secrets of the Athenians. Remember the immense importance of your present decision, and do not hesitate to send an expedition to Sicily. By dispatching a fraction of your forces to co-operate

in Sicily you may save great interests, and may overthrow the
Athenian power once and forever. And so henceforward you may
dwell safely yourselves and be leaders of all of Greece.

Alcibiades intends to regain his country and makes the claim that a
true patriot is willing to attack his own country out of a "warmth of his
affection." The very idea that doing evil to fellow Athenians, even killing
them by whatever means necessary, is somehow an expression of caring is
deeply twisted and indicative of how Alcibiades's mind functions. Athens
has injured Alcibiades, and now to prove his love, he will injure them back.
I would like to remind you, the reader, the reason we are following Alcibiades is that Socrates, his former teacher, will be blamed, whether rightly
or wrongly, for his misdeeds. It is important to understand the reasons for
the wrath that will be later directed at Socrates.

Regardless of Alcibiades's motives, the Spartans see an advantage in it
for themselves and enthusiastically adopt Alcibiades's plan. The Spartan
forces are quickly dispatched to Syracuse under the command of Gylippus.
They land in Sicily at the farthest point from Syracuse.[4] Here they follow
Alcibiades's original plan of attack from when he was an Athenian general, except this time the target is not Syracuse itself but the Athenians
surrounding Syracuse. Gylippus assembles an ever-increasing force from
local tribes as he stealthily and swiftly moves toward Syracuse.

He is a tsunami coming in the deep of night.

22

The Tide Turns

A dispirited Syracusan Assembly meets to discuss the details and wording of the final capitulation agreement being made with Nicias.[1] A messenger comes rushing in and tells the Assembly that the Spartans have sent an army to aid them and that Gylippus will be arriving shortly.[2] The Syracusans leap to their feet to meet the Spartans. Gylippus is a man of singular focus and marches his army directly at the unsuspecting Athenian encampment, which at this point sits safely behind a more than two-kilometer (a mile and a half) long wall. Gylippus stops short and in an act of supreme confidence sends a messenger to tell Nicias that the Spartans will grant the Athenians a truce and safe passage back to Athens, if the Athenians will leave Syracuse as soon as possible.[3] Nicias, doubled over in pain, hears the relayed message but makes no reply. He doesn't have to. He is not a man prone to quick decisions anyway, and he is safely protected by his long wall. Gylippus establishes his camp where he can keep an eye on the Athenians. He notes the Syracusans are in disarray, so he takes them under his command and organizes them to better effect.[4]

Nicias is deeply disturbed by the sudden appearance of the Spartan forces. He is so close to defeating Syracuse, and now he faces a truly formidable foe in Gylippus. Nicias has taken too much time, his personality and the kidney stones to blame for the slow progress.

He is, however, an assiduous planner and sends a message back to Athens calling for reinforcements.[5] Athens quickly sends a small fleet, with a larger one to follow as soon as possible.[6] While Nicias sits and waits for more reinforcements, Gylippus seizes a nearby but outlying Athenian garrison that holds its stores of food, supplies, and monies. This cuts off the Athenians' supply chain.[7] Gylippus is a strategic nightmare for Nicias. Next, Gylippus attacks and destroys some of Athens's ships in the harbor.[8] Nicias, as always, holds his cards, not overly exposing his troops to danger, which seems a poor ploy in the face of an aggressive and surgically strategic adversary. That is, until the Athenian reinforcements arrive under the command of Demosthenes: seventy-three ships of war, five thousand fresh soldiers, and three thousand archers, javelineers, and slingers.[9] The sight of his tremendous fleet surely disheartens the Syracusans and Spartans.

In the Athenian camp a dispute arises between Demosthenes and Nicias. Demosthenes wants to attack at once, and Nicias wants to wait, as per usual. The other leaders side with Demosthenes, and he launches a surprise night attack on the Spartan position. Demosthenes's infantry slays the first group they encounter and presses on, but meets stiffer resistance as they advance.[10] The leading edge of the Athenian attack starts to take heavy casualties, and some turn to retreat, but they run into the advancing Athenian rear guard, who because of the darkness cannot distinguish friend from foe, and Athenians end up fighting other Athenians. Panic and confusion spread.[11] They thrash out violently in the darkness. The curse of the gods—Hermes, Demeter, and Persephone—is upon them. The bewildered Athenians give ground, and the Spartans attack from all sides. The Athenians scatter in every direction. Some of the Athenians die at the hands of their pursuers, others by one another's hands, and still others by plunging down the cliffs.[12] When dawn comes, the scattered and wandering Athenians are overtaken and cut to pieces by the Syracusan horsemen. All told, Demosthenes loses two thousand soldiers in his ill-fated nighttime raid.[13]

Nicias is furious but also physically feeble.

The Athenian generals meet to try to figure out what to do next. The defeated Demosthenes now just wants to sail back to Athens, which in retrospect might have been the best course of action, but an eclipse occurs and the generals are so spooked that they decide to wait another lunar cycle before making a move. These are very superstitious times. In a turn of even worse luck, sickness spreads through the Athenian camp.[14] Soldiers get fevers, chills, fatigue, aches, nausea, and vomiting. They are probably suffering from some combination of cholera and malaria, but at this moment in history the sickness is seen only as the disfavor of the gods, the profanation of the Eleusinian Mysteries and the mutilation of the Hermes sculptures still hovering over the expedition. The soldiers can hardly stand up, much less fight. The stench of contagion and fetid bodily fluids permeate the camp.

Nicias takes more time, too much time, but he has no choice. He needs for his men to recover. Gylippus takes advantage of the moment and has his ships seal off the entrance to the harbor, blocking in the Athenian fleet. He then launches a full-out attack on the Athenian ships in the harbor, and Nicias is forced to rush his sick troops down to the shore to protect the fleet.[15] The Athenians fight valiantly, but they are just too ill, and Gylippus routs them and tows away their surviving ships.[16] Athens's vaunted navy has failed, the harbor is blocked, and the sickened army of Nicias is now trapped on land and sits exposed. The ailing Athenians have no choice but to try to make an escape overland.[17] Nicias, still racked by kidney stones, is a pitiful sight but draws the fortitude to stand tall and lead his troops onward.[18] Gylippus swiftly has his men cut off the Athenian escape route: they occupy roads, fortify river crossings, cut away bridges, and post their cavalry in flat open ground.[19] The Athenians are forced across ever rougher terrain, and their line gets strung out as the ill fall behind. The Spartans pick off the stragglers one by one. The detachment under Demosthenes can't keep up and is captured.[20] The bedraggled Athenians march for eight straight days without water. I can't imagine how Nicias was able to do this. Thoughts of his original arguments against the Sicilian Expedition and his well-reasoned explanations for why it would fail echo in his mind as he leads his beleaguered men.[21]

Nicias sends a messenger to Gylippus to propose a truce, which would permit the Athenians to peacefully leave Sicily in exchange for handing any hostages back over to the Syracusans and offering to repay them for all the expenses they incurred for the war.[22] Gylippus does not entertain the proposal and makes no reply, in much the same way that Nicias did not reply to Gylippus's original offer to let the Athenians leave Syracuse. Nicias understands the situation.

The desperate Athenians arrive at a river and abandon all order as they fall to their knees to slake their driving thirst. The forces of Gylippus ambush them and butcher them as they drink. Savage carnage rages, and the river runs red with blood. Nicias falls down at the feet of Gylippus and cries:[23]

> NICIAS: Have pity, Gylippus, now that you are victorious, not on me at all, though my great successes have brought me name and fame, but on the rest of these Athenians. Remember that the fortunes of war are common to all, and that the Athenians, when we were in good fortune, used it with moderation and gentleness toward you.

Gylippus feels some compunction, because he remembers that the Spartans were treated fairly by Nicias when the Peace of Nicias was made, and besides, he thinks it would increase his own fame if he should bring home alive the Athenian generals he had defeated.[24]

Gylippus raises up Nicias and gives him his word.[25]

The Syracusans, however, do not care what Gylippus has agreed to, and after some debate, they execute Nicias and the other Athenian commanders. Nicias's dead, emaciated body is thrown out into the road.[26] Animals pick it apart. Flies lay eggs in his flesh. The remainder of the Athenians troops are put into stone quarries and die of disease and starvation, except for those who are sold into slavery.[27] Almost none of the soldiers make it back to Athens alive. All told, Athens loses more than two hundred ships, its best generals, more than fourteen thousand soldiers, and perhaps as many as thirty thousand rowers.

The Athenian expedition to Sicily is a total loss.

The Athenian expedition had been Alcibiades's idea originally, but he won the war for the other side, for Sicily, by sending the Spartans to the aid of Syracuse. Alcibiades may not have physically fought in Sicily, but he is still largely responsible for Athens's defeat. Nicias and Athens had been on the cusp of victory, in fact mere hours from Syracuse's total surrender, when the Spartans intervened and caused the eventual destruction of the entire Athenian army. The elimination of the able commander and statesman Nicias was a personal objective of Alcibiades. Mission accomplished. But at such a terrible cost.

As a reminder, the reason we are following Alcibiades is because Socrates will eventually be blamed for Alcibiades's treachery. As his former teacher, Socrates will be an easy target for Athens's anger. Those tens of thousands of dead Athenian soldiers had families.

23

Double Betrayal

Alcibiades's strategic advice to Sparta, however, does not stop with coming to the aid of Syracuse. He adds other prongs to his plan to take revenge on his home city of Athens:[1]

ALCIBIADES: . . . You should also fortify Decelea. The Athenians are always in particular dread of this. To them it seems to be the only peril they have not faced in the course of war. And the way to hurt an enemy most surely is to inform yourself exactly about the weak points of which you see that he is conscious, and strike at them. For every man is likely to know best himself the dangers which he has most to fear. I will sum up briefly the chief though by no means all the advantages which you will gain, and the disadvantages which you will inflict, by the fortification of Decelea. The whole wealth of Athens will fall into your hands. The slaves will come over to you of their own accord; what there is besides will be seized by you. The Athenians will at once be deprived of the revenues which they obtain from the silver mines of Laurium, and of all the profits

which they make by the land, and above all, the customary
tribute will cease to flow in . . .

Decelea is about eighteen kilometers (eleven miles) north of Athens. It
sits at the entrance to a pass through the Parnes Mountains and overlooks
the Athenian plain, occupying a logistically critical juncture to a number of
Athenian enterprises. If the Spartans can occupy it, as Alcibiades suggests,
it will cause major disruptions to Athenian life: Athens's access to its silver
mines will be cut off, depriving Athens of its source of wealth. The slaves
who work the mines will be able to flee. Remember who the largest owner
of Athens's silver mine concession is: Callias. Those slaves belong to him.
Alcibiades's plan will injure Athens in general, but pointedly, it specifically targets the source of Callias's wealth. By controlling the trade routes
near Decelea, Sparta will also be able to reduce the amount of tribute that
can flow into Athens from adjoining states. Without access to silver and
diminished tribute, Athens will have great difficulty raising the money to
rebuild its navy. This is of huge strategic value to Sparta. But it's not just
money that flows through the area, it is also the path by which crops and
livestock are delivered to Athens. Spartan control of Decelea will cut off
Athens's supply to food.

Once Decelea is in Spartan possession, they will be able to control
other nearby routes across the plain, including the road from Athens
to Eleusis.[2] This is perhaps the most important aspect of the plan from
Alcibiades's perspective, as it cuts off Athens's land route to the temple
of the Mysteries of Eleusis, which is the other major source of Callias's power, and specifically the power Callias used to try to eliminate
Alcibiades. The great pomp and religious significance of the procession
from Athens to Eleusis cannot happen if the Spartans fortify the route.
Alcibiades is giving Sparta strategic guidance, but unbeknownst to
them, he is also using them to take revenge on Callias. Alcibiades will
cut off Callias from his silver mines and Eleusis. Callias will be reduced
to nothing. In Alcibiades's mind this is fair, since Callias used his position with the Eleusinian Mysteries to sentence him to death. These two

"half" brothers use the power of religious, governmental, and military institutions to injure each other.

The final part of Alcibiades's plan is for Sparta to directly attack a weakened Athens.

The Spartan king, Agis, enthusiastically adopts Alcibiades's plan and sets it into action.[3] The Spartans seize Decelea and fortify it. With the total loss of the Athenian forces in Sicily, Athens is depleted, and there is little they can do to stop them. All the provisions that Athens needs now have to come by boat, which takes longer and is more expensive, just at a time when Athens no longer has two of its major sources of income, silver mines and tribute. Spartan ground forces surround Athens and blockade it by land. Food becomes scarce, famine follows, and Athens suffers terribly.[4] Now Sparta is the boa constrictor wrapping itself around Athens. In the daytime, the Athenians guard the battlements by relay, ever concerned the Spartans will attempt to breech the walls, and at night every man is on guard at the gates and on the walls.[5] This includes Socrates, who, like all Athenian males, is guarding the ramparts day and night. Socrates is an ever-vigilant defender of Athens, and it is not lost on him that his Athens is being destroyed at the direction of his former student Alcibiades, a man without virtue. Socrates, as you may recall from Alcibiades's earlier testimonial, has incredible fortitude and stamina, an unnatural ability to go without sleep, rest, and food. He is well-suited to endure the privations of war and defend Athens. Years later, he offers this recollection of the siege:[6]

SOCRATES: During the siege, while others were pitying themselves, I lived in no greater poverty than when the city was at the height of its prosperity. And while others were used to getting delicacies from the market at great cost, I got mine from the sustenance of the soul, which was more sweet than theirs, and procured without expense.

Mind over matter. Socrates can be insufferable, and part of what makes him so unbearable is that he is so often right. It can wear on people's nerves.

In reality, the siege would not have been easy on Socrates despite his fortitude, for one very important reason: his growing three-year-old son needs
to eat and food is scarce.

Callias is also very aware of what Alcibiades has done to him, undercut-
ting Eleusis and depriving him of his money. If Callias survives the siege,
there will be consequences. Between the privation, hunger, and lack of
sleep, Athens is exhausted and on the verge of collapse. Athenians are dying
because of Alcibiades; Athens is dying because of Alcibiades.

As a reminder, the reason that we are following the actions of Alcibiades
is to impress upon you, the reader, why Athenians will have very strong feelings about Alcibiades and why they will eventually look to blame somebody,
anybody, for his treachery. His old teacher Socrates will be a convenient
scapegoat. If Socrates will eventually be blamed for Alcibiades's sins, then
we need to know what Alcibiades's sins were. And there were many.

Just as Athens reaches a most desperate point, a seed planted in a foreign
land shifts the balance. Timaea, the queen of Sparta, is showing unmis-
takable signs of being pregnant. Now, the Spartan king Agis is older and
knows that he hasn't had sex with his wife in some time. King Agis con-
fronts Queen Timaea, and she unabashedly tells him that the child belongs
to Alcibiades.[7] From her perspective she has nothing to be ashamed of; her
needs weren't being met, and there was an incredibly handsome man in
Alcibiades who was willing to serve her. Agis does not take this news very
well: word of his anger swiftly spreads throughout the ranks. Alcibiades
is, however, not in Sparta when his affair with Timaea is revealed; he's at
sea.[8] Orders are issued to the other Spartan generals to capture Alcibiades
and execute him.[9] Alcibiades somehow learns of the orders, perhaps from
Timaea. Fearing for his life, he flees. (Just like he did from Athens.) But
where can he go? He's now under death sentences in both Athenian and
Spartan domains.

All of Greece wants him dead.

24

Persian Power

Alcibiades resurfaces at the court of Tissaphernes, a provincial governor of the powerful Persian Empire, which is ruled by King Darius II.[1] The Persian Empire is headquartered in modern-day Iran but sprawls from the Indus Valley in India to the Balkan Mountains in Europe and across the Levant to Egypt in North Africa. It is among the largest empires the world will ever see, dwarfing Athens and Sparta combined. The Persian Empire has a long-standing interest in expanding to the west, and even tried to conquer Greece twice before, about seventy-five and sixty-five years earlier. The first Persian invasion of Greece included the famous Battle of Marathon, where a smaller Greek force repelled a much larger Persian army. The second Persian invasion of Greece included the famous Battle of Thermopylae, where a small contingent of Greeks, "The 300," held off a Persian army of perhaps more than a hundred thousand soldiers for three days at a narrow pass. Ultimately, the Persian army found a way through and captured much of Greece and burned Athens to the ground. The allied Greeks, including Spartans and Athenians alike, realigned and eventually won victories over Persia at Salamis and Plataea, effectively pushing the Persians out of Greece. This occurred about a decade before Socrates was born, so he would have grown up hearing stories about these events.

Even though the Persian Empire has not invaded Greece for many decades, it still keeps a keen eye on the situation, ever looking for another opportunity. Persia's provincial governor, Tissaphernes, oversees an area of what is now modern-day Turkey, which allows him to monitor his Greek neighbors and meddle in their affairs where possible. Governor Tissaphernes grants an audience to Alcibiades, because Alcibiades has significant information about the current happenings in Greece between Athens and Sparta. Tissaphernes wants intelligence he can use.

The court of Tissaphernes is opulent, the fantastic wealth of the Persian Empire on full display, with impressive architecture and art, extensive gardens, luxurious carpets and pillows, resplendent clothing and jewelry, fine wine and fruits, exotic delicacies and feasts, and a bevy of attendants and courtesans to indulge any appetite. Alcibiades, ever the chameleon, swiftly assimilates to the lavish lifestyle of pomp and excess, which is a stark contrast to the regimented existence he once had in Sparta and even outstrips the aristocratic excess he once enjoyed in Athens.[2] Alcibiades knows how to do pleasure. The ever-watchful Tissaphernes is impressed with how well Alcibiades fits in.

Tissaphernes is renowned for his guile, his cruelty, and, above all, his hatred of the Greeks.[3] Alcibiades incurs very real risk when he updates Tissaphernes on the status of the Athenian/Spartan conflict. His detailed knowledge about what is happening and why, and more importantly how the leaders of both sides think and act makes a strong impression on the hard-hearted Tissaphernes. Alcibiades will be of use. They are, Tissaphernes and Alcibiades, in fact, very alike. Completely ruthless. Alcibiades ingratiates himself to the governor, working his charm on Tissaphernes, and becoming his constant adviser.[4] They become so close that Tissaphernes even names his most beautiful park after Alcibiades.[5] Alcibiades Park—with its stunning gardens, a lovely stream, beautiful meadows, stately pavilions, and exquisite adornments—is a testament to the bond between the two. It even seems like a bit of a romantic gesture, too, but it's unknown whether they had that sort of relationship. In confidence, Alcibiades offers strategic advice to Tissaphernes:[6]

> ALCIBIADES: First, it is to your advantage to let Sparta and Athens wear each other out, so that any future Persian incursion would meet little resistance from the two depleted city-states. The Spartans are now dominating the Athenians, and if Sparta defeats them and subsumes them, they will unite all of Greece under one banner, and Persia will have no possibility of claiming any Greek lands ever; but this danger could be easily averted at a little cost and at no risk to you, Tissaphernes, if you simply foster a more even match between Sparta and Athens so the internal strife in Greece can continue to consume them. You won't even have to commit your own troops, and eventually there will be no one left standing to obstruct your designs . . . Do not let the whole power both by sea and land fall into the same hands, as Sparta is about to accomplish. Let the dominions remain divided—Sparta the army and Athens the navy—then, whichever of the two rivals is troublesome, Persia might always use the other . . . Just extend some well-placed expenditures, on bribes and military pay, increase it here and decrease it there. Weaken Sparta's hold on its territorial possessions just enough to level the competitive balance between Sparta and Athens; left alone and evenly equipped they will kill each other off. Let them do your work.

Tissaphernes is swayed by Alcibiades's elegant line of thinking and takes up the plan to injure the Spartan cause.[7] He keeps the Spartans ill-provided, pays bribes to encourage parts of the Spartan domain to break away, and at the same time refuses to let Sparta fight at sea, insisting that they must wait until the Phoenician ships arrive.[8] In this manner, he ruins the efficiency of Sparta's navy, which had once been first-rate.[9]

Alcibiades, of course, has ulterior motives. If Sparta can be weakened, then they will have greater difficulty hunting him down and executing him. Sparta hates him for a reason, and reflexively, Alcibiades hates them back. Alcibiades can be spiteful and punitive, as evidenced by what he did to Athens after his death sentence there. He will use Persia, if he can, to punish Sparta and free himself. If, somehow, he can get Persia to take control of Sparta, he could effectively eliminate the Spartan execution order. Likewise, if Persia takes control of Athens, then he can eliminate that death sentence, too. If Persia takes all of Greece, he can be free of both executions and position himself to be the obvious choice for provincial governor. Of course, if he ever became governor, he would lead a revolt against Persia. Alcibiades, ever the egomaniac, still holds out hope that he will be the leader of all of Greece, or at least parts of it, primarily his home city of Athens. It's a driving obsession, even after all he has been through and all he has put Athens and now Sparta through. His almost delusional fixation with supreme leadership is borderline pathological. Persia is a means to an end for Alcibiades, an improbable fairy tale of an end, and yet he still labors for it.

Socrates trained Alcibiades to be a philosopher-king, and while he has abandoned the philosopher part, he still clings to the king part.

25

The Offer

Athens itself is besieged and starving, largely due to Alcibiades's treachery, but a group of Athenian aristocrats has escaped Athens and is hiding out on the island of Samos with the remains of the Athenian fleet. Alcibiades is familiar with these people, having grown up in the same circles, and fought beside them in the military. He is also aware of their desperation and sends a message to them saying that he is now a trusted adviser of Tissaphernes and that he can bring Persia to the aid of Athens. A small group of the desperate but intrigued aristocrats crosses over and secretly meets the well-fed and beautifully dressed Alcibiades.[1] He explains how he, and he alone, can get Persia, with all its wealth and power, to Athens's side, if and only if, Athens replaces its messy democracy with a clean oligarchy (rule by the few), which the king prefers, and most importantly, he is allowed safe return to Athens.[2] Change the government and drop the Eleusis charges, and Alcibiades will make Persia the ally of Athens.

Time is running out.

Sparta will soon crush Athens.

The convinced aristocrats return to Samos and gather their colleagues. They relate how the king of Persia would be their friend, and would provide them with money, if Alcibiades is restored and the democracy abolished. Many are irritated at the thought of changing government, but they clearly see the advantage of pay from the king.[3] There is much discussion, as they examine and reexamine Alcibiades's proposal.[4] These aristocrats, who also suffered severely from the Spartan siege, now entertain great hopes of getting the government into their own hands and of triumphing over Sparta. However, one of the leaders has some misgivings:[5]

> ATHENIAN GENERAL: Alcibiades, who we all know, cares no more for an oligarchy than for a democracy, he only seeks to change the institutions of our country in order to get himself reinstated. Our job is not to do Alcibiades's bidding, but to avoid disunion. Moreover, it is not in the Persian king's interest to go out of his way to side with we Athenians whom he does not trust, and aggravate the Spartans . . . The proposition of Alcibiades, and the intrigues now in progress, should not be approved.

The group, however, does not heed this sage advice and accepts Alcibiades's proposal. They send a man named Peisander and few others back to beleaguered Athens to pitch the plan.[6]

At the Athenian Assembly, Peisander makes a speech before the people, giving a brief summary of his views and particularly insisting that, if Alcibiades is recalled and the democratic constitution is changed, they could have the king of Persia on their side, and they would finally be able to repel Sparta.[7] A number of speakers oppose the idea of an oligarchy outright; the unnamed enemies of Alcibiades cry out against his restoration, what a scandal, and a violation of the constitution; and the priests of the Mysteries of Eleusis protest on behalf of the two goddesses, the very cause of his banishment, and even call upon the goddesses to forbid the recall of Alcibiades.[8] The priests of Eleusis, as you well know, include Callias, who after having been robbed of his wealth by Alcibiades's strategic instructions to the Spartans, is even more set against Alcibiades (if such a thing is possible), but he also sees the misery of Athens's situation (he hungers, too).

Quietly, he realizes if Alcibiades comes home, he will be easier to locate, isolate, corner, and kill. Callias still plans to win the day. Peisander, in the midst of these heated arguments, comes forward, and asks the Athenian Assembly a penetrating question:[9]

> PEISANDER: How is there any hope of saving our state, unless someone can somehow induce the king of Persia to come over to our side?

None of the people could answer that they knew of any way to save Athens, other than gaining the support of the king of Persia. He then plainly says to them:[10]

> PEISANDER: We cannot gain the king's trust unless we have a more reasonable form of government, and confine the power of office to a smaller number. Let us not dwell on the form of our constitution, which we can always change back later. The very existence of Athens is at stake. We must immediately restore Alcibiades, who is the only man living capable of saving us.

The Assembly is, at first, highly skeptical at the mention of an oligarchy, but upon understanding clearly from Peisander that this is the only option left, they give way and vote for an oligarchy, but not before taking counsel of their fears and promising to someday change the government back to a democracy.[11] (There is no record of anyone consulting Socrates on this plan.) The Assembly then votes that Peisander should sail with ten others and bring the news to Alcibiades that an oligarchy has been installed and that he has been restored. Their mission is to make the best arrangements they can with Tissaphernes as quickly as possible.[12]

The Athenian envoys with Peisander arrive at the court of Tissaphernes to confer with him about the proposed agreement.[13] They are welcomed, but in a bizarre power play, Alcibiades speaks for Tissaphernes, who sits by in measured silence.[14] Alcibiades makes extravagant demands of the

Athenians, who for a long while agree to whatever he asks—they are desperate, after all. He requires the whole of Ionia be ceded to Persia. They agree. He requires all the adjacent islands be ceded to Persia. They agree. Alcibiades makes the concessions even more painful.[15] He next requires them to allow Persia to build ships and sail along Athens's coast with as many ships as it wants, whenever it wants. At this the Athenians yield no further. They realize that Alcibiades has deceived them, and furious, they storm out of the meeting and return to their hideout in Samos.[16] Alcibiades knew all along that Tissaphernes was not going to agree to any terms, and so he tried to make it appear that Tissaphernes had already been persuaded to join them but that the Athenians were not conceding enough to him in exchange.[17]

Athens had undone its democracy based on a lie.

Persia would never come to the aid of Athens, and Alcibiades knew it all along. Tissaphernes was only interested in making Sparta as weak as Athens, not in strengthening Athens (this was Alcibiades's advice to him, after all). Alcibiades's lie benefits one person and one person only: himself. He gets what he wanted; he is restored, and his death sentence is lifted by the order of the Athenian Assembly.

At long last, he has thwarted Callias.

26

Trapped

M eanwhile in Sparta, Timaea gives birth to a son.[1] The boy is named Leotychides, but in private, she and her attendants call him Alcibiades by whispers.[2] Alcibiades soon learns of his son's birth.[3]

> ALCIBIADES: I did not do this act out of wantonness of insult nor to gratify passion, but so that my line might one day become kings of Sparta.

King Agis, however, does not acknowledge Leotychides as his son, and the boy is barred from the line of succession.[4] Agis makes sure that the seed of Alcibiades will never be king of Sparta. Agis redoubles his effort to find Alcibiades and kill him. He needs to talk to Tissaphernes.

In 411 B.C.E., with the failure of the attempt to bring Persia to Athens's side, the people of Athens try to reassert their beloved democracy, but unsurprisingly, the newly minted oligarchs, known as "The 400," refuse to give up power.[5] Oligarchies are, in Socrates's estimation, designed to amass wealth for the few and leave the rest of the populace in poverty. Why would any oligarch want to give up such an opportunity? The disparities of wealth and power cause internal conflict, "There is an inevitable division: such a State is not one, but two States, the one poor, the other rich; and they live in the same place and always conspire against one another . . ."[6] Socrates questions the logic of an oligarchy, where wealth is the main qualification for leadership.[7]

> SOCRATES: . . . Just think what would happen if boat pilots were chosen according to their wealth, and a poor man were refused permission to steer, even though he were a better pilot?

> GLAUCON: You mean that they would shipwreck?

> SOCRATES: Yes; and is not this true of the government or anything?

> GLAUCON: I should imagine so.

The ship of state can be wrecked, too. The people who speak out against the 400 are swiftly rooted out and put to death.[8] This is, of course, how oligarchies work. A violent civil war erupts between Athens's pro-democracy forces and the oligarchs.

Sparta can just sit back and watch Athens destroy itself.

Alcibiades's blatant lie about bringing Persia to Athens's aid causes a civil war and even more destruction and privation in Athens. This is just another item in the long list of his offenses, from which Athenians will be able to draw when looking to blame someone for his actions.

Socrates, Xanthippe, and their now five-year-old son try to survive the civil war as best they can.

The democratic faction, in a bizarre twist, calls for Alcibiades to take control of the remains of the Athenian navy at Samos and come back to Athens to drive out the oligarchs and save democracy.[9] The democratic forces even give back to Alcibiades his former title: general.[10] Did they forget that Alcibiades was the person who lied to them and came up with the idea to turn Athens into an oligarchy in the first place? Alcibiades is seen as both the cause and the solution to Athens's many problems.

Alcibiades immediately takes command of the Athenian ships at Samos. At long last he has control over the Athenian fleet, and he doesn't have to share power with Nicias. But in another betrayal in a string of betrayals, Alcibiades doesn't sail back to Athens to save democracy. In fact, he doesn't bring his ships anywhere near Athens. Alcibiades is rightfully leery about returning to Athens. Callias is still there, and even if the Assembly reinstated him, Callias will just find another way to get him. He grew up with Callias; he knows him better than almost anyone. He knows his guile and his wickedness. He has seen the "evil genius" operate firsthand. Besides, much of Athens will still be furious with him for helping Sparta destroy the Athenian expedition to Sicily. If Alcibiades is ever going to go back to Athens, which is a long shot, he would need to make amends to a lot of people, to change hearts and minds, and that sort of thing doesn't come quickly, if it's even possible at all. Alcibiades has another agenda anyway—vengeance. He takes the Athenian ships under his command and goes hunting for Spartans. If they are going to kill him, then he's going to kill as many of them as he can first.

Sometimes the best defense is a good offense.

Alcibiades receives intelligence that Mindarus, a Spartan admiral, is sailing with his whole army into the Hellespont.[11] The Athenian ships rush to intercept Mindarus, save for the eighteen galleys under Alcibiades's command, which are several hours behind.[12] The fleets engage near Abydos, and the brutal but fairly even fight lasts till night. When Alcibiades finally arrives in the darkness, the Spartans are encouraged because they think their reinforcements have arrived.[13] But Alcibiades suddenly raises the Athenian colors in the admiral ship and falls upon the Spartan ships.[14] He soon chases away the Spartan galleys and follows them so closely that they are forced to shore. Pharnabazus, a Persian governor from a different province than Tissaphernes, brings his troops by land to support the Spartan fleet and protects their sailors on shore.[15] The Athenians win a decisive sea victory, losing none of their ships while capturing thirty Spartan ships.[16] This is the first good news Athens has had in a very long time.

Flush with pride from his victory and still trying to curry favor with Persia, Alcibiades delivers a single ship laden with gifts and treasure to Tissaphernes, who gladly accepts the plunder but then throws Alcibiades in jail.[17] Tissaphernes has lost interest in Alcibiades's schemes and is making further alliances with Sparta. Alcibiades, who remains under an execution order from Sparta, is now imprisoned by Persia. He is running out of bridges to burn. As each day of imprisonment passes, Alcibiades's position worsens. Will Tissaphernes kill him? Will Tissaphernes turn him over to Sparta and let them kill him? What sort of negotiations are going on? Is Tissaphernes squeezing concessions out of Agis in exchange for him? Is Callias involved? Did the rescission of his death sentence in Athens spur Callias to use his position as proxenus to Sparta to work with Agis? How many people and states are involved? Alcibiades's mind is spinning with possibilities. Weeks pass, and soon he has been held for a month. What is going on? Alcibiades is distressed, something is coming, and it can only be bad.

27

Vengeance at Sea

I t takes four months of bitter warfare before democracy is reinstalled in Athens. It is accomplished without any direct help from Alcibiades. (The oligarchs, however, enjoyed the brief taste of power. They will be back.)

The Spartans remain in control of all land routes to Athens, and supplies can come in only by boat. Athens, regardless of its form of government, continues to deal with privation.

In the meantime, a window of opportunity cracks open for the jailed Alcibiades. He launches an escape. The ancient sources do not explain exactly how he attempts it, other than to say that he somehow gets a horse.[1] Clearly it is difficult to get a horse when incarcerated. Alcibiades may have used brute force (he is a physical specimen, after all) to overpower a guard; or he may have simply talked his way out (he is a master manipulator); or he may have used his considerable libido to gratify someone sexually; or any combination of these to gain his freedom. He gets out by whatever means, and now he must come up with a plan. He's rightfully reluctant to go back to Athens, and Sparta and Persia are clearly allied against him. He's running out of options.

Alcibiades outraces his Persian pursuers on land and sea and finds his way back to the protection of the Athenian camp at Samos. Alcibiades comes rushing into camp, breathing heavily, muscles pumped from heavy exertion, his handsome jaw clenched, and his gorgeous eyes flashing with rage. His soldiers rejoice at his reappearance. They furnish him with food and water and gather around, eager to hear of his miraculous escape from Tissaphernes. They hang on to his every word: he is legend. But Alcibiades wants information from them, too. He needs an update on the happenings he missed and the current status of the conflict. His loyal troops tell him that the forces of the Spartan admiral Mindarus and the Persian governor Pharnabazus are gathered together at a place called Cyzicus, a strategic point located in modern-day Turkey.[2] Alcibiades, flush with fury, decides to attack them immediately. There's an oft-repeated truism that a person who's just narrowly avoided death feels most alive. Alcibiades just escaped certain execution by Tissaphernes and now feels deeply appreciative of the air in his lungs, the blood coursing through his veins, and the clarity of his thoughts. The gods have granted him a reprieve from death, and he means to take full advantage of the opportunity. Alcibiades addresses his soldiers:[3]

ALCIBIADES: We will take the fight to the enemy: we shall fight at sea, on land, and even lay siege to fortifications. We must win in every way by any way . . .

(Here we have some lineaments of Winston Churchill's famed "We Shall Fight on the Beaches" speech. Again, know the classics.[4]) Alcibiades's motivated soldiers swarm on to the ships. He leads them toward Cyzicus. Along the way they seize all small trading craft they pass and keep them under guard, so the enemy does not learn of their approach.[5] As they approach Cyzicus, a fortuitous dark storm rolls in that further conceals the oncoming Athenian fleet.[6] Alcibiades holds the rest of the fleet back and out of view of the enemy, and he advances toward them with a mere forty ships. The Spartans are deceived by the relatively small number of Athenian ships and attack at once, but as soon as they are engaged, the rest of the Athenian fleet bears down on them.[7] The terrified Spartans flee to shore. Alcibiades's group chases them, disembarks, and overtakes the Spartans on land. Alcibiades and his men slaughter a great number of Spartans, including the Spartan admiral Mindarus, in a veritable orgy of bloodlust. The Persian governor Pharnabazus flees and saves himself. The corpses of dead Spartans litter the shore. A triumphant and blood-spattered Alcibiades surveys the scene: he is alive, and he is winning. It feels good.

The soldiers of Alcibiades are flush with pride at their success, feeling for the moment almost invincible.[8] The Athenians take all the Spartan ships, destroy the Spartan garrison, secure the area, and take control of the sea.[9] This battle gives the Athenians control of the shipping lanes through the Black Sea, allowing them to get, for the first time in a long time, supplies of grain and other food staples efficiently to Athens. (And you can file this under "the more things change, the more they stay the same": grain shipments coming across the Black Sea from Europe's "breadbasket," which is modern-day Ukraine, remain a critical route for feeding the region and a geopolitical flash point to this very day.) For many in Athens, the ill will they had for Alcibiades and all he had done to injure them in the past is forgotten the moment food meets their famished mouths.

Alcibiades is saving Athens. (Never mind that he's the one who caused the blockade and starvation in the first place.) Like all Athenians, Callias and Socrates are glad to have food again, but they are also wary; they know that whenever Alcibiades does good it brings future harm. Alcibiades's agenda is to injure Sparta because of his death sentence there, but a byproduct of defeating Spartans in battle is that it starts to change some minds in Athens about him. He pursues Spartans relentlessly and piles up victories. Winning battles leads to winning hearts back in Athens.

Pharnabazus's massive Persian force of cavalry and foot soldiers attacks the Athenian position at Abydos, and the Athenians look to be overrun when Alcibiades sweeps in from the side and routes Pharnabazus, who again flees.[10] The next day, the Athenians lay waste to much of Governor Pharnabazus's province. Alcibiades is sending a message to Tissaphernes by putting the hurt on the adjacent Persian province. Next, Alcibiades attacks Bithynia, which is terrified at the sight of his force and swiftly turns over tribute and enters into an alliance with him.[11] He then goes to Chalcedon, which had once been part of the Athenian Delian League but had revolted and joined Sparta, and lays siege upon it.[12] A regrouped and determined Pharnabazus comes to the aid of Chalcedon, but Alcibiades forces Pharnabazus to flee yet again and slays the Chalcedonian leader. Alcibiades then takes Selymbria without a fight, receives tribute, and stations an Athenian garrison there.[13] Pharnabazus, who is by now utterly sick of Alcibiades, grudgingly enters into a treaty with him, which gives Athens a sum of money and control of Chalcedon in exchange for a commitment not to attack Pharnabazus's province ever again.[14]

Each supply ship coming into Athens carries word of Alcibiades's successes. Alcibiades is, bit by bit, reconstituting the Delian League, returning the vassal states to Athenian control, and rebuilding Athens's realm one battle at a time—so much winning. The people of Athens are both elated and tempered in their feelings about Alcibiades:

They yearn for him, they hate him, they want him back.[15]

28

Return Home

After eight years in exile, Alcibiades, at long last, sets sail for Athens. His fleet of ships are adorned with the shields of his vanquished foes and other spoils of war. They tow behind them many captured enemy galleys bearing ornaments and figureheads, the carved sculptures from the prows of still other enemy ships that had been sunk and destroyed.[1] This show of accomplishment and military might has two important purposes: first, to impress his fellow Athenians, and second, to intimidate his enemies within Athens, Callias most of all. Alcibiades ventures into the harbor gripped with fear, an emotion not natural to him, because he knows full well all the horror and suffering he had brought upon Athens and the ill will it created, but also the very real risk of the old scores that would have to be settled. He would need a fresh start with Athens, and that would be difficult work, in fact, a task more daunting than all he had faced and overcome before. After eight years in exile, this situation calls for conciliatory word and deed, of which he is unaccustomed. He is used to running away; now he has to learn to come home.

Standing on the deck of his ship, he comes close to the Athenian shore but does not dock. He feels trepidation—is this a trap? Callias is clever.

Alcibiades sees a cousin on land, along with a group of old friends and acquaintances, enthusiastically beckoning him to come to shore.[2] A throng of well-wishers gathers. The look of expectation and adoration in their faces puts him at ease.

It is safe.

Alcibiades steps on land and is immediately embraced and engulfed by the joyous crowd. People come rushing from every direction to welcome him, and they crown him with garlands and sing his praises.[3] Some bystanders even weep with a happiness born from the miseries they had long endured.[4] His sailors come ashore, too, some after many years away, and reunite with their families: hugs, tears, sighs, laughter, and relief. The port becomes the site of an epic celebration and deep emotional release. Athens is whole again.

The Assembly is quickly called to session. Alcibiades enters, and as he had both hoped and dreaded, the priests of Eleusis are in attendance. Their solemnity stands in stark contrast to the exuberance of the crowd. He makes eye contact with Callias. Has he changed? Can he forgive? The boisterous throng falls to a hush as Alcibiades collects himself and steps to the dais.[5]

> ALCIBIADES: Lo, fellow Athenians, you have not come to hear me lament my travails in the many years that I have been kept away from you. You well know that I was banished without just cause, but rather because I was plotted against by those who had less power than me and connived their political doings for their own private gain, whereas I was always only ever concerned with advancing our commonwealth, both by my own means and by the power of the state. If I had been brought to trial at once on these spurious charges—I did not commit sacrilege against the Mysteries of Eleusis—then I would have won acquittal, but my enemies, as you well know, postponed the trial, which was obviously my right, and then, when I was absent, robbed me of my homeland; but they also robbed you, if I had remained in

command of the Sicilian Expedition we would have won, and
our people and army would have remained strong, and we would
have the wealth of Sicily to support us, but in exile I was help-
less as a slave and in danger of my life every day, and so I was
forced to align myself with those I hated most. From abroad,
I saw those who were dearest to me, my fellow-citizens and
kinsmen of Athens, making mistakes, but I was in no position
to help you.

Yet, I do not blame the people of Athens for my difficulties, I only fault my own bad fortune and ill fate, and the
few plotters, who for their own lust for power, killed and
banished our best men, thus cheating Athens of what it most
needed—leadership.

I gently admonish you, my fellow citizens, to not again fall
prey to the slanders of the wicked; we must be united to contend
with the powerful enemies outside our walls: the Syracusans,
Spartans, and Persians. While their armies are great, their supe-
riors are poor, plodding along with the same predictable tactics.
Their weakness is in the mind, which is our greatest strength.
By our wiles we have restored our dominion over the sea, and
by such means we will also be victorious over our enemies
everywhere on land. Hear me, Athens, never since the time of
my guardian Pericles, have our prospects been so auspicious; fix
your eyes on the greatness of Athens, my friends, for today is
the first day of a new Golden Age.

The Assembly is roused with hope and courage. They place a crown of
gold on Alcibiades's head and elect him autocrat, with sole military power
over land and sea.[6] (This is significant, because military power was traditionally divided among several generals.) The people clearly accept his
contention that he was unjustly framed for the profanation of the Eleusinian
Mysteries, which brings up a looming issue that must be addressed and
resolved immediately. The Assembly votes to restore all the property that

was taken from him when he was convicted of profaning the Eleusinian Mysteries, and they compel the priests of Eleusis to immediately revoke the curses they had put on him before.[7] Callias's reaction is not recorded, but the high priest Theodorus hedges:[8]

> THEODORUS: Nay, I invoked no evil upon him, if he does no wrong to the city.

The implication being: if Alcibiades wrongs the city again, great evil will fall upon him. Remember, this is a time and place in history where curses from priests carry significant weight. If Alcibiades did not profane the Mysteries, then the Assembly's judgment is redemption and the case is closed, but if he did do it, then he just got away with it right in front of the priests of Eleusis, while insulting them as plotters, and there will be future consequences. It's only a matter of who gets to whom first.

Alcibiades has decisively won the day: he is named autocrat, his property is restored, and the curses against him are, at least, quasi-revoked. He has finally attained his lifelong goal of becoming the leader of Athens's military, assuming the legacy of Pericles. Now it's his turn to improve upon his guardian's contributions to Athens. But even if his problems with Eleusis and its two patron goddesses, Persephone and Demeter, are subdued for the moment, he has a new and unforeseen problem with another goddess to deal with: an ill omen in the house of Athena, the patron goddess of Athens. He landed on the day of the ritual calendar when the robes are taken off the great sculpture of Athena and washed; in the interim she is covered in a shroud. This is considered the unluckiest day of the year.[9] The attendants of the cult of Athena see this as a bad sign: Athena veiled herself and did not look favorably upon Alcibiades.[10] The prodigal son will have to earn his way back into her good graces.

Alcibiades sees pretty clearly that while he may be the favorite of the majority of people, the priests of Eleusis still view him with suspicion. This could be dangerous. The first order of business is to win over

both them and the portion of the populace still leery of him by publicly making amends to Persephone and Demeter. He needs to redeem
himself in the eyes of the goddesses, to redeem himself in the eyes of
the people.

There is no surviving record of Socrates's perspective on the return of
Alcibiades, but it's difficult to imagine he wouldn't have had thoughts on
the matter. Perhaps he was hopeful that Alcibiades had somehow learned
virtue and would become the philosopher-king he had trained him to be,
but he probably knew better. Just as Alcibiades, Athens's prodigal son,
must deal with Athena, the patroness goddess of Athens, Socrates's own
son, young Lamprocles, is having difficulty dealing with his mother,
Xanthippe. Socrates tries to straighten the boy out.[11]

> LAMPROCLES: No soul on earth could endure my mother's
> temper.

> SOCRATES: Really? Do you think it would be harder to bear
> a wild beast's savagery or a mother's?

> LAMPROCLES: To my mind, a mother's—at least if she's
> like mine.

> SOCRATES: Dear me! And has this mother ever done you
> any injury—such as people frequently receive from beasts, by
> bite or kick?

> LAMPROCLES: No, she uses words. You would rather sell
> your life than listen to her.

> SOCRATES: And how many annoyances have you caused your
> mother, night and day, since you were a little boy with peevish
> words and brattish acts? How much sorrow and pain have you
> caused? How much worry when you were ill or hurt?

LAMPROCLES: Well, I never said or did anything to bring a blush to her cheeks.

SOCRATES: Oh, come now, child! . . . Whatever your mother says, she does not mean you harm. She is actually wishing blessings to descend upon you. Or do you really believe that your own mother is set against you?

LAMPROCLES: No, I don't think that.

SOCRATES: Then this mother, who is kindly disposed to you, and takes such tender care of you when you are ill to make you well again, and to see that you want for nothing which may help you; and, more than that, perpetually prays for blessings and offers her vows to the heavens on your behalf—can you say that she is too harsh? It seems to me, that if you cannot tolerate such a mother, then you cannot tolerate a good thing.

Socrates explains that we owe, in general, gratitude to others commensurate with the benefit we've received from them. To Socrates's way of thinking, there is no one who has done more for Lamprocles than his mother, Xanthippe. She brought him into this world with "travail and pain, and the risk of her own life."[12] She fed him with her own food in the womb, and once born, she nursed him and watched over him with tender affection. She endures never-ending toil raising the child. "What return does she receive for all her trouble?"[13] And once the child is old enough to learn, the parents teach the child as a guide to life and provide for its formal education. The parents watch over their children, doing all in their power to enable them "to grow up to be as good as possible."[14]

Socrates's description of the role of parents and the obligation a child owes to its mother applies as much to Alcibiades as it does Lamprocles.

In an ancient Athenian context, every citizen owes the gods, particularly Athena, the patron goddess of Athens. She is the divine source of all that Athens has achieved. What does Alcibiades owe her? How can he make up for all the harm he has caused? Will she be as harsh with him as Xanthippe is with Lamprocles? Or worse? Much worse?

29

Road to Eleusis

Alcibiades determines that he should reopen the road to Eleusis and guard the sacred procession. The Spartans, however, still occupy the road, blocking the way from Athens to the temple of Eleusis, which, if you will recall, they did at Alcibiades's direction. This endeavor to reopen the route will not be without risk for Alcibiades; the Spartan soldiers of King Agis are quartered there and are still under orders to execute Alcibiades on sight.

Alcibiades sends a messenger to inform the priests of Eleusis about his plan. We have no record of how they received the news or what discussions they might have had about it, but assuredly it would not have gone without remark. The priests have been denied the procession for years, and if the person who blocked the route can reopen it, then so be it. Neither is there any record of Socrates's opinion on Alcibiades's plan to reestablish the procession. I would like to think that Socrates advised Alcibiades to make amends to Eleusis, but that would be mere conjecture. There is no record of them talking to each other at this time. Regardless, Alcibiades is, at least publicly, trying to right himself with the goddesses.

On the morning of the procession, Alcibiades stations sentries on the heights and sends out an advance guard.[1] Alcibiades, aboard his impressive steed, leads his soldiers to join the crowd of eager initiates, priests, and other officials gathered by the Eleusinion, a small satellite sanctuary located on the slopes of the Athenian Acropolis. (You can visit the ruins of the sanctuary to this day.) The high priest Theodorus delivers an invocation to the throng. Callias stands by his side along with the other priests of Eleusis. He warily eyes Alcibiades. The initiates recite the prayers. Alcibiades has his soldiers form a protective wall around them. Callias instinctively bristles. Alcibiades makes a gesture, and the procession officially begins, moving out slowly and solemnly along the Panathenaic Way, with the initiates chanting the customary verses. The rhythm of the songs and the coordinated footfalls of the march are almost hypnotic. As they travel, Alcibiades keeps a close eye on the surroundings; Callias keeps a close eye on him. So devout is the bearing of Alcibiades that he seems more like a high priest than a general.[2] We do not know if the priests were impressed or threatened by the spectacle of Alcibiades as a sincere devotee. Surely some did not believe it at all: the man is a chameleon.

The procession passes out of the city gates and through the cemetery, which is thematic given that they are making a symbolic journey to the realm of the dead. They slowly climb Mount Aegaleo and look down on the fertile Thriasio plain. The road they are to follow across the plain appears as a thin ribbon, passing by, there in the distance, a Spartan fortification. Slowly the procession marches on, down into the plain, and approaches the Spartan stronghold. Alcibiades prepares for a field battle and moves his men into position. He has unspoken hopes that the Spartans will bring the fight so he can slay them in full view of the Athenian procession. A military victory with civilian witnesses would be a rare political opportunity. The procession slows down. All eyes are on the Spartan fort. The Athenian soldiers draw their spears and swords and cautiously edge forward. Alcibiades proudly, even defiantly, picks up the pace. The time has come; he rides his horse right up to the Spartan walls.

But the Spartans do not engage. They remain safely tucked away inside, ominously silent. The Spartans are disciplined. Alcibiades respects them for it.

Puzzled, Alcibiades leads the procession onward. The initiates are relieved that they were not subject to an armed conflict and hail praises to Alcibiades. But Alcibiades, glancing back, is concerned. Maybe the Spartans are waiting to attack them on the return trip. Maybe they were just watching to see how he arranged his troops, so they could devise a more effective attack when he comes back through. He leaves scouts to keep a distant eye on the Spartans. How would the Spartans react to the formation that he showed them? What would be their counter? How can he counter their counter?

The procession makes it to the temple of Eleusis, and the initiates begin the process of ritual bathing and spiritual purification as they prepare for the rites. Alcibiades and his officers huddle to the side and discuss defensive alignments for the return trip. When night comes, the initiates drink the sacred elixir of the goddesses and file into the temple. Alcibiades and his army stand guard outside. The rites proceed in their usual manner. In the morning, the exhausted but uplifted initiates spill out of the temple.

They have earned an eternal afterlife in heaven, but how soon will they meet it?

Alcibiades gathers the initiates and organizes them for the return trip to Athens. The soldiers encircle the procession once again, and Alcibiades leads them forward. The Spartans will certainly bring resistance this time. Alcibiades is ready. When they draw within sight of the Spartans, Alcibiades deploys his troops. His soldiers are alert, focused, and ready for action.

The Spartan fortification is again eerily quiet.

The Athenians press on.

The advance guard passes through without resistance. The encircled initiates, led by Alcibiades, pass through, then the rear guard. The Spartans do not show themselves. Alcibiades looks back and wonders what Sparta is up to. Now that Athens is on a more even footing with Sparta, is King Agis in support of his leading Athens? Could he broker a Peace of

Alcibiades? Or did Callias somehow negotiate a deal using his station as proxenus to Sparta? Alcibiades looks at Callias, but Callias does not return his gaze. He considers the possibility that Callias has robbed him of a chance at victory.

Regardless, the initiates sing that Alcibiades has defeated the Spartans without even drawing his sword. The Spartans have been twice humbled by the mere threat of Alcibiades. The road to Eleusis is open, and Alcibiades is a hero. The army is exalted in spirit and feels itself invincible under his command.[3] The people are so captivated by his leadership that they are filled with an amazing passion for him to be their tyrant.[4] (A tyrant is, of course, a person with sole political power, which, when matched with his sole military power as autocrat, would make Alcibiades more like a king than a general.)

The Mysteries sent him away, the Mysteries kept him away, and now the Mysteries bring him home.

But has Alcibiades really reformed? One school of thought is that he has matured, the long years of hardship in exile leading him to right himself and take Athens's best interest to heart, even after causing many of Athens's most difficult problems. He is earnestly making restitution to his home city. The other way to look at his triumphant return to Athens is that he is the same old Alcibiades that he has always been, and he is using extravagant public displays to get people to trust him again, but he will invariably sell them out. He's an opportunist and likely psychopath, a type that doesn't readily change. Either way, he is back and Athens is going to have to figure out how to handle him. The playwright Aristophanes describes Athens's dilemma with Alcibiades in a famous metaphor:[5]

A lion is not to be reared within the state; But, once you've reared him up, consult his every mood.

Athens is in a quandary, and ultimately Athena will be its judge. That is, unless another goddess—Persephone, via Callias—takes matters into hand first. Callias is not mentioned by name in the ancient texts about

Alcibiades's return to Athens, even though the priests of Eleusis, of which he is one, figure prominently. This is typical of Callias; he is more comfortable in the shadows. There is no indication of how he views Alcibiades's return or the procession to Athens; he simply does not reveal his thoughts or plans; evil geniuses like him are not wont to public display. He will make his moves behind the scenes; in this way he is never implicated, blamed, or praised for his actions.

He is the opposite of Alcibiades.

30

Stripped

What Alcibiades thinks about the idea of being named tyrant is unknown, but it frightens many of Athens's most influential citizens.[1] Perhaps Callias most of all: imagine the sort of dread that would be triggered by the thought of a psychopath being given the power of a tyrant, particularly since this would-be tyrant has already profaned your religion, stolen your money, punched your father, possibly murdered your sister, and certainly plotted your own assassination. Anyone, but especially Callias, must have grave concerns about what Alcibiades would do with unchecked power. Callias had grown up with Alcibiades; he knew him better than anyone else, knew his nature and his malevolence.

There is no word on Socrates's feelings about the chatter of Alcibiades being named tyrant, but Socrates's perspective on tyrants in general is well-recorded by Plato. To Socrates, the flaw of democracy is its vulnerability to tyrants.[2] The populace—the mob, as he calls them—are gullible and can easily fall under the spell of a charismatic leader. Alcibiades certainly fits the bill. In Socrates's estimation, the tyrant first appears as a protector.[3] The people have something they fear, either inside or outside of the state, either real or imagined, from which the tyrant claims he can guard them.

He will make them the "victors." The people flock to him of their own accord, for he pays them in lies, lies they want to hear, lies they want to believe. They are "superior"; they are "true patriots." His favorite tools are false accusations and unleashing his mob against the "threat."[4] In time, the tyrant erases any and all opposition, "with unholy tongue and lips tasting the blood of his fellow citizens."[5] He and his supporters are empowered by the purge, "and the more detestable his actions . . . the greater devotion he requires from his followers."[6] These words are as true in the modern world as they were in ancient Athens.

Many countries today still struggle with this structural defect of democracy: the majority of the populace in a democracy may elect a tyrant, who will invariably disassemble the democracy that elected him—a democracy can make a tyrant, but a tyrant can unmake a democracy. The weak portion of the populace yearns to be strong, so they attach themselves to a strong man; such is the allure of the bully, the appeal of the despot, the attraction of the tyrant. Ancient Athens is where democracy first began and first fell, and so can teach us lessons that are, unfortunately, still applicable. But for Socrates, the would-be tyrant is Alcibiades, who is, at least partially, one of Socrates's own making. Alcibiades had once before caused Athens to take down its democracy based on his outrageous lie and install an oligarchy that sparked a civil war. And he wasn't even in Athens at the time. Now he's in Athens and well positioned to take down Athens's democracy once again, but this time to replace it with his own tyranny. Leading members of the Assembly are deeply concerned with the idea of Alcibiades being named tyrant and quickly vote to send him on a mission.[7]

This buys them time to sort it out.

The mission probably comes as something of a relief to Alcibiades. He is far more comfortable with war than with peace, with soldiers than with civilians. He likely also realizes that his words and even his deeds, particularly his act of protecting the procession to Eleusis, have not won over the priests of Eleusis and may have, in fact, hardened their resolve against him. Athens is a dangerous place for him to be, even as autocrat, even more so as tyrant: "Uneasy lies the head that wears a crown."[8] His oldest enemies are close at hand. Alcibiades leaves Athens with one hundred ships bound for the island of Andros.[9]

This buys him time to sort it out.

At Andros, he defeats the islanders in battle, as well as the Spartans who are stationed there, but he does not capture the city.[10] His enemies back in Athens use this "failure" to bring fresh charges against him.[11] The ancient source texts do not name the enemies of Alcibiades, but we can understand that Callias is their leader. And Callias will always be able to marshal allies, because, bear in mind, this is Alcibiades and there is no telling who else in Athens he may have previously betrayed, injured, robbed, or belittled; or whose wives or husbands he may have slept with. Alcibiades, over his lifetime, has earned the contempt of many well-placed people. These enemies of Alcibiades are able to use the expectation of sure success against him. One ancient source explains:[12]

> . . . if ever a man was ruined by his own exalted reputation, it was Alcibiades. His continuous successes gave him such a reputation for unbound daring, that when he failed in anything, they suspected his inclination; they would not believe in his inability. If he were only inclined to do a thing, they thought, nothing could escape him. So, they expected to hear that the Chians also had been taken, along with the rest of Ionia. They were therefore incensed to hear that he had not accomplished everything at once and speedily . . .

The practical hinderance to a quick accomplishment of Athens's military goals is a lack of money.[13] Alcibiades has to make frequent stops to levy and/or pillage townships for rations and wages for his sailors, whereas the Spartan fleet, now under the command of Lysander, is well-provisioned and financed by the Persian Empire. Lysander pays his sailors a hefty four obols a day, while Alcibiades has to constantly scrounge to pay his sailors a mere three obols a day.[14] Alcibiades sails off with some of his ships to look for money and supplies and leaves the fleet under the charge of a captain with explicit instructions not to engage the enemy. The captain, however, takes two triremes out and, finding the Spartan fleet, curses and goads them. At first, Lysander sends a few ships to chase the Athenian captain away, but when the Athenian fleet comes to aid the captain, Lysander sets his whole Spartan fleet upon them.[15] The Spartans slay the captain and capture many Athenian ships.

Alcibiades returns, is disgusted by the news, and gives chase to Lysander, but Lysander just sails off, pleased with his victory.[16] A messenger, more of a mole, actually, goes back to Athens and informs the Assembly of the defeat and blames Alcibiades for leaving incompetent people in charge while he was out cruising around collecting money and allegedly enjoying excesses of drunkenness and revelry with courtesans.[17] This sounds completely plausible to the Assembly given Alcibiades's licentious ways and voracious sexual appetites. The Assembly votes to strip Alcibiades of his generalship and replaces him with other generals. When news of his demotion reaches Alcibiades, he is genuinely afraid for his own safety.[18] It is all falling apart so quickly. He leaves the Athenian camp immediately, assembles a troop of mercenaries, and heads to the Thracian frontier, a land without a king, where he keeps a castle as a refuge against trouble. He realizes that his fantasy of ruling Athens is impossible. Athens has changed and yet stayed the same, ever consumed by petty grievances, susceptible to slanders, and always ready to send innocent people to death and banishment on the flimsiest of accusations. He is lucky to have made it out of Athens alive; had he stayed, Callias would surely have gotten him. The quick demotion proves that. Ultimately, Alcibiades had achieved his goal of being leader of Athens, brief though it was, and now he will have to do without Athens, and Athens without him.

This round goes to Callias. Athena has rejected Alcibiades.

31

Clash at Aegospotami

For the next two years Athens and Alcibiades lead separate lives, during which time Persia continues to build up the Spartan military. The person in charge of funneling money to Sparta is Cyrus, the son of King Darius II. Cyrus meets with the Spartan general Lysander and provides him with enough money to pay the wages of all his sailors.[1] Meanwhile, the Athenian navy is preparing their fleet near Samos.[2]

A battle is imminent.

But King Darius II falls ill back in Persia and Cyrus is beckoned to return to the palace, but before he goes, he gives Lysander another tranche of money as well as an instruction: do not engage the Athenian fleet unless the Spartans have superior numbers.[3] The Persian financial support will be sufficient to outfit Sparta with many more ships and sailors.

The Athenian commanders muster all their ships, nearly 180 of them, near a place off the coast of Thrace called Aegospotami.[4] The Athenian troops spend most of their time on land whiling away in general disorder, just waiting for the call to action. In a bizarre twist of fate, the Athenian navy is anchored in the vicinity of Alcibiades's castle. Alcibiades observes them but does not like what he sees, so he rides his horse down to the water and summons the Athenian commanders.[5] He gives them some unsolicited advice:[6]

ALCIBIADES: Hail, comrades, this is not a good place to anchor. This is an open shore, with no city nearby, and you are fetching your provisions from Sestus, a distance of fifteen stadia, while the enemy, are harbored near a city, where they can get everything they need. You should shift your anchorage to Sestus and thus gain the advantage of a harbor and a city; for if you are there, you will be able to fight on your own terms. Secondly, you cannot permit your crews, whenever they're on land, to wander about at their own sweet wills, when the Spartans are trained to do everything silently at a word of absolute command.

COMMANDER ONE: Go away, Alcibiades. You're no longer a general.

COMMANDER TWO: But we are. Now be off.

Alcibiades is escorted out of camp.

Lysander has been watching the Athenians, too, noting the way they disembark from their ships and freely disperse on land. He sees an opportunity. He sends his entire fleet at top speed to the Athenian position. When the Athenians see the Spartans coming, they rush to their ships, but since they are scattered here and there, some of the ships get only two banks of oars manned, some but one, and some are entirely empty.[7] Lysander captures more than 170 Athenian ships and all the Athenian crews still on land.[8] Only nine Athenian ships get away. This is a tremendous victory for Sparta and a debilitating defeat for Athens.

Alcibiades, sitting idly in his castle, watches it all happen.

Back in Athens and unaware of the battle, Xanthippe gives birth to another son.

Socrates beams with joy.

Lysander now has almost three thousand Athenian prisoners of war to deal with. What to do with them? He puts them all to death, cutting the throats of the Athenian generals he despises.[9] Lysander then sails around to other provinces that have Athenian garrisons and gives the Athenian soldiers a choice: die right now or peacefully go back to Athens. Almost all accept his offer of safe passage back to Athens.[10] Athens is soon overpacked with returnees. Lysander sails into Athens with more than two hundred ships and closes Athens's harbor.[11] The Spartan infantry, under the command of King Agis, marches in from Decelea and surrounds Athens. Athens has no way to get provisions, either by land or sea. The Spartan boa constrictor has Athens tightly in its grip. Athens bravely attempts to hold out initially, steadfast in its determination to withstand the Spartans, but hunger slowly grips the city.

Seeing the futility of its situation, Athens sends ambassadors to Agis, declaring their wish to make a treaty with Sparta.[12] But the Spartans are not interested in listening to Athens's offer and send them back. Time is on Sparta's side. The Athenians try again and send a man named Theramenes to Sparta to find out if the Spartans intend to sell the Athenians into slavery (among other potential treaty details), but Lysander simply holds him, taking him prisoner for three months, knowing full well that each day of delay makes the Athenians more desperate.[13] After months without food, Athens is now a place of hopeless, starving, gaunt, ghostlike people slowly moving past emaciated corpses laying in the streets. Even Socrates's substantial belly has withered away and flattened. His mind is still sharp, and he bears the famine better than most, but he feels it, too. He has to sacrifice to keep Xanthippe and their eleven-year-old son and infant son alive. There is nothing quite as awful as the cry of a starving baby. Every day, the famine inexorably kills more Athenians. Callias, because of his wealth, is holding out better than most. He knows that he is likely to fare well under Spartan rule as he is close to their ambassadors. Sparta likes hierarchy, chain of command, and order. Aristocrats like Callias can expect to fill the upper echelon of the new government.

After more back-and-forth and strategic foot-dragging, the Spartans finally offer peace on the following conditions: the long walls of Athens will be destroyed, Athens will surrender all its ships except twelve, all exiles will be allowed to return, Athens will have the same allies and enemies as Sparta, and Athens will follow the Spartans both by land and by sea wherever they should lead them.[14]

Theramenes has no choice but to accept the terms.

Teams of Spartan soldiers tear down Athens's long walls, block by block. Once-proud Athens sits defenseless.[15] And now that Athens is under Spartan control, it needs to be provisioned. Goods from the countryside are allowed to be delivered overland to the markets of Athens for the first time in a very long time. Spartan guards wave in cart after cart overflowing with fruits, vegetables, and grains, followed by herdsmen with their livestock. The desperate denizens of Athens trudge, hobble, and crawl to the carts, grabbing whatever they can reach, filling their dry mouths and tasting food, actual food, again. Many can only swallow a few bites before they are overfull, as their stomachs have become too taut to absorb anymore. The Athenians have lost their freedom but gained sustenance, and in this moment that is all that matters.

Sparta removes Athens's democratic government and replaces it with an oligarchy, selecting thirty leading members of Athens aristocracy to rule. This group is known as the "Thirty Tyrants," or simply "The Thirty." An aristocrat named Kritias becomes the de facto leader of the Thirty. He has been mentioned in this book twice before, but only in passing. He is a former student of Socrates and was accused in the profanation of the Eleusinian Mysteries/mutilation of the Hermes sculptures episode along with Alcibiades, but he was acquitted. Kritias also appeared alongside Alcibiades during a discussion Socrates had at Callias's house.

Kritias, like Alcibiades, was a potential philosopher-king, trained by Socrates to lead the just state.

32

The Thirty Tyrants

The Thirty, however, unleash a reign of terror on Athens, purging, at first, pro-democracy supporters, and then anyone of prominence, executing them, confiscating their property, and distributing it among themselves.[1] More than a thousand are executed, and thousands more are exiled. As carnage of the Thirty goes on, Socrates makes an observation:[2]

> SOCRATES: It would be sufficiently extraordinary if the keeper of a herd of cattle who is continually decreasing the numbers in his herd did not admit to himself that he is a poor herdsman, but that a ruler of the state who is continually decreasing the number of citizens should neither be ashamed nor admit himself to be a poor ruler is more extraordinary still.

But Socrates is not alone; the cruelty of Kritias even shocks another important member of the Thirty, Theramenes, the man who negotiated the alliance with Sparta. Theramenes addresses the rest of the Thirty:[3]

THERAMENES: It is unreasonable to put respectable people, who have never done anything wrong in their lives, to death simply because they once enjoyed influence and honor under the democracy. Why, you and I, Kritias, also said and did many things for the sake of appealing to the people.

KRITIAS: There is no other choice, dear Theramenes, but to get rid of those who are in a position to hinder us.

The killings go on, day after day, and the list of persons put to death for no just reason grows ever longer.[4] Theramenes rises to speak again:

THERAMENES: We have to keep a sufficient number of competent people alive just to be able to conduct the affairs of society, if not our oligarchy will certainly come to an end . . . I see we are trying to do two things, which are diametrically opposed; we are manufacturing a government, which is based on force, and at the same time inferior in number to those whom we propose to govern. The present course is making it dangerous for us.

Kritias runs out of patience with Theramenes, now viewing him as an obstacle to his ambitions and the long-term success of the oligarchy.

KRITIAS: If any member of this council, here seated, imagines that an undue amount of blood has been shed, let me remind him that with changes of constitution such things cannot be avoided. It is the rule everywhere, but more particularly in Athens. It is inevitable that there are a large number of people who are sworn foes to any constitutional change in the direction of oligarchy . . . Now, as to two points we are clear. The first is that democracy is a form of government detestable to persons like ourselves; the next is that the people of Athens were never willing to become friends with our saviors, the Spartans. But on the loyalty of the better classes the Spartans can count. And that is our reason for establishing an oligarchical constitution with their concurrence. That is why we do our best to rid us of everyone whom we perceive to be opposed to the oligarchy; and, in our opinion, if one of ourselves should elect to undermine this constitution of ours, he would deserve punishment. Do you not agree? And the case is no imaginary one. The offender is present—Theramenes. And what we say of him is, that he is bent upon destroying yourselves and us by every means in his power . . .

Why, this is the very man who originated our friendly and confidential relations with Sparta. This is the very man who authorized the abolition of the democracy, who urged us on to inflict punishment on the earliest batch of prisoners brought before us. But today all is changed; now you and we are out of favor with the people, and he accordingly has ceased to be pleased with our proceedings.

I contend that this man is fairly entitled to render his account, not only as an ordinary enemy, but as a traitor to yourselves and us . . . There he stands unmasked; he has forfeited our confidence for evermore . . .

. . . If you are wise, spare yourselves, not him. For what does the alternative mean? I will tell you. His preservation will cause the courage of many who hold opposite views to rise; his destruction will cut off the last hopes of all our enemies, whether inside or outside the city.

With these words Kritias sits down, and Theramenes rises and speaks:

THERAMENES: . . . Well, then! Up to the moment at which you were formed into a governmental body, when the magistracies were appointed, and certain notorious "informers" were brought to trial, we all held the same views. But later on, when our colleagues began to hale respectable honest people to prison and to death, I, on my side, began to differ from them. From the moment when Leon of Salamis, a man of high and well-deserved reputation, was put to death, though he had not committed the shadow of a crime, I knew that all his equals must tremble for themselves, and, so trembling, be driven into opposition against us. In the same way, when Niceratus, the son of Nicias, was arrested; a wealthy man, who, no more than his father, had never done anything that could be called popular or democratic in his life; it did not require much insight to discover that his friends would be converted into our foes. But to go a step further: when it came to Antiphon dying at our hands—Antiphon, who during the war contributed two fast-sailing ships out of his own resources, it was then plain to me, that all who had ever been zealous and patriotic must eye us with suspicion. Once more I could not help speaking out in opposition to my colleagues when they suggested that each of us ought to seize a person. For what could be more certain than that their death warrant would turn the whole population into enemies of the oligarchic constitution . . .

. . . Much more truly may the imputation be retorted on those who wrongfully appropriate their neighbors' goods and put to death those who have done no wrong. These are they who cause our adversaries to grow and multiply, and who in very truth are traitors, not to their friends only, but to themselves, spurred on by sordid love of gain.

. . . Yes! Kritias, I am, and ever have been, a foe of those who think that a democracy cannot reach perfection until slaves and those who, from poverty, would sell the city for a drachma, can get their drachma a day. But not less am I, and ever have been, a pronounced opponent of those who do not think there can possibly exist a perfect oligarchy until the State is subjected to the despotism of a few. On the contrary, my own ambition has been to combine with those who are rich enough to possess a horse and shield, and to use them for the benefit of the State. That was my ideal in the old days, and I hold to it still. If you can imagine when and where, in conjunction with despots or demagogues, I have set to my hand to deprive honest people of their citizenship, pray speak. If you can convict me of such crimes at present, or can prove my perpetration of them in the past, I admit that I deserve to die, and by the worst of deaths.

A loud murmur and even applause marks the favorable impression of Theramenes's speech. It is clear to Kritias that if he allows Theramenes's fate to be decided by formal voting that Theramenes will escape punishment. Kritias orders the guards with the daggers to stand close to the bar in full view of the oligarchs.

KRITIAS: I hold it to be the duty of a good president, when he sees his colleagues about to be made dupes of some delusion, to intervene. That at any rate is what I propose to do. Indeed, our friends here standing by the bar say that if we propose to acquit a man so openly bent upon the ruin of the oligarchy, they do not mean to let us do so. Now there is a clause in the new code forbidding any of the approved people to be put to death without your vote; but the Thirty have power of life and death over all outside that list. Accordingly, I herewith strike this man, Theramenes, off the list; and this with the concurrence of my colleagues. And now, we condemn him to death.

Hearing these words, Theramenes springs to his feet:

THERAMENES: And I, sirs, appeal to you for the barest forms of law and justice. Let it not be in the power of Kritias to strike either me or any one of you off the list. But in my case, in what may be your case, if we are tried, let our trial be in accordance with the law we have made concerning those on the list. I know all too well, that this dais will not protect me; but I will make it plain that these men are as impious toward the gods as they are nefarious toward people. Yet I do marvel, good sirs and honest gentlemen, for so you are, that you will not help yourselves, and that when you see the names of every one of you is as easily erased as mine.

The guards seize Theramenes.

KRITIAS: We deliver Theramenes, who has been condemned according to the law. Take him and lead him away to the proper place, and do there with him what remains to do.

Theramenes is dragged out of the proceeding, protesting loudly, and through the agora. He is put to death.

Oligarchies do not allow dissenting opinions, even from the oligarchs.

Kritias and his associate Charicles draft a law in which they insert a clause making it illegal "to teach the art of words." This is pointed at Socrates, Kritias's former teacher. They send for him and show him the law.[5]

SOCRATES: Is it allowed to ask for an explanation, in case I fail to understand this command in any point?

KRITIAS and CHARICLES: Certainly.

SOCRATES: I am prepared to obey the laws, but to avoid transgression of the law through ignorance I need instruction: Is it on the supposition that the art of words tends to correctness of statement or to incorrectness that you bid us abstain from it? For if the former, it is clear we must abstain from speaking correctly, but if the latter, our endeavor should be to correct our speech.

CHARICLES: (*angrily*) In consideration of your ignorance, Socrates, we will frame the prohibition in language better suited to your intelligence: you are forbidden to hold any conversation whatsoever with the young.

SOCRATES: To avoid all ambiguity then, or the possibility of my doing anything else other than what you command, may I ask you to define up to what age a human being is to be considered young?

CHARICLES: Anyone too young to sit as a member of the Council, as not having attained the maturity of wisdom. Accordingly, you will not converse with anyone under the age of thirty.

SOCRATES: Even when I want to buy something? Will I not be able to ask what the price is, if the vendor is under the age of thirty?

CHARICLES: Yes, you may in things of that sort, but you know, Socrates, you have a way of asking questions, when all the while knowing how the matter stands. There will be no questions of that sort.

SOCRATES: Nor answers either, I suppose, if the inquiry concerns what I know, as, for instance, where does Charicles live? Or where is Kritias to be found?

CHARICLES: Oh yes, of course, things of that kind.

KRITIAS: But at the same time you had better be done with your illustrations with shoemakers, carpenters, coppersmiths, and the like. These are worn-out by this time, considering the circulation you have given them.

SOCRATES: And am I to stay away from the topics they illustrate also—the just, the holy, and the like?

CHARICLES: Most assuredly, and from cattle herders in particular; or else you may lessen the number of your herd.

Clearly Kritias and Charicles have heard Socrates's earlier statement comparing them to bad cattle herders. There is a death threat implied in Charicles's last line, and this is a very real threat; the Thirty are in the business of butchery. Socrates is in a difficult situation: he has two young sons, and Xanthippe is pregnant again. They are all at risk.

The Thirty may have concerns about Socrates's words but they are utterly terrified of the possibility of Alcibiades's deeds. The Thirty are fraught with anxious thoughts and desperate inquiries to find out where Alcibiades is and what he might be doing and planning.[6] Kritias fears Alcibiades's military prowess and his ever-lingering popularity among some quarters in Athens, notwithstanding that Athens has twice rejected Alcibiades and he might have little interest in coming back again. Kritias worries that when Alcibiades learns of the carnage in Athens he might be furious enough to attack. Kritias and Alcibiades know each other well. The Thirty formally banish the already exiled Alcibiades, perhaps at the urging of Callias, but Kritias would prefer that Alcibiades just be killed. Kritias tells Lysander, the Spartan general, that as long as Alcibiades remains alive, many Athenians will hold out hope of his return and resist Spartan control.[7] About the same time, Lysander receives renewed orders from Sparta to hunt down and execute Alcibiades. King Agis still wants his pound of flesh. Lysander sends a message to the Persian provincial governor Pharnabazus.

33

Ambush

Alcibiades leaves his fortified castle in Thrace and camps in Phrygia, which is a Persian province under the control of Governor Pharnabazus, who Alcibiades had humiliated in battle many times in the past. Why Alcibiades would venture away from Thrace is unknown, especially with the Spartans in control of Athens and in league with the Persians. His enemies are united, their purposes aligned. Perhaps he is on his way to reach the Persian king to offer his services.[1] Alcibiades is already on the wrong side of two Persian governors, Pharnabazus and Tissaphernes, and might see an opportunity to cozy up to their boss, the king, as a way to gain control over them. There is no real information on this point. Either way, he is in Phrygia with a woman named Timandra. As he sleeps, he has a dream in which he wears women's garments and Timandra is holding his head while putting makeup on his face.[2] The next night, he awakes abruptly, coughing; the place is on fire. He quickly gathers up garments and bedding and throws them on the fire.[3] Someone is burning him out. Who? He wraps his cloak around his left arm, and drawing his sword with his right, he bursts outside, untouched by the fire.[4] Flush with adrenaline and panic, he is ready to slay whoever might be lurking in the darkness.

But there is no one there.

Shhhk, shhhk, shhhk, shhhk, shhhk. A hail of arrows strikes him from seemingly every direction. He instinctively contorts his body to try to protect himself, but the arrows pierce deep into his back, torso, neck, arms, and legs. He can no longer maintain his grip on his sword, and it falls to the ground. He staggers and drops. Writhing in the dirt, he gasps for air, wheezing from his punctured lungs. His eyes wildly search the darkness for the faces of his assassins. He tries to say something, hurl a curse, but he has no breath and emits only a snarling rasp. Blood pours from his chest. His body goes limp; his eyes glaze over.

Alcibiades is dead.

The unseen team of assassins quietly slip away. Timandra takes up his body, wraps it in her own garments, and gives it as honorable a burial as she can provide.[5] This was a well-planned and expertly coordinated attack. Pointedly, no party takes credit for the assassination of Alcibiades. Various ancient writers ascribe the assassination to different individuals and groups: the Thirty, Lysander, Pharnabazus, but also other Phrygians, and possibly even the brothers of Timandra.[6] Or put another way, some Athenians, Spartans, Persians, and Phrygians were implicated, whether individually or collectively. Alcibiades had made so many enemies over the years.

How Timandra made it out of the fire and how her clothes were not burned are unresolved questions. Possibly she was not in the tent when it was set on fire, which would implicate her in the plot. And yet none of the self-aggrandizing political and military figures purportedly involved—not Tissaphernes, not Agis, not Pharnabazus, not Kritias, not Lysander—claimed the glory. At this time, leaders erect markers and trophies at the sites of successful operations to advertise their triumphs and send heralds far and wide to announce their accomplishments. Why would these leaders, so practiced in the art of public displays of victory, remain quiet when it came to taking credit for an achievement as monumental as the assassination of the fearsome and famous Alcibiades?

Why the silence?

Silence, if you will recall, is the way and law of the goddess Persephone. The goddess always achieves her mark by stealth. This is how the Mysteries operate, in secret. Do not forget that Callias is still acting as proxenus to Sparta and is well-positioned to facilitate the flow of secret information between Athens and Sparta, between his old companion Kritias, who will make the township of Eleusis his own personal fortress, and Spartan diplomats. Callias, as a priest of Eleusis, holds authority outside and beyond the ranks of government and is interconnected with the priests of other Mystery religions that predominate the entire Mediterranean sphere, Phrygia included. And Callias harbors the oldest and deepest reasons to eliminate Alcibiades. The covert nature of the murder of Alcibiades may indicate that Callias, by the hand of the goddess, has finally gotten rid of Alcibiades, regardless of how many other parties were involved in the logistics. One "brother," after everything, has finally killed the other.

But it is Callias and not Alcibiades who is left standing.

The assassination of Alcibiades brings to a close the life of one of the most outlandish, colorful, charming, talented, troubled, and cruel characters that Athens, or even all of history, has ever seen. Those who loved him would long remember his bravery. Those who hated him would always remember the incredible destruction, damage, and injury he left in his wake. Callias probably felt both triumph and relief at Alcibiades's death: at long last, his sister Hipparete had been avenged. But many more people still would look back upon Alcibiades with ambivalence, seeing both the good and the bad, but mostly the squandered potential. Oh, what Alcibiades might have been, if he had only listened to Socrates . . .

Meanwhile, back in Athens, the Thirty order Socrates and four other men to go apprehend an upstanding citizen and bring him back for execution. This is part of the way the Thirty involve others in their crimes.[7] Shared but forced culpability is the art of oligarchy.

Socrates balks.

When the other four go to arrest the man, Socrates simply goes home.[8] Socrates's only concern is doing what is right, just, and holy; regardless of any possible adverse consequences. The Thirty are probably going to execute him, but they cannot scare Socrates into doing anything unjust.[9] Socrates, throughout his life, has not much cared what other people thought of him, but as he ages, he cares less and less. The Thirty will do what they do. He will simply lead his life in the best way he can for as long as he can.

He will not compromise.

34

Civil War

Theramenes's prediction comes true; the excesses of the Thirty turn many people against the oligarchy, particularly exiled Athenians who are at liberty to organize themselves. The exiled Athenian general Thrasybulus marshals a fighting force of exiles. He attacks and seizes the Fort of Phyle, an Athenian outpost nineteen kilometers (twelve miles) north of Athens.[1] The army of the Thirty marches out toward Phyle to regain the fort and sets up camp south of Phyle. Just before dawn Thrasybulus's army of exiles quietly surrounds the encampment of the army of the Thirty. When the wake-up call is given, the soldiers of the Thirty roust and groggily stumble off into the bushes to urinate. At this moment, Thrasybulus's men sweep in, catching the soldiers of the Thirty with only their penises in their hands.

With this daring dawn raid, Thrasybulus's troops rout the army of the Thirty and send them scrambling back to Athens.[2] Kritias starts to realize the precariousness of his situation and makes the township of Eleusis, where the temple of the Mysteries of Eleusis is located, his fallback position if the Thirty are ever forced to flee Athens.[3] A few days later, Thrasybulus, now leading a corps more than a thousand strong, proceeds to Athens. They mean to reclaim their home. The forces of the Thirty are waiting for them. Just before the battle, Thrasybulus addresses his troops:[4]

> THRASYBULUS: Fellow citizens, I wish to inform some, and to remind others of you, that of the men you see advancing beneath us, the right division are the very men we routed and pursued in Phyle only five days ago; while on the extreme left you see the members of the Thirty themselves. These are the men who have robbed us of our city, though we did no wrong; who have hounded us from our homes; who have set the seal of banishment on our dearest friends. But today the wheel of fortune has turned; that has come about which least of all they looked for, which most of all we prayed for . . . Today, the gods do visibly fight on our side . . . they have brought us to a place where the steep ascent hinders our foes from reaching us with lance or arrow farther than our foremost ranks; but we with our volley of spears and arrows and stones cannot fail to reach them with terrible effect. Had we been forced to meet them vanguard to vanguard, on an equal footing, who could have been surprised? But as it is, all I say to you is, let your arrows fly with a brave will . . . But let me call upon you so to bear yourselves that each shall be conscious that victory should be won by him and him alone. Victory, God willing, will on this day, restore to us the land of our fathers, our homes, our freedom, our children, and our wives. As conquerors we shall look upon this as the gladdest of all days. No less fortunate is the man who falls today. Not all the wealth in the world shall purchase him a monument so glorious. At the right instant I will strike the keynote of the paean; then, with an invocation to the god of battle, and in answer to the wanton insults they have put upon us, let us with one accord wreak vengeance upon them.

Thrasybulus's army of exiles is ready; every soldier is on edge and focused on the enemy below. The call pierces the air, and the exiles, taking advantage of their advantageous topographical position, rain arrows and spears down upon the oligarchs, killing and injuring many in this opening salvo. The army of the Thirty responds by launching its own aerial barrage, but their arrows fall short of the exiles, harmlessly lodging in the ground or ricocheting off the rocks. The archers of the oligarchs see the futility of their aerial strike and quickly join the infantry hiding under their shields in a collective defensive formation. The army of the Thirty is, for the moment, blind to what's happening on the other side of their wall of shields. The exiles seize the moment and swiftly rush to the edge of the oligarchs' army. Thrasybulus's archers instantly stop shooting arrows. The oligarchs peek out from behind their shields, only to see the thrusting tips of the exiles' swords. The exiles overrun the oligarchs and force them into disarray. Fierce hand-to-hand fighting follows. Kritias, the leader of the oligarchs and chief author of the executions and banishments, is the main target. They intend to cut off the head to kill the body. Kritias fights valiantly, but there are just too many swords being swung at him from too many directions. He is slashed, pierced, and hacked to pieces. The exiles slay several other oligarchs, and the army of the Thirty is forced to retreat.

The inspired pro-democracy forces of Thrasybulus hold the day and rewin their beloved city.

The remaining members of the Thirty withdraw to their stronghold at Eleusis and send a message to Sparta pleading for help.[5] Sparta jumps into action. The Spartan general Lysander goes to Eleusis to draw up a battle plan with the Thirty, who at this point are more like the Twenty. The Spartan political powers are, however, fairly leery of spending their resources dealing with Athens's internal strife, particularly when a much bigger issue has recently developed—Persian king Darius II has died and there is a war of succession brewing between two of his heirs, Cyrus (the old friend of Sparta) and Artaxerxes II (the rightful new king), and Sparta will likely be dragged into it. The Spartans send a team of ambassadors to Athens to effect a reconciliation in the best way possible.[6] From the

Spartan perspective, Athens is an annoyance; without its protective walls or its navy, it no longer poses any threat to Sparta, while the problems in Persia are an existential danger. To keep the peace in Athens, the Spartans decide that the pro-democracy forces can keep Athens and the Thirty can stay at Eleusis.

So ends the civil war in Athens.[7]

Sparta also establishes some very important reconciliation measures to speed up the healing process for war-torn Athens. An amnesty agreement bars all charges for crimes committed during or before the reign of the Thirty. (This amnesty agreement will play an important, if underappreciated, role in the later trial of Socrates.) The death of Kritias and the defeat of the Thirty could not have come at a better time for Socrates, who surely would have been executed had they remained in power. Socrates was not going to stop speaking.

Socrates, Xanthippe, and their two sons somehow survive these gruesome years, and they even welcome a new healthy baby. They are a family with a young teenager, a toddler, and an infant all intact and well. But two of Socrates's most prominent former students, Alcibiades and Kritias, do not survive. Their deaths mark both the triumphs and failures of democracy and oligarchy, and perhaps Socrates's teachings. In the coming years, Athens will try to come to terms with the great damage caused by these two former students of Socrates. Some Athenians will look to blame Socrates for their ruinous actions.

35

The Charges and the *Clouds*

In 399 B.C.E., five years after the assassination of Alcibiades and four years after the death of Kritias, and at a time of relative stability after decades of war, famine, disease, and political upheaval, an indictment is sworn out against Socrates, then age seventy, accusing him of impiety and corrupting the youth.

Hopefully, as you have read the preceding chapters, it has been pressed into your mind that ancient Athens was a place where innocent people were routinely put to death or banished for no just cause, whether under an oligarchy or a democracy. Extreme plays for political power or mere petty jealousies were enough to end a person's life. Athens was a city of slander, grudges, and ambition. So, the question is not why Socrates was inexplicably charged at age seventy, but rather why he hadn't been charged many times before, like seemingly everyone else. First off, many of the cases Athenians brought against each other were barely veneered acts of covetousness or retribution for prior acts of covetousness. People wanted what other people had and were willing to lie to get it. Socrates had few possessions and dressed shabbily, which insulated him from such intrigues. Nobody wanted Socrates's estate. The other reason he had not been charged before, which is the entire point of this book, is because he hadn't yet committed heresy. His *Allegory of the Cave*, which I have argued is a brazen disparagement of the Eleusinian Mysteries, is the reason for the impiety charge, the predictable result of words that came straight out of Socrates's mouth. The description of people fettered in darkness believing in shadows cast by sculptures held before a great fire comes way too close to the actual ritual operations of the manifestation of the goddess Persephone as light at the hallowed Mysteries of Eleusis. The *Allegory of the Cave* is the triggering event to the charges, even if old grudges also come into play. The second part of the charges, "leading the youth astray," takes advantage of the misdeeds of his former and wayward students, among them Kritias, but Alcibiades most of all.

There are two other important episodes that affect the charges against Socrates. According to Plato, the comedic play *Clouds* by Aristophanes, which was written long before all the troubles and lampooned Socrates and a young Alcibiades, influenced the sentiments of Athenians and left many with the lasting impression that Socrates was a petty con man.[1] And the other was the trial of Andocides, which occurred a few months before the Socrates trial, where Andocides was spuriously charged by Callias with profaning the Eleusinian Mysteries. The trial of Andocides helps to shape the prosecutorial strategy against Socrates: the lessons learned in the Andocides case will be applied to Socrates's case.

The play *Clouds* was first performed in 423 B.C.E., or about eight years before the disastrous Syracuse Expedition that Alcibiades devised and twenty-four years before the trial of Socrates. In the play, Socrates is portrayed as a hilariously absurd scam artist and young Alcibiades, under another name, as his highborn dupe. *Clouds* came in third place in a play competition behind a play titled *Konnos*, which also skewered Socrates (unfortunately, this play has been lost). Clearly making a mockery of Socrates was in fashion at the time and all in good sport. Socrates is said to have attended the plays, and when some foreigners asked who Socrates was, he stood up, to everyone's delight.

The three main characters in *Clouds* are Socrates, Strepsiades, and Phidippedes. (Sorry for the difficulty of these two names, but that's part of the humor: Strepsiades = "cheater" and Phidippedes "saves horses.") Strepsiades is the stepfather of Phidippedes, a stand-in for Alcibiades, who is a wastrel who spends too much money on horses. Recall how much money Alcibiades spent on horses. Also, Phidippedes's mother in the play is a relative of the great leader Megacles, just like Alcibiades's real mother. Strepsiades is worried about his mounting debts and encourages Phidippedes to attend Socrates's "Thinkery" to learn arguments that he can use against his creditors. Phidippedes initially agrees but then backs out, so the stepfather, Strepsiades, joins the Thinkery himself. Eventually, Phidippedes also joins the Thinkery and is able to ward off creditors with superior arguments, but he becomes too emboldened and starts to physically beat his stepfather, Strepsiades. Remember that Alcibiades hit a number of male authorities, including Callias's father Hipponicus. Strepsiades blames Phidippedes's insolent turn on Socrates and burns down the Thinkery. Two of the more famous bits from the play, to give you a real sense of the satire involved, are "Gnat's Butt" and "Clouds as Gods." Both are comic gold.

When Strepsiades first makes an inquiry about joining Socrates's Thinkery, he meets a student who tells him of the genius of Socrates:[2]

> STUDENT: A person asked Socrates whether he thought gnats buzzed through their mouths or their asses.

> STREPSIADES: What did Socrates say about the gnat?

> STUDENT: He said the intestine of the gnat was narrow and that the gas went forcibly through it, being slender, straight to the butt; and then that the rump, being hollow where it is adjacent to the narrow part, resounded through the violence of the gas.

> STREPSIADES: The butt of a gnat then is a trumpet! Oh, how happy his sharp-sightedness! Surely a defendant

might easily get acquitted who understands the intestines
of a gnat.

The student then brings Strepsiades into the Thinkery, where Socrates's
students are on all fours with their heads pressed into the ground and their
backsides in the air. The student explains that they are looking for roots
(causes) below the ground while their butts learn astronomy independently.
Socrates floats in a basket above the students. Strepsiades asks Socrates
what he's doing.

SOCRATES: I am walking in the air, and speculating about
the sun.

STREPSIADES: And so you look down upon the gods from
your basket, and not from the earth?

SOCRATES: For I should not have rightly discovered things
celestial if I had not suspended the intellect, and mixed the
thought in a subtle form with its kindred air. But if, being on
the ground, I speculated from below on things above, I should
never have discovered them. For the earth forcibly attracts to
itself the meditative moisture. Watercresses also suffer the very
same thing.

STREPSIADES: What do you say? Does meditation attract the
moisture to the watercresses? Come then, Socrates, descend to
me, that you may teach me those things, for the sake of which
I have come.

Socrates lowers himself to the ground, gets out of his basket, and measures up Strepsiades.

SOCRATES: And for what did you come?

STREPSIADES: Wishing to learn to speak; for by reason of usury, and most ill-natured creditors, I am pillaged and plundered, and have my goods seized for debt . . .

Socrates sits Strepsiades on a sacred couch. And the conversation continues about the Thinkery.

STREPSIADES: Then what shall I gain by joining the Thinkery?

SOCRATES: You shall become in oratory a tricky rogue, a clever tongue, a slick speaker. But keep quiet . . .

Socrates goes on to further explain the benefits the divine clouds confer to men such as them.

SOCRATES: . . . heavenly clouds, great divinities to idle men; who supply us with thought and argument, and intelligence and nonsense, and circumlocution, and the ability to con and comprehend . . .

Socrates leads Strepsiades further into the clouds.

SOCRATES: Did you not, however, know nor yet consider, these clouds to be goddesses?

STREPSIADES: No, by the gods! But I thought them to be mist, and dew, and smoke.

SOCRATES: For you do not know that these feed very many sophists, soothsayers, practicers, lazy-long-haired-onyx-ring-wearers, song-twisters for the cyclic dances, and meteorological quacks. They feed idle people who do nothing, because such men celebrate them in verse . . .

The illustrations lead ever deeper into thicker clouds of absurdity.

SOCRATES: Have you ever, when you looked up, seen a cloud like a centaur, or a panther, or a wolf, or a bull?

STREPSIADES: By the gods, yes have I! But what of that?

SOCRATES: They become all things, whatever they please. And then if they see a person with long hair, a wild one of these hairy fellows, in derision of his folly, they liken themselves to centaurs. .

STREPSIADES: Why, what, if they should see Simon, a plunderer of the public property, what do they do?

SOCRATES: They suddenly become wolves, showing up his disposition.

STREPSIADES: For this reason, then, when they yesterday saw Cleonymus the renegade, they became stags, because they saw this most cowardly fellow.

SOCRATES: And now, too, because they saw Clisthenes, you observe, they became women . . .

And then for the coup de grâce:

STREPSIADES: Who is it that compels the clouds to move along? Is it not Zeus?

SOCRATES: By no means, but ethereal Vortex.

STREPSIADES: Vortex? It had escaped my notice that Zeus did not exist, and that Vortex now reigned in his stead.

Here the character of Socrates has replaced the old divinities with clouds, actual atmospheric entities, replacing, in a manner of speaking, religion with observational science. This idea is absurd in the context of the prevailing orthodoxy of the time: the gods had human forms. None of this blatantly blasphemous text is based on anything Socrates actually said or thought. The playwright Aristophanes took Socrates's method of inquiry and blew it out to laughable extremes. This is how good comedy works.

Clouds offers a rough sketch of the charges against Socrates, comically inventing new gods at the expense of the old gods and corrupting the youth. But at the point of the initial performance, Alcibiades had not yet plotted the assassination of Callias, cheated on Hipparete and possibly killed her, profaned the Eleusinian Mysteries, been banished, turned traitor, directed the death of the entire Athenian army, crippled Athens, caused starvation, nor lost the fleet. *Clouds* is from a more innocent time. The interpretation of *Clouds* becomes more sinister only in retrospect, because of Alcibiades's many subsequent outrages. Most importantly, Alcibiades's offenses in the play are attributed to Socrates's teachings at the Thinkery. Plato's contention is *Clouds* leaves an impression that still lingers in the minds of many Athenians some twenty-four years later when Socrates is charged. And *Clouds* wasn't even the best play that year that mocked Socrates. Between these two plays and some written in other years, the notion of Socrates as maker of gods and corrupter of the youth becomes cemented in the minds of at least some Athenians.

Of all the youths who were potentially corrupted, Alcibiades is far and away the most corrupt.

36

Trial of Andocides

A few months before the trial of Socrates, a man named Andocides (who you might remember was previously charged in the profanation of the Eleusinian Mysteries in 415 B.C.E., and whose incarceration was discussed in Chapter Sixteen) was again charged by Callias with profaning the Eleusinian Mysteries. This time Andocides stands accused of placing a bough on the altar, which is a big ritual sin for some reason. Andocides is, like Callias, a wealthy aristocrat well-versed in the art of argumentation. He had beaten Callias before. Andocides offers his account of what happened.[1]

> ANDOCIDES: . . . When we had returned to Athens from Eleusis, and the information had been presented and the Archon had made his appearance, to deliver, as is the custom, his report on the performance of the Mysteries of Eleusis, they notified both Cephisius and me to be present at the Eleusinium. For the officials were about to sit there, according to the law of Solon which commands them to sit in the Eleusinium upon the day after the performance of the Mysteries. We were in attendance, as we were commanded.

According to Andocides's explanation, once a quorum is assembled, Callias then stands up in his official priestly garments and makes an announcement.

CALLIAS: Someone placed a suppliant branch upon the altar.

HERALD: Who placed it there?

No one answers. Callias then makes a declaration:

CALLIAS: There is an ancient law that instantly, and without trial, orders to be put to death anyone who puts a suppliant branch on the altar at the temple. My father, Hipponicus, made this clear to the Athenians during his time. I have it on good authority that Andocides, who is standing here, is the one that committed this brazen act.

One of the attendees springs to his feet and cries out:

ATTENDEE: Oh Callias, you wicked man! In the first place, you, an official light-bearer, are not the reader of interpretation. In the second place, you refer to an ancient law, while the very tablet of the law rests at your side and commands only the payment of one thousand drachmae by anyone who deposits a suppliant branch on the altar. And furthermore, from whom did you hear that Andocides had placed the bough? Summon that person before us, in order that we may hear his testimony.

The law is read, and Callias is unable to say who witnessed Andocides placing the bough on the altar. It becomes evident to the officials that Callias put the suppliant branch upon the altar himself.[2] With the charge refuted, Andocides sets forth to expose Callias's motivation for falsely accusing him:[3]

ANDOCIDES: Now, gentlemen, perhaps you would like to hear with what intent Callias placed the sacred branch on the altar? I will explain why he plotted against me.

Andocides goes into great detail about how he became engaged to marry a woman.

ANDOCIDES: Having become aware of my engagement, Callias entered a claim on behalf of his son, in order that he might prevent me from marrying her. Then, during the last ten days of the month, that is to say, during the performance of the Mysteries, he gave Cephisius a thousand drachmae to falsely accuse me and bring me up to this trial. When he saw that I remained for trial, he deposited the suppliant branch upon the altar with the intention of putting me to death or driving me into exile without a trial and of taking from me my intended. Then, learning that even as it was, his plan could not be carried out without incurring a legal trial, he went to my friends and told them that if I were willing to give up my intended, he was ready to stop the case against me, to buy off Cephisius, and to pay me compensation . . . please summon the witnesses to prove what I have said. [Witnesses testify.]

Having refuted the charges and established Callias's motive, Andocides now goes after Callias in a truly vicious character assassination.[4]

ANDOCIDES: . . . Callias married his wife and, after living with her for scarcely a year, he took her mother as a lover, too, and—wretched man—lived with both mother and daughter. Here was the priest of Eleusis, a leader of the Mother and Daughter Mysteries of Persephone and Demeter; living with a mother and daughter and keeping them both in his bed! Truly, he felt no shame, nor did he fear the two Goddesses! But his wife could no longer bear it and preferred to die rather than live this way, and so attempted to hang herself, but was stopped in the act. On her recovery she was driven from the house by her mother, who in turn, was driven out by Callias when he became tired of her. But the mother was, by then, pregnant by him. Later, when she bore him a son, he denied the child was his.

Subsequently, Andocides describes what happened at the feast of Apaturia, where Callias himself was the priest conducting the ceremony. The relatives of the mother of his wife take the infant to the altar, offering the child as a victim for sacrifice:

CALLIAS: Whose child is this?

FAMILY: It is the child of Callias, the son of Hipponicus.

CALLIAS: But I am Callias, the son of Hipponicus.

FAMILY: This is your son.

CALLIAS: (*laying his hand upon the altar*) I swear that I have no son except Hipponicus, by the daughter of Glaucon. If this is not so, may my house be cursed.

Callias does not acknowledge his paternity of the child, but neither is the child given in sacrifice.

ANDOCIDES: After this, gentlemen, he fell in love with his wife's mother again, and welcomed the old woman back into his house. When his former son was grown, he introduced him among the Ceryces as his son. Callides opposed his admission, so the Ceryces voted, according to their law, that his father might introduce him if he swore that he was his own son. Then Callias placed his hand upon the altar, and swore that the child, whom he had previously denied upon oath, was his own son. Please call the witnesses who will testify the truth of this. [Witnesses testify.]

. . . Now, gentlemen, consider if such a deed has ever been committed among the Greeks—that a man, having already married a woman, would lay with her mother . . . But tell me what do you call the son? . . . Is the child not a son, a brother, or an uncle to himself? . . .

Callias, a man ever in the shadows, has stepped out into the light and been scorched. His personal affairs are the subject of open ridicule. Andocides calls a small group of high-standing citizens to act as his character witnesses, among them is the powerful Anytus,[5] who holds great sway because of his role in overthrowing the Thirty. Anytus had become the moral compass of Athens.

The jury acquits Andocides.

The Andocides trial shows Callias using his powers as a priest of Eleusis to achieve personal goals, much as he had done with Alcibiades. Callias was planning to have Andocides eliminated through official means, so that his son could marry a woman who was already engaged to Andocides. This is a humiliating defeat for Callias that teaches him some harsh but important lessons. First, he had paid a man, Cephisius, to be the lead proxy accuser, among other secondary accusers, which was his normal manner of behind-the-scenes operation, but he had made a mistake when he himself accused Andocides in front of a small group of officials, which exposed him to counterattack. Going forward, it would be better and safer for him to stay offstage and use proxy accusers solely, but not Cephisius, who had failed him. He would need to promote one of his team of secondary accusers to the lead spot. Certainly, there would be other people to accuse in the future. In fact, he already had a list. Second, the specificity of the charges made them easier to refute. He would need to embrace some level of nebulousness to be more effective. Finally, he saw rather clearly that he would need to get Anytus on his side, on the prosecution's side, to make any accusation stick. Fortunately, Anytus had long-standing grudges against certain Athenians.

The lessons of the Andocides trial will be applied to the Socrates trial.

37

Socrates's Accusers

hree official accusers bring charges against Socrates. They are
Anytus, Lycon, and Meletus.

Anytus, the defender of Andocides, was a former lover of Alcibiades,
who Alcibiades had treated badly, as was often the case with Alcibiades's lovers. Alcibiades had spurned Anytus's advances while he remained
fixated with Socrates. At one point, Anytus had invited Alcibiades over
to a party at his house, but Alcibiades declined the invitation. Alcibiades
then led his friends over to Anytus's banquet and stole half of the gold and
silver drinkware and took it home with him. Anytus's party guests were
shocked. But Anytus, still completely smitten with Alcibiades, is said
to have remarked that Alcibiades had actually been kind, because he might
have taken all there was but had left them with half.[1] It is understandable
that Anytus might have carried some lingering resentment toward Socrates,
blaming him for his difficulty in winning Alcibiades. Anytus would go
on to father a son who would eventually become a student of Socrates (much
to Anytus's chagrin). Anytus wanted his son to spend his time learning
a profitable craft, which Socrates argued against.[2] Ultimately, the young
man became a drunk.[3] The disappointing outcome of Anytus's son would

certainly have given Anytus another reason to despise Socrates. In addition, Anytus and Socrates had a dustup or two over the years, one of which Plato describes in his work *Meno*, where Socrates, Meno, and Anytus discuss the teachability of virtue (yes, the same old topic). They are deep in the dialogue as Socrates chronicles a list of great Athenians who were unable to teach their children virtue when Anytus takes offense:[4]

> SOCRATES: Now, can there be any doubt that Thucydides would have taught his children to be good men, which would have cost him nothing, if virtue could have been taught? Will you reply that he was a mean man, and had not many friends among the Athenians and allies? Of course not, but he was of a great family, and a man of influence in Athens and in all Greece, and, if virtue could have been taught, he would have found some Athenian or foreigner who would have made good men of his sons, if he could not himself spare the time from cares of state. Once more, I suspect, friend Anytus, that virtue is not a thing which can be taught?

> ANYTUS: (*seething*) Socrates, I think that you are too ready to speak evil of men: and, if you will take my advice, I would recommend you be careful. Perhaps there is no city in which it is not easier to do men harm than to do them good, and this is certainly the case at Athens, as I believe you already know.

Anytus storms out.

> SOCRATES: Oh Meno, I think that Anytus is angry. And he may well be in a rage, for he thinks, in the first place, that I am defaming these great men; and in the second place, he is of the opinion that he is one of them. But someday he will know what the meaning of "speaking evil" is, and if he ever does, he will forgive me . . .

(Hint: he won't.)

Oh, the tongue of Socrates: "He is of the opinion that he is one of them" may be one of the most cutting put-downs in all of history. Socrates speaks the truth, and sometimes it can sting. Socrates and Meno carry on the conversation at some length, arriving at a conclusion that touches upon Anytus:[5]

> MENO: And I think, Socrates, that you are right; although very likely our friend Anytus has taken offense at your words.
>
> SOCRATES: I don't care. As for Anytus, there will be another opportunity to speak with him . . .
>
> MENO: Very well.
>
> SOCRATES: Then, Meno, the conclusion is that virtue comes to the virtuous by the gift of God. But we shall never know the certain truth of how virtue is granted, until we inquire into the actual nature of virtue itself. I must leave now, but since you are persuaded to this fact, please persuade our friend Anytus. Do not let him be so exasperated. If you can persuade him, you will be doing a great service to all Athenians.

Clearly Meno is never able to persuade Anytus, who disagrees with Socrates about the teachability of virtue, as a father trying to teach his son, a son Socrates will lead, in his opinion, to idleness and alcoholism. As the years go by, Anytus builds a list of grievances against Socrates. When it comes time to charge Socrates, which would have taken some consultation and agreement among interested parties, Anytus stands ready to be named an accuser. After all, his own son was among the youth who had been led astray.

The next accuser is Lycon, who you may recall from Callias's dinner party (which was discussed in Chapter Ten and set decades earlier), where

Callias hosted a group of friends to engage in a philosophical discussion about how to improve the citizens of Athens. In it, Lycon is portrayed as being friendly if deferential to Socrates and very close to Callias. In fact, Lycon's son Autolycus is also there and would become, at least for a time, a lover of Callias. The entanglements of ancient Athenians are quite remarkable. Young Autolycus was murdered by the Thirty.[6] If Lycon rightly blamed the loss of his beloved son on Kritias, the leader of the Thirty, then it follows that he might blame Kritias's former mentor, Socrates, for the ideas that caused his son's death, notwithstanding that Socrates was very much at odds with the Thirty and would likely have been executed, too, if they had remained in power. Lycon and Callias had been very close for decades. Their shared history together, and the pain of Lycon's loss, makes Lycon an obvious choice to be among the accusers of Socrates.

The last accuser, Meletus, is in some ways the first. He is the lead prosecutor even though he has no history with Socrates. In fact, when the charges are first announced, Socrates says Meletus is little known to him.[7] But Meletus is well-known to Callias. Meletus was paid by Callias to be one of the secondary accusers to levy the charges against Andocides in the bough incident just months before.[8] Meletus is a hired gun, a man with a gift for spoken word and a taste for Callias's money. Meletus has won a promotion, moving from a secondary accuser in the Andocides trial to the lead accuser in the Socrates trial. Meletus sees an opportunity, not only to line his pockets but also to elevate his name.

Callias has done his research and assembled a formidable team, and likely, as was his wont, paid them handsomely: the prominent Anytus, who bears a deep grudge against Socrates for the dissipation of his son; his old friend Lycon, who blames the murder of his son indirectly on Socrates; and Meletus, the X factor, a man with no relationship to Socrates, who was hired because he was deemed to have the best skills, intellectually and oratorically, to stand toe to toe with Socrates and spar with him in an argument. If Andocides could make a strong argument, then Socrates could make one stronger still.

The charges against Socrates, not unlike the assassination of Alcibiades, are the result of an alignment of enemies and agendas. Both required significant coordination; both, I offer, had Callias pulling the strings. In the Socrates trial, Meletus would deliver the arguments and Anytus and Lycon would deliver the votes. Unlike the charges against Andocides, which were instigated before a smaller and more discerning group of officials and council members, the trial of Socrates would occur in the Assembly with a jury of five hundred citizens.

Venue and jury pool matter.

Callias needs Anytus and Lycon to deliver 251 votes to secure the conviction of Socrates, and undoubtedly, Callias's money will help ensure the jury's cooperation. Anytus had famously bribed an entire jury seven years earlier,[9] so he has some experience in the practice. The votes were likely mustered and counted in advance; if Callias didn't have the votes in his pocket, then he wouldn't have moved forward with the charges. But he had done his homework this time, unlike the Andocides trial, and positioned his team to win even before the accusation was submitted. Preparation is the key to battle, on the battlefield and in the courtroom.

38

The Big "Why"

What remains to be answered is why Callias chose this specific
point in time to put together his team and go after Socrates. Two
of the official accusers had issues with Socrates that dated back years if
not decades. Why now? A deeper dive into the charges themselves may
shed some light on the matter. The official indictment accuses Socrates of
impiety, lack of reverence for state-recognized gods, and leading the youth
astray, which seems completely lifted from the script of Aristophanes's
comedy play *Clouds*, because there's nothing specific in any of it. Callias
had learned his lesson about the dangers of undue specificity with the
Andocides trial, but there is much more to it than that. Socrates's *Allegory
of the Cave*, the likely trigger for the charges, puts Callias in an awkward
position. Only a few people, the priests of Eleusis and maybe their most
trusted attendants, would recognize the *Allegory of the Cave* as describing
the ritual process by which the sacred vision of the goddess Persephone
was produced at the height of the Mysteries of Eleusis. Socrates was not
allowed to have this information. The initiates into the Mysteries would
be familiar with the vision but were absolutely unaware of the means of its
manufacture. Clearly there had been a leak. But given Socrates's long life,

there is no telling when and from whom he learned of the secret process. It may have been before Callias was even born, or it may have circled back around through Alcibiades and back to Callias himself. Regardless of how Socrates acquired the information, he clearly had it, and that meant he had to be gotten rid of. But how? If Callias charged Socrates with profanation of the Mysteries of Eleusis, then he would risk others learning the secret, which would jeopardize the entire enterprise. (Think Toto pulling back the curtain on the deceptive operation of the great and powerful Wizard of Oz.) The vague impiety charge is calculated to protect the majesty of the Mysteries while holding Socrates accountable. Socrates won't be able to answer questions about Eleusis if none are asked. He won't be able to refute Eleusis if it's not mentioned. He will have no solid opponent; Socrates will swing at shadows . . . or clouds.

The influence of *Clouds*, and the other comedies, on the charges against Socrates is perhaps somewhat blunted by the number of Athenians who had seen the play in 423 B.C.E. but did not survive to see the trial of Socrates in 399 B.C.E.[1] Think of how many Athenian men were killed during the Sicilian Expedition, in the many battles with Sparta, in the famines during the blockades, the purges of the Thirty, and the civil wars. Two and a half decades of strife had wiped out generations of Athenians. How many were left alive in 399 B.C.E. who had even seen the play twenty-four years before? But perhaps the plays saw renewed popularity after the war was over and civic stability had been reestablished. In retrospect, the charge against Socrates of leading the youth astray makes some sense, although it would have been rather long in coming. Two of Socrates's former students, Alcibiades and Kritias, had brought great suffering upon Athens, as thoroughly documented in prior chapters. These two had abandoned Socrates's teachings for the pursuit of power and self-gain. Both had been dead for a few years by the time Socrates was charged with leading the youth astray in 399 B.C.E.: Alcibiades was slain in 404 B.C.E. and Kritias in 403 B.C.E. Moreover, it would have been difficult to label either Alcibiades or Kritias "youths" had they been alive in 399 B.C.E.; they would have been fifty-one and sixty-one years old, respectively. In addition, when democratic

government was reestablished in 403 B.C.E., a reconciliation measure called
the Act of Oblivion was passed, which was designed to heal the wounds
of years of political upheaval and prevented prosecution for crimes that
occurred prior to 403 B.C.E. Even if Socrates had been liable for the sins of
his former students, Alcibiades in particular, the amnesty law forbade his
being charged. The question then becomes, what did Socrates do to subvert
the gods of the state and lead the youth astray after 403 B.C.E.? We do not
know when Socrates first said the *Allegory of the Cave*—Plato wrote it down
some two decades after Socrates's death—but based on the circumstances, it
was probably delivered a few months after the Andocides trial. The people
who heard the *Allegory* are the new youths being corrupted.

The charge of not worshipping the state gods but divinities of his own
invention was thought to refer to Socrates's lifelong practice of following
his "inner voice," which warned him against taking wrong action. The issue
with the "inner voice" is that it is part of a divinely assigned mission given to
him by the Oracle at Delphi, who is the voice of the god Apollo, to examine
people to search out the wisest person, albeit in vague and poetic terms.
The "inner voice," which stems to some extent from a state-recognized god,
in no way precluded his worship of the many other state-recognized gods.
Socrates was known to have been dutifully attentive to Athenian religious
observances. The only words attributed to Socrates where he appears to
dismiss a state-recognized god and then places favor with a new "divinity"
are in the *Allegory of the Cave*, where he depicts the goddess Persephone as
a meaningless and deceptive shadow and then shows the released prisoner
the true light of the sun itself, in this way deifying the intellect.

This is heresy, plain and simple.

Again, ancient Athens was not a place where any person had to wait
around to make charges against someone else. As I'm sure you've noticed
by now, people got charged for alleged offenses, big and small, all the time,
which helps further distort the picture of the trial of Socrates. If *Clouds*
was enough to prompt charges, then they didn't need to wait twenty-four
years to do so. The plays were not in and of themselves enough to cause
charges to be brought against Socrates, even if they did contribute to their

ultimate success. If his "inner voice" was sufficient to trigger the charges, then there was a more than fifty-year time frame to charge him with that, but he couldn't really be charged with following the Oracle at Delphi. That was what people were supposed to do. Clearly the "inner voice" was not enough standing on its own. If the actions of Alcibiades were blamable in the least on Socrates, then there was ample opportunity over the decades to launch charges against Socrates. They could have picked any of Alcibiades's many outrageous acts to blame on Socrates. And yet they didn't while he was alive. If Kritias's actions were likewise the fault of Socrates, then there may have been a window of opportunity after the fall of the Thirty to charge Socrates, at least up until the Act of Oblivion was passed. But again, Socrates was very much at odds with the Thirty. The point is, the causes usually cited for the charges against Socrates—*Clouds*, "inner voice," Alcibiades, and Kritias—are important contributing factors, elements that enhance the odds of successful prosecution, but they miss the main factor—the sheer heresy of the *Allegory of the Cave*. I cannot emphasize this point enough, that these are the only words attributed to Socrates where he appears to impugn a state-recognized god, portraying Persephone as a worthless shadow and replacing her with the intellectual light of truth from the sun itself, making philosophy the one true god. Socrates comes far too close to the ritual miracle of the Mysteries of Eleusis, the most divine secret in the ancient Greek world. A secret guarded by the stealthy Callias at the time, as well as hundreds of other priests just like him over the almost two thousand years the Mysteries of Eleusis were in force.

This is a game of shadows, a dispute about shadows, fought in the shadows. Socrates's case will be tried back in the cave. Socrates, a lover of the light of truth and a basker in the true reality of the sun, will be out of his philosophical element. His jury will be a group of prisoners chained to a wall staring at shadows. Hidden behind that wall will be Callias holding his puppets in front of the fire.

39

Trial of Socrates

T he trial of Socrates has always seemed like something of a riddle, because the prosecution's case was not recorded. His accusers talked for three hours, and we have not a single word of their presentation. Our only understanding of their remarks comes from inferences in Socrates's rebuttal to them. However, now that you have read the preceding chapters, you should have a much better understanding of the events, persons, and agendas at play. Even if you have read Plato's version of the trial of Socrates before, as many have, you will now see it with fresh eyes and a deeper appreciation of what was really happening. You will be able to read between the lines and more fully apprehend this remarkably well-choreographed dance of shadows.

Socrates begins:[1]

> SOCRATES: I cannot tell how you have felt, my fellow Athenians, at hearing the speeches of my accusers, but I know that their persuasive words almost made me forget who I was, and yet they have hardly spoken a word of truth. But many as their

falsehoods were, there was one of them, which quite amazed me—I mean when they told you to be upon your guard, and not to let yourselves be deceived by the force of my eloquence, they ought to have been ashamed, because they were sure to be detected as soon as I opened my lips and displayed my inelo-quence . . . unless by the force of eloquence they mean the force of truth; for then I do indeed admit that I am eloquent . . .

Based on Socrates's response, it seems clear the accusers have warned the jury about Socrates's ability to deliver convincing arguments. Although Socrates is not prone to flowery speeches or emotional displays, he never-theless presents a compelling case in a straightforward manner:

SOCRATES: . . . I am more than seventy years of age, and this is the first time that I have ever appeared in a court of law, and I am quite a stranger to the ways of this place; therefore, please regard me as if I were really a stranger, whom you would excuse if he spoke in his native tongue, and after the fashion of his country. I think this is a fair request. Never mind the manner, which may or may not be good; but think only of the justice of my cause, and give heed to that. Let the judges decide justly and the speaker speak truly.

Next, Socrates addresses his accusers, dividing them into two types: old and new, which is a strong indication that something new has happened. He begins with the accusers of old, the people who have slandered him in the past:

SOCRATES: . . . And first, I have to reply to the older charges and to my first accusers, and then I will go to the later ones. For I have had many accusers, who accused me of old, and their false charges have continued during many years; and I am more afraid of them than of Anytus and his associates, who are dangerous, too, in their own way. But far more dangerous are the oldest accusers, who began when you were children, and took possession of your minds with their falsehoods, telling of Socrates, a wise man, who speculated about the heaven above, and searched into the earth beneath, and made the worse appear the better cause. These are the accusers whom I dread, for they are the circulators of rumors that inquirers and philosophers such as myself do not believe in the gods. And these accusers are many, and their charges against me are very old, and they made them in days when many of you were impressionable—in childhood or in youth—and these lies were accepted by default, for there was no one to protest them. And, hardest of all, I do not know and cannot tell you the names of theses slanderers; except perchance the comic poet Aristophanes. But the main group of these slanderers, who from envy and malice have affected you, are most difficult to deal with, because I cannot call them up here to cross-examine them, and therefore I must simply fight with shadows in my own defense . . .

Socrates understands that he is dealing with a long-held feeling of discomfort about his philosophizing and he's attempting to address it early and cut it off at the root. He is none of the things he is popularly mischaracterized to be; he is not the satirized version of Socrates but a living, breathing person who has sought truth only. But in this instance, he cannot call his oldest accusers to the stand since many have already passed away. Socrates is seventy years old in a time and place where reaching seventy was extremely rare. His oldest accusers, his elders and many of his contemporaries, are dead. Socrates is fighting shadows on several levels.

Next, Socrates attempts to distinguish himself from professional teachers, sophists, who take pay for their services. Socrates has never taken pay: he is just a man who likes to ask questions. To make this distinction between himself and the sophists, he chooses an interesting person to use as an example—Callias.

SOCRATES: . . . I heard about a foreign philosopher residing in Athens, and I came to hear of him in this way: Callias, as you well know, has spent a world of money on the Sophists to educate his sons. I asked him, "Callias, if your two sons were foals or calves, there would be no difficulty in finding someone to supervise them; we should hire a trainer of horses or a farmer probably who would improve and perfect them in their own proper virtue and excellence; but as they are human beings, whom are you thinking of placing in charge of them? Is there anyone who understands human and political virtue? You must have thought about this as you have sons; is there anyone?" "There is," he said. "Who is he?" I asked. "And of what country? And what does he charge?" "Evenus the Parian," he replied; "he is the man, and his charge is five minae." Happy is Evenus, I said to myself, if he really has this wisdom, and teaches at such a modest charge. Had I the same, I should have been very proud and conceited; but the truth is that I have no knowledge of the kind.

Socrates, at least the way Plato portrays him here (remembering that when Plato wrote about the trial of Socrates he was under the same societal rules about the Mysteries and probably had to tone down his version of Socrates's defense), distances himself from a sophist while also demeaning neither him nor Callias. In reality, Socrates could be very judgmental about sophists and Callias. Also note, the topic the teachability of virtue is one of the main themes of Socrates's discussions one of which occurred at Callias's house at Callias's urging. Everyone knows that Socrates does not believe in the teachability of virtue. Given the background, there is a subtle dig in Socrates's words, which would not have been lost on Callias or his entourage. To Socrates, the type of knowledge Callias seeks and dispenses has no value. Clearly Socrates does not go after Callias in the same brutal way that Andocides had, tearing into his personal life. But it is significant that Socrates uses Callias, a hereditary official of the holy Eleusinian Mysteries, as an illustration of someone paying sophists to educate his children, and he does so in front of five hundred jurors who honored and feared the priests of Eleusis and the goddess Persephone. In this time, it was widely believed that a single person's insult to a god could cause that god to withdraw its favor and visit calamity on the entire population. All things good and bad came from the gods. Socrates's jab at Callias is measured. The fact that Socrates brings up Callias at all is noteworthy: it shows that Socrates is aware of the game that's being played.

Socrates then turns to the subject of his "new" accusers and calls Meletus to the stand.

> SOCRATES: You think a great deal about the improvement of youth?

> MELETUS: Yes, I do.

> SOCRATES: Tell the judges, then, who is it that improves the youth; for you must know, as you have taken the pains to discover their corrupter, and are citing and accusing me before them. Speak, then, and tell the judges who their improver is.

Meletus, unsure what to say, does not respond.

> SOCRATES: Observe, Meletus, that you are silent, and have nothing to say. Is this not rather disgraceful, and a very considerable proof that you have no interest in the matter? Speak up, friend, and tell us who their improver is.

> MELETUS: The laws.

> SOCRATES: But that, my good sir, is not my meaning. I want to know who the person is, who, in the first place, knows the laws.

MELETUS: The judges, Socrates, who are present in court.

SOCRATES: What do you mean to say, Meletus, that they are able to instruct and improve youth?

MELETUS: Certainly they are.

SOCRATES: What, all of them, or some only and not others?

MELETUS: All of them.

SOCRATES: By the goddess, that is good news! There are plenty of improvers, then. And what do you say of the audience—do they improve them?

MELETUS: Yes, they do.

SOCRATES: And the council members?

MELETUS: Yes, the council members improve them.

SOCRATES: But perhaps the members of the citizen assembly corrupt them? Or do they, too, improve them?

MELETUS: They improve them.

SOCRATES: Then every Athenian improves and elevates them; all with the exception of myself; and I alone am their corrupter? Is that what you affirm?

MELETUS: That is what I stoutly affirm.

SOCRATES: I am very unfortunate if that is true. But suppose I ask you a question: Would you say that this also holds true in the case of horses? Does one man do them harm and all the world good? Is not the exact opposite of this true? One man is able to do them good, or at least not many, the trainer of horses, that is to say, does them good, and others who have to do with them rather injure them? Is not that true, Meletus, of horses, or any other animals? Yes, certainly. Whether you and Anytus say yes or no, that is no matter. Happy indeed would be the condition of youth if they had one corrupter only, and all the rest of the world were their improvers. And you, Meletus, have sufficiently shown that you never had a thought about the young: your carelessness is seen in your not caring about matters spoken of in this very indictment . . .

. . . But still I should like to know, Meletus, in what I am supposed to corrupt the young. I suppose you mean, as I infer from your indictment, that I teach them not to acknowledge the gods which the state acknowledges, but some other new divinities or spiritual agencies in their stead. These are the lessons of which I allegedly corrupt the youth, as you say?

MELETUS: Yes, that I say emphatically.

SOCRATES: Then, by the gods, Meletus, of whom we are speaking, tell me and the court, in somewhat plainer terms, what you mean! I do not as yet understand whether you affirm that I teach others to acknowledge some gods, and therefore do believe in gods and am not an entire atheist, this you do not lay to my charge, but only that they are not the same gods which the city recognizes. The charge is that they are different gods or do you mean to say that I am an atheist simply, and a teacher of atheism?

MELETUS: I mean the latter, you are a complete atheist.

SOCRATES: That is an extraordinary statement, Meletus. Why do you say this? . . .

MELETUS: I assure you, judges, that he does not believe in them . . .

SOCRATES: Friend Meletus, do you think that you are accusing Anaxagoras? And do you have such a low opinion of the judges to consider them ignorant to such a degree as not to know that these doctrines you mention are found in the books of Anaxagoras, not me . . . And so, Meletus, you really think that I do not believe in any god?

MELETUS: I swear by Zeus that you believe absolutely in none at all.

SOCRATES: You are a liar, Meletus, not believed even by yourself. For I cannot help thinking, my fellow Athenians, that Meletus is reckless and impudent, and that he has written this indictment in a spirit of mere wantonness and youthful bravado . . . For he certainly does appear to me to contradict himself in the indictment as much as if he said that Socrates is guilty of not believing in the gods, and yet of believing in them, but this surely is a piece of fun.

I should like you, men of Athens, to join me in examining what I conceive to be his inconsistency; and you, Meletus, answer. And I must remind you that you are not to interrupt me if I speak in my accustomed manner.

Throughout his defense, Socrates repeatedly asks the jury not to interrupt him, which seems to indicate that he is being interrupted quite regularly. There is no record of what the members of the jury were saying to him, but it does give a sense of the mood of the jury. Socrates continues:

SOCRATES: Did ever man, Meletus, believe in the existence of human things, and not of human beings?

Meletus does not answer.

SOCRATES: . . . I wish, men of Athens, that he would answer, and not be always trying to get up an interruption. Did ever any man believe in horsemanship, and not in horses? Or in flute-playing, and not in flute-players? No, my friend, I will answer to you and to the court, as you refuse to answer for yourself. There is no man who ever did. But now please to answer the next question: Can a man believe in spiritual and divine agencies, and not in spirits or demigods?

MELETUS: He cannot.

SOCRATES: I am glad that I have extracted that answer, by the assistance of the court . . .

Evidently the judges ordered Meletus to answer.

SOCRATES: . . . Nevertheless you swear in the indictment that I teach and believe in divine or spiritual agencies (new or old, no matter for that); at any rate, I believe in spiritual agencies, as you say and swear in the affidavit; but if I believe in divine beings, I must believe in spirits or demigods; is not that true? Yes, that is true, for I may assume that your silence gives assent to that. Now what are spirits or demigods? Are they not either gods or the sons of gods? Is that true?

MELETUS: Yes, that is true . . .

SOCRATES: . . . You say first that I don't believe in gods, and then again that I do believe in gods; that is, if I believe in demigods. For if the demigods are the illegitimate sons of gods, whether by the Nymphs or by any other mothers, as is thought, that, as all men will allow, necessarily implies the existence of their parents. You might as well affirm the existence of mules, and deny that of horses and asses. Such nonsense, Meletus, could only have been intended by you as a trial of me. You have put this into the indictment because you had nothing real of which to accuse me. But no one who has a particle of understanding will ever be convinced by you that the same man can believe in divine and supernatural beings, and yet not believe that there are gods and demigods and heroes.

I have said enough in answer to the charge of Meletus: any elaborate defense is unnecessary . . .

Meletus is released from the stand. Socrates deftly avoids the question of old gods, those recognized by the state, and new gods of his own invention by framing the matter as atheism versus theism and showing the absurdity of being both simultaneously. Meletus's silence and his attempts to induce outbursts from the jury indicate that he knows he is in over his head. Socrates's examination of Meletus, and his refutation of the charges as written, is meant to persuade members of the jury who do not know what's actually going on. Callias remains hidden even from those who do his bidding. By now, Socrates has made his own vote count based on those who have been interrupting him. He just needs to flip a little over thirty votes out of five hundred to win acquittal, but the looks on the jury members' faces give him pause:

SOCRATES: . . . I certainly have my share of enemies, and this is what will be my destruction if I am destroyed, of that I am certain, not by Meletus, nor yet Anytus, but the envy and disparagements of the world, which has been the death of many good men, and will probably be the death of many more, there is no danger of my being the last . . .

But Socrates, sensing his problem with the jury math, has to draw a line, has to make a stand: he was not cowed by the Thirty nor will he be intimidated his accusers, the judges, or this jury:

> SOCRATES: . . . Oh men of Athens, I say to you, do as Anytus bids or not as Anytus bids, and either acquit me or not; but whatever you do, know that I shall never alter my ways, not even if I have to die many times . . .

The force of this statement leads him to a surefire winning line of argumentation:

> SOCRATES: . . . For if I am really corrupting the youth, and have corrupted some of them already, those of them who have grown up should come forward as accusers and take their revenge; and if they do not like to come themselves, some of their relatives, fathers, brothers, or other kinsmen, should say what evil their families suffered at my hands. Now is their time. Many of them I see here in court . . . any of whom Meletus should have produced as witnesses in the course of his speech. And let him still produce them, if he has forgotten. I will make way for him. And let him say, if he has any testimony of the sort which he can produce . . .

Meletus offers no witnesses. The prosecution avoids the easiest way to corroborate the charges. This is telling, as it signals that the charges are about something else entirely, and this trial is a sham, a foregone conclusion from the get-go. Socrates concludes his defense with the assertion that he firmly believes in the gods:

> SOCRATES: . . . I do believe that there are gods, and in a far higher sense than that in which any of my accusers believe in

them. And to you and to God I commit my cause, to be determined by you as is best for you and me.

The court herald calls for the jury to make its judgment. All five hundred
jurors slowly line up, sandaled feet shuffling across marble floors, and one
by one deposit little bronze discs into marked urns, guilty and not guilty . . .
plink, plink, plink . . . After the last juror has voted, a select handful of jurors
tally the discs. Socrates's defense offered a compelling counternarrative to
the unrecorded case made by his accusers. Somehow it proves unpersuasive.

The jury, voting 280–220, finds Socrates guilty.

Callias and Anytus had done their math correctly.

40

Sentencing

The prosecution and the defense are then given the opportunity to make proposals for sentencing. The prosecution suggests the death penalty. Socrates counters:[1]

> SOCRATES: . . . My fellow Athenians, there are many reasons why I am not grieved at the vote of condemnation. I expected it, and am only surprised that the votes are so nearly equal. I had thought that the majority against me would have been far larger; but now, had thirty votes gone over to the other side, I should have been acquitted. And I may say that I have escaped Meletus, as is evident, for without the assistance of Anytus and Lycon, he would not have had one-fifth of the votes . . .

Socrates acknowledges the role of Anytus and Lycon in delivering votes but feels vindicated that he would have bested Meletus had it just been a one-on-one contest. In Socrates's estimation, the accusers had prevailed not by the force of their reasoning but by the number of their political allies. Next, Socrates proposes a very different "punishment."

SOCRATES: . . . And so he proposes death as the penalty. And what shall I propose on my part, dear Athenians? Clearly that which is my due. And what is that which I ought to pay or to receive? What shall be done to the man who has never been idle during his whole life, but has not cared for what the many care about: wealth, military offices, political offices, plots, and parties . . . What would be a reward suitable to a poor man who is your benefactor, who desires leisure that he may instruct you? There can be no more fitting reward than maintenance in the heroes' banquet hall, oh Athenians, a reward which he deserves far more than the citizen who has won the prize at Olympia in the horse or chariot race, whether the chariots were drawn by two horses or by many. For I am poor, and he has enough; and he only gives you the appearance of happiness, and I give you the reality. And if I am to estimate the penalty justly, I say that maintenance in the heroes' banquet hall is the just return . . .

To be clear, Socrates is suggesting that his "punishment" be free food and drink at the heroes' banquet hall for the rest of his days. This is beyond bold, even impudent, given the situation. It enrages his condemners, but he is just being honest, since he doesn't see that he deserves any punishment at all, much less the death penalty.

SOCRATES: . . . I say again that the greatest good is to converse about virtue daily, and all that you hear of me examining myself and others—that the life which is unexamined is not worth living—that you are still less likely to believe. And yet what I say is true, although a thing of which it is hard for me to persuade you. Moreover, I am not accustomed to think that I deserve any punishment . . .

Of the many quotes from Socrates, however translated, "the unexamined life is not worth living" is among the finest and most repeated. However, the jury is in no mood to listen to his admonishments. Socrates's allies in the jury, sensing the danger, bid him to change his tact.

> SOCRATES: . . . If I had money I might have proposed to give you what I had, and have been none the worse. But you see that I have none, and can only ask you to proportion the fine to my means. However, I think that I could afford a minae, and therefore I propose that penalty . . .

This is a paltry sum of money, and is more of an insult to the court than a proper fine. Socrates's friends in the jury urge him to be more reasonable.

> SOCRATES: . . . Plato, Crito, Critobulus, and Apollodorus, my friends here, bid me say thirty minae, and they will be the sureties. Well then, say thirty minae, let that be the penalty; for that they will be ample security to you.

Socrates concludes his sentencing proposal. He has gone from proposing a hero's treatment and a banquet in his honor to offering to pay a small fine. This is quite a reversal, likely prompted by the mounting concern his friends feel for him, and shows how perilous his position has become. The jury then votes between the proposed sentences of the prosecution and the defense.

The majority of the jury votes in favor of the accusers' sentencing proposal.

The herald announces that Socrates is officially condemned to death.

41

Closing Remarks

As is the custom, the condemned man is afforded the opportunity to make his final remarks:[1]

> SOCRATES: . . . Not much time will be gained, Athenians, in return for the evil name which you will get from the detractors of the city, who will say that you killed Socrates, a wise man; for they will call me wise when they want to reproach you. If you had waited a little while, your desire would have been fulfilled in the course of nature. For I am far advanced in years, as you may perceive, and not far from death.

Socrates questions the rationale for putting an elderly man to death. He is going to die soon anyway; all his accusers and convictors have gained is the mark of evil on their eternal souls.

> SOCRATES: I am speaking now only to those of you who have condemned me to death . . . nor do I now repent of the manner

of my defense, and I would rather die having spoken after my manner, than speak in your manner and live. For neither in war nor yet at law ought any man use every way of escaping death. For often in battle there is no doubt that if a man will throw away his arms, and fall on his knees before his pursuers, he may escape death; and in other dangers there are other ways of escaping death, if a man is willing to say and do anything. The difficulty, my friends, is not in avoiding death, but in avoiding unrighteousness; for that runs faster than death. I am old and move slowly, and the slower runner has overtaken me, and my accusers are keen and quick, and the faster runner, who is unrighteousness, has overtaken them. And now I depart hence condemned by you to suffer the penalty of death, and you the jury, too, go your ways condemned by the truth to suffer the penalty of villainy and wrong; and I must abide by my award, and let you abide by yours . . .

Having addressed his condemners he turns to address his supporters, his friends who voted for acquittal, espousing the possibilities of what lies beyond the mortal vale:

SOCRATES: . . . Let us reflect in another way, and we shall see that there is great reason to hope that death is a good, for one of two things: either death is a state of nothingness and utter unconsciousness, or, as men say, there is a change and migration of the soul from this world to another. Now if you suppose that there is no consciousness, but a sleep like the sleep of him who is undisturbed even by dreams, death will be an unspeakable gain. For if a person were to select the night in which his sleep was undisturbed even by dreams, and were to compare with this with the other days and nights of his life, and then were to tell us how many days and nights he had passed in the course of his life better and more pleasantly than this one, I think that any man, I will not say a private man, but even the great king, will not find many such days or nights, when compared with the others. Now if death is like this, I say that to die is to gain, for eternity is then only a single night . . .

If death be nothingness, then he will enjoy its long night of deepest slumber. Next, he addresses the possibility of a migration of the immortal soul to a great beyond.

SOCRATES: . . . But if death is the journey to another place, and there, as men say, all the dead are, what good, my friends and judges, can be greater than this? If indeed when the pilgrim arrives to the other side, he is delivered from the so-called purveyors of justice in this world, and finds the true judges who are said to give judgment there, sons of God who were righteous in their own life, that pilgrimage will be worth making. What would not a man give if he might converse with Orpheus and Musaeus and Hesiod and Homer? Indeed, if this be true, let me die again and again. I, too, shall have a wonderful interest in a place where I can converse with Palamedes, and Ajax the son of Telamon, and other heroes of old, who have suffered death through an unjust judgment; and there will be no small pleasure, as I think, in comparing my own sufferings with theirs. Above all, I shall be able to continue my search into true and false knowledge; as in this world, so also in that; I shall find out who is wise, and who pretends to be wise, and is not. What would not a man give, oh judges, to be able to examine the leader of the great Trojan expedition; or Odysseus or Sisyphus, or numberless others, men and women, too! What infinite delight would there be in conversing with them and asking them questions! For in that realm they do not put a man to death for this; certainly not. For besides being happier in that world than in this, they will be immortal, if what is said is true . . .

He continues to paint the death in the brightest of possible terms, seemingly in an attempt to cheer up his weeping colleagues.

> SOCRATES: . . . Be of good cheer about death, and know this is true: that no evil can happen to a good man, either in life or after death. He and his are not neglected by the gods; nor has my own approaching end happened by mere chance. But I see clearly that to die and be released is better for me; and therefore, the oracle gave no sign. For which reason also, I am not angry with my accusers, or my condemners; they have done me no harm, although neither of them meant to do me any good; and for this I may gently reprove them . . .

Socrates concludes his remarks:

> . . . The hour of departure has arrived, and we go our separate ways; I to die, and you to live. Which is better only God knows.

His friends gather around him, many weeping.[2]

> APOLLODORUS: But the hardest thing of all to bear, dear Socrates, is to see you put to death unjustly.

> SOCRATES: Would you rather, my dear friend, see me put to death justly?

Socrates smiles and comforts Apollodorus. Socrates is then led away to his jail cell and his followers are left devastated. His defense had been a sweeping explanation of the role of the philosopher in society, the height of oratory, among the greatest and most widely read speeches in human history, but it wasn't enough to win acquittal.

Over the course of the last two thousand years, hundreds of millions of people from around the globe have read translations of the trial of Socrates, including most students today, and many have come away with great sympathy for Socrates, inspired by his fortitude, but also with a lingering sense that something is missing, the accusers' case, obviously, which has long hindered an understanding of what this trial was actually about. The trial was set in the context of ancient Athenian society, and like every society it had its idiosyncratic mores. It is difficult for us, more than two thousand years removed from the trial, to grasp the references, inferences, and idioms that relate to topics that were so woven into the culture that they went almost without saying to ancient Athenians. The role religion played in the society, especially the Mysteries of Eleusis with all its secrecy, cannot be overstated. The trial of Socrates, not unlike the assassination of Alcibiades, is the result of an alignment of enemies and agendas. Callias had a religious reason for eliminating Socrates, and he most likely did not share that reason with his team of accusers, who had their own personal reasons to get rid of Socrates, except for Meletus, who was just a hired prosecutorial mercenary. Anytus and Lycon delivered blocs of jurors who were tied to their agendas. These jurors didn't know Callias's rationale for the charges and may not have even known he was involved. Socrates's *Allegory of the Cave* and its scathing critique of the Mysteries of Eleusis was dangerous to the religious establishment, and they used others to do their bidding and silence him. Many members of the jury didn't know what the trial was really about. So the nebulousness of the trial, as you read it today, is understandable, because it was nebulous at the time. By design.

Callias, hidden behind the wall, had deftly maneuvered his puppets.

42

The Wait

U nder normal circumstances, Socrates would have been whisked away to jail and put to death later that same day. However, Socrates's trial took place at the beginning of the holy season of the pilgrimage to Delos, when executions were not allowed.[1] The priests of Apollo had crowned the stern of the pilgrims' ship, the official opening of the holy season, the day before Socrates's trial, and the holy season would last until the pilgrims returned from Delos, which could be delayed by sea conditions or storms.[2] Socrates languishes in prison for several weeks, not knowing when the ship would return but knowing full well that when it did, he would die.

This interlude allows his friends and family to visit him in jail, which is a nondescript low-slung building not far from the agora. (You can visit the site of the jail the next time you're in Athens.)

Plato records a visit Socrates receives from his friend Crito.[3] Socrates awakens in the morning to find Crito sitting across from him.

SOCRATES: (*rousing*) Crito? Did you just get here?

CRITO: No, I've been here little while.

SOCRATES: Then why didn't you wake me up?

CRITO: Why, indeed, Socrates. I myself would rather not have all this sleeplessness and sorrow, but I have been wondering at your peaceful slumber, and that was the reason why I did not wake you up, because I wanted you to be out of pain. I have always thought you happy in the calmness of your temperament, but never did I see the like of the easy and cheerful way in which you bear this calamity.

SOCRATES: Why, Crito, when a man has reached my age he shouldn't fear death.

CRITO: And yet when other old men find themselves with similar misfortunes, age does not prevent them from fretting.

SOCRATES: That may be. But you have not told me why you have come so early in the morning.

CRITO: I come to bring you a message which is sad and painful; not, as I believe, to yourself but to all of us who are your friends, and saddest of all to me.

SOCRATES: What! I suppose that the ship has come from Delos, on the arrival of which I am to die?

CRITO: No, the ship has not actually arrived, but she will probably be here late today, as persons who have come from there tell me; and therefore tomorrow, Socrates, will be the last day of your life.

SOCRATES: Very well, Crito; if such is the will of God, I am willing . . .

CRITO: . . . But, oh Socrates, let me ask you once more to take my advice and escape. For if you die, I shall not only lose a friend who can never be replaced, but there is another evil: people who do not know you and me will believe that I might have saved you if I had been willing to give money, but that I did not care. Now, can there be a worse disgrace than this—that I should be thought to value money more than the life of a friend? For the many will not be persuaded that I wanted you to escape, and that you refused.

SOCRATES: But why, my dear Crito, should we care about the opinion of the many? Good people, and they are the only persons who are worth considering, will think of these things truly as they happened.

CRITO: But do you see, Socrates, that the opinion of the many must be regarded, as is evident by your own case . . . Tell me, Socrates, whether you are not acting out of regard to me and your other friends. Are you afraid that if you escape, we may get into trouble with the law for having stolen you away, and lose either the whole or a greater part of our property; or that even a worse evil may happen to us? Now, if this is your fear, be at ease; for in order to save you, we ought surely to run this or even a greater risk; be persuaded, then, and do as I say.

SOCRATES: Yes, Crito, that is one fear which you mention, but by no means the only one.

CRITO: Well, my friend, do not fear. There are persons who at no great cost are willing to save you and bring you out of prison; and as for any would-be informers, you may observe that they are far from being exorbitant in their demands; a little money will satisfy them. My means, which, as I am sure, are ample, are at your service, and if you have a scruple about spending

all mine, there are others among us who will give you the use
of their money; and one of them has brought a sum of money
for this very purpose; and many others are willing to spend their
money, too. I say, therefore, do not hesitate about making your
escape . . . Nor can I think that you are justified, Socrates, in
betraying your own life when you might be saved; this is playing
into the hands of your enemies and destroyers; and moreover, I
should say that you are betraying your children; for you might
bring them up and educate them; instead of which you will leave
them, and they will have to take their chance; and if they do not
meet with the usual fate of orphans, there will be small thanks to
you. No man should bring children into the world who is unwilling
to persevere to the end in their nurture and education . . . Make
your mind up then, or rather have your mind already made up,
for the time of deliberation is over, and there is only one thing to
be done, which must be done, if at all, this very night, and which
any delay will render all but impossible; I beseech you therefore,
Socrates, to listen to me and do as I say.

Alcibiades would have taken this deal in an instant, but Socrates is far
more discerning.

SOCRATES: Dear Crito, your zeal is invaluable, if a right one;
but if wrong, the greater the zeal the greater the evil; and therefore
we ought to consider whether these things shall be done or not . . .

Socrates wants to explore the premises of Crito's proposition, before
rendering a decision to flee or not:

SOCRATES: . . . Let us argue the question whether I ought or
ought not to try to escape: and if I am clearly right in escaping,
then I will make the attempt; but if not, I will abstain. The
other considerations which you mention, of money and loss of

character, and the duty of educating children, are, I fear, only the ideas of the many, who would be as ready to call people to life, if they were able, as they are to put them to death—and with as little reason. The only question which remains to be considered is whether it is right to escape, and if not, then death or any other calamity which may ensue on my remaining here must not be allowed to enter into the calculation.

CRITO: I think that you are right, Socrates. How should we proceed?

SOCRATES: Let us consider the matter together, and either refute me if you can, and I will be convinced; or else cease, my dear friend, from repeating to me that I ought to escape: for I am extremely desirous to be persuaded by you, but not against my own better judgment. And now please consider my first position, and do your best to answer me.

CRITO: I will do my best.

SOCRATES: Are we to say that we are never intentionally to do wrong, or that in one way we should do wrong and in another way we shouldn't do wrong? Or is doing wrong always evil and dishonorable? Are all our conclusions which we made in the last few days just to be thrown away? And have we, at our age, having earnestly discoursed with one another all our life long only to discover that we are no better than children? Or are we to rest assured, in spite of the opinion of the many, and in spite of consequences whether better or worse, of the truth of what was then said, that injustice is always an evil and dishonor to him who acts unjustly? Shall we affirm that?

CRITO: Yes . . .

Socrates then launches into a long discourse about the implied agreement, or covenant, between the state and its citizens. He freely chose to live his life in Athens, and thus, under the rules of Athens. He could have moved to another place if he didn't like Athens, but he stayed and fathered three children as Athenian citizens, which shows his acceptance of the social contract. Socrates changes the voice of his dialogue, speaking as the laws of Athens to himself.

> SOCRATES: "... Moreover, you might, if you had liked, have fixed the penalty at banishment in the course of the trial. The State which refuses to let you go now would have let you go then. But you pretended that you preferred death to exile, and that you were not grieved at death. And now you have forgotten these fine sentiments, and pay no respect to us, the laws, and are doing what only the miserable would do, running away and turning your back upon the compacts and agreements which you made as a citizen. Answer this question: Are we right in saying that you agreed to be governed according to us in deed, and not in word only? Is that true or not?"
>
> How shall we answer that, Crito? Must we not agree?

> CRITO: There is no help, Socrates.

Socrates continues to speak to himself as the voice of Athens.

> SOCRATES: "... Just consider, if you transgress and err by escaping, what good will you do, either to yourself or to your friends? That your friends will be driven into exile and deprived of citizenship, or will lose their property, is tolerably certain ... Say that you wish to live for the sake of your children, that you may bring them up and educate them; will you take them away and deprive them of Athenian citizenship? Is that the benefit which you would confer upon them? Or are you under

the impression that they will be better cared for and educated
in Athens if you are still alive, although absent from them,
because your friends will take care of them? Do you think that
if you're the inhabitant of some other land your friends will
take care of them, but if you are an inhabitant of the realm of
the dead your friends will not take care of them? . . ."

Socrates clearly understands that if he escapes, then his friends will be
put at considerable risk, a greater risk than, perhaps, they even realize.
To protect them, they must remain ignorant of his actual crime. Socrates
attacked the Mysteries in a scathing philosophical critique, which was a
capital offense; he punched Callias in the nose, philosophically speaking.
While Socrates knows full well what the charges were about, Crito and
the rest do not. Given the circumstances, escape is really not an option,
despite what Crito proposes. Socrates asks whether there is a place outside
of Athens where death cannot go.[4] If Socrates flees, he will be hunted
down and killed, just like Alcibiades, and any friends involved in the
escape will suffer harsh penalties, which Socrates simply cannot allow.
Callias may be hoping that Socrates flees, so he can have Socrates and
his whole lot of friends eliminated, too, in one fell swoop. If Socrates's
friends are exiled or killed, then there will be no men left to look after his
children, which would put them in a considerably worse set of circumstances. The best way for Socrates to protect his friends and family is to
take his punishment. Socrates stops talking as the "Laws" and addresses
Crito directly:

> SOCRATES: This is the voice [the laws of Athens] which I
> seem to hear murmuring in my ears . . . which prevents me
> from hearing any other. And I know that anything more which
> you will say will be in vain. Yet speak, if you have anything
> to say.

> CRITO: I have nothing to say, Socrates.

SOCRATES: Then let me follow the intimations of the will of God.

Socrates's rationale for not escaping, while noble on its surface, is intended as a justification on philosophical terms—Socrates simply cannot consciously do an unjust deed—which Crito grudgingly understands. Socrates's real goal of the conversation is to dissuade Crito, while also not involving him in any past or future crimes.

43

Execution

On the day of the execution, a number of Socrates's friends visit him in his jail cell. They get into a discussion about the afterlife. Socrates is never one to shy away from a pressing topic, regardless of how painful it may be to his listeners or himself. He equates the Theory of Forms (which was discussed in the beginning of the book) with the idea of an immortal soul. He draws parallels between the Abstract Plane, the intellectual heavens that hold an imperishable/immutable form or idea of every physical object, with the Supernatural Realm, the immaterial "beyond" where deities and the dead dwell. This is Socrates's last and perhaps most important philosophical discourse, even though it's not often discussed today. It offers a reconciliation of the Abstract Plane and the Supernatural Realm. And it's not even slightly blasphemous.[1]

> SOCRATES: Is an idea or form, which we may define as an essence of true existence, liable to change to some degree over time? Or is it always what it is, having the same simple, self-existent, and unchanging form with no variation at all, in any way, at any time?

CEBES: The form must be always the same, Socrates.

SOCRATES: And what would you say of the form of "beauty," as it applies to humans, horses, or garments or anything else. Even if the form of beauty is unchanged do the beings and objects themselves remain unchanged? May they not rather be described as almost always changing whether quickly or slowly?

CEBES: The latter, they are always in a state of change.

SOCRATES: And these things you can touch and see and perceive with the senses, but the unchanging forms you can only perceive with the mind. Forms are invisible and are not directly seen?

CEBES: That is very true.

SOCRATES: Well, then, let us suppose that there are two sorts of existences, one seen, the other unseen. The seen is the changing, and the unseen is the unchanging. And, further, is not one part of a person a physical body and another part the soul?

CEBES: To be sure.

SOCRATES: And to which class may we say that the body is more like?

CEBES: Clearly to the seen. No one can doubt that.

SOCRATES: And is the soul seen or not seen?

CEBES: Not seen, Socrates . . .

SOCRATES: . . . And which does the soul resemble?

CEBES: The soul resembles the divine and the body the mortal; there can be no doubt of that, Socrates.

SOCRATES: Then reflect, Cebes, is not the conclusion of the whole matter this: that the soul is in the very likeness of the divine, immortal, intelligible, indissoluble, and unchangeable; and the body is in the very likeness of the human, mortal, dissoluble, and changeable. Can this, my dear Cebes, be denied?

CEBES: No, indeed.

SOCRATES: But if this is true, then is not the body liable to speedy dissolution? And is not the soul almost or altogether indissoluble?

CEBES: Certainly . . .

SOCRATES: . . . Suppose the soul, which is invisible, passes to the afterlife, pure and noble, and on its way to the good and wise God (to which, if God wills, my soul will also soon go), the soul perishes immediately on leaving the body as some say? That can never be, dear friends. The truth rather is that the soul which is pure at its departing draws after it no taint of the body . . . And what does this mean but that the soul has been a true disciple of philosophy and has practiced how to die easily? And is not philosophy the practice of death?

CEBES: Certainly.

This is an interesting concept, philosophy as the practice of death, which relates to the religious concept of leading a ritually well-practiced and righteous life in preparation for the afterlife, which, of course, first requires the death of the body.

> SOCRATES: That soul, I say, is invisible, departs to the invisible world to the divine realm of the immortal and rational: and arriving there, it lives in bliss and is released from human error and folly, their fears and wild passions and all other human ills, and forever dwells, as they say of the initiated, in company with the gods. Is not this true?

> CEBES: Yes, beyond a doubt . . .

Note: when Socrates speaks here of the "initiated," he is speaking of those people who have been initiated into the Eleusinian Mysteries. Socrates is tying the core concept of the Eleusinian Mysteries, a blissful afterlife, to the concept of the Theory of Forms, the abstract heavens.

> SOCRATES: . . . Those also who are remarkable for having led holy lives are released from this earthly prison, and go to their pure home. And those who have duly purified themselves with philosophy live henceforth altogether without the body, in mansions far better than these, which may not be described, and of which the time would fail me to tell . . .
> . . . Fair is the prize, and the hope great. I do not mean to affirm that the description which I have given of the soul and its heavenly mansions is exactly true. A person of sense ought hardly to say that. But I do say that, inasmuch as the soul is shown to be immortal, we may venture to think, not improperly or unworthily, that something of the kind is true. The venture is a glorious one, and we should comfort ourselves with words like these. I say, let a man be of good cheer about his soul, who has cast away the adornment of the body, and has followed after the pleasures of knowledge in this life; who has adorned the soul

in its own proper jewels, which are temperance, justice, courage, nobility, and truth. In these the soul is arrayed and ready to go on its journey to the other world . . .

This discussion of the soul is well-placed under the circumstances. Socrates's final dialogue, out of the many he had during his long lifetime, is a summation of sorts, the Abstract Plane and Supernatural Realm in harmony. The reason this final dialogue is so rarely discussed is not because it is valueless or was later refuted and forgotten, but rather because it became so widely accepted. Socrates spoke these words about four hundred years before the birth of Jesus of Nazareth and the subsequent writing of the Greek Scriptures (New Testament). Moreover, much of the actual assembly of the Hebrew Scriptures (Old Testament) from various sources occurred during the lifetime of Socrates. Understand that the concept of an immortal soul was not a significant part of the Jewish tradition at this time. It had quite enough of the idea back in the afterlife-obsessed realm of Pharaonic Egypt.

The ancient Greek, or Hellenistic, influence on the core concepts of the Abrahamic tradition is its own established branch of theological study. This is not to say that the ancient Greeks invented the concept of an afterlife, which was widespread and vastly predates them and perhaps goes back more than one hundred thousand years (based on grave goods from the Paleolithic), but rather that the ancient Greeks perfected the ritual performance of the afterlife with the Eleusinian Mysteries, and that Socrates, in his final dialogue, gave it intellectual justification. What Socrates says in his final dialogue was revolutionary at the time, even if many people living today take its ideas for granted and don't recognize it for its monumental importance. Socrates's explanation of the immortal soul went a long way toward promoting the idea and helping it become incorporated into subsequent traditions. Most people living today learned of the idea of an immortal soul from other sources without knowing the outsized role the Mystery religions and Socrates played in the popularization and dissemination of the concept. Socrates's final dialogue, while mostly forgotten, may be his most influential.

The final dialogue is both intellectually abstract and deeply spiritual, but Socrates cannot dwell in the realm of otherworldly speculation for too long; he has an earthly concern to address:

> SOCRATES: . . . Soon I must drink the poison, and I think that I better take a bath first, in order that no one will have to deal with washing my body after I am dead.

Yes, a man who spent most of his life going around unbathed and stinky takes a sudden interest in personal hygiene just as he nears death's door.

> CRITO: Yes, but first, do have you any commands for us, Socrates?
>
> SOCRATES: Nothing particular, only, as I have always told you, look discerningly at yourselves; this will always be a service to me and mine as well as to yourselves . . .
>
> CRITO: We will do our best. Now, how do you wish to be buried?
>
> SOCRATES: In any way that you like; only you must catch me first, and take care that I do not walk away from you. (*Smiling*) I cannot make Crito believe that I, the Socrates who has been talking to you, is not the same as the dead body you will soon see. Crito asks, "How shall he bury me?" I have spoken many words in the endeavor to show you that when I drink the poison, I shall leave you and go to the joys of the blessed beyond. These words of mine, with which I comforted you and myself, have had, I perceive, no effect upon Crito. And therefore I want you to be surety for me now, as he was surety for me at the trial: but let the promise be of another sort; for he was my surety to the judges that I would remain, but you must be my surety to him

that I shall not remain, but go away and depart; and then he will suffer less at my death, and not be grieved when he sees my body being burned or buried . . . Be of good cheer, then, my dear Crito, and say that you are burying my body only, and do with that as is usual, and as you think best.

Socrates goes to the bathing room. His friends wait in the jail cell. Phaedo describes how he feels at this moment:

PHAEDO: We wait, talking and thinking of the subject of discourse, and also of the greatness of our sorrow; he is like a father of whom we are being bereaved, and we are about to pass the rest of our lives as orphans.

After Socrates has taken his bath and dressed, his family enters. Xanthippe and their three sons, two of whom are still quite young, embrace Socrates, and he speaks with them for some time. Their conversation was not recorded, but we might imagine that it was heartfelt. At this point, Xanthippe may be the only person who truly understands why Socrates took the stand he did and why he mounted the defense he did. He was, in his way, looking after them. The family will not be allowed to witness the execution for obvious reasons. The appointed hour of sunset draws near, and they must say their goodbyes, husband to wife, father to sons.[2]

Socrates's male friends remain in the cell with him. The jailer enters and addresses Socrates:

JAILER: To you, Socrates, whom I know to be the noblest and gentlest and best of all who have ever come to this place, I will not impute the angry feelings of other men, who rage and swear at me when, in obedience to the authorities, I bid them drink the poison. I am sure that you will not be angry with me; for others, as you are aware, and not I, are the guilty cause. And so fare you well, and try to bear lightly what must needs be. You know my errand.

SOCRATES: (*to Jailer*) I return your good wishes, and will do as you bid.

The jailer bursts into tears, turns away, and goes out. Socrates addresses his friends:

SOCRATES: How charming the jailer is: since I have been in prison he has always been coming to see me, and at times he would talk to me, and was as good as could be to me, and now see how generously he sorrows for me. But we must do as he says, Crito; let the cup be brought, if the poison is prepared: if not, let the attendant prepare it.

CRITO: Yet, the sun is still upon the hilltops, and many a condemned person has taken the drink later, and even after the announcement has been made to him, he has eaten and drunk, and indulged in delights. Do not be in such a hurry, there is still time.

SOCRATES: Yes, Crito, and they of whom you speak are right in doing thus, for they think that they will gain by the delay; but I am right in not doing that, for I do not think that I should gain anything by drinking the poison a little later; I should be sparing and saving a life which is already gone: I could only laugh at myself for this. Please then do as I say, and do not refuse me.

Crito makes a sign to the servant, and the servant goes out. He is gone for some time.

The jailer enters the room, carrying the poison in a cup. He moves steadily, even solemnly; he is well-practiced.

SOCRATES: Sir, you understand these things, how does this go?

JAILER: Just drink it. Then walk around until your legs feel heavy. Then lay down. The poison will run its course.

He hands the cup to Socrates, who, in the easiest and gentlest manner, without the least fear or change of color or feature, takes the cup and offers a toast.[3]

SOCRATES: I must pray to the gods to bless my journey from this to that other world. May my prayer be granted.

Then, holding the cup to his lips, quite readily and cheerfully, he drinks the poison.[4] The jailer is both saddened and relieved; he's used to having to hold people down and force the hemlock into their mouths. The gathered friends are unable to control their sorrow: Phaedo begins to weep; Crito is likewise unable to restrain his tears; Apollodorus breaks out in a loud cry.[5] Socrates alone remains calm.

SOCRATES: What is this strange outcry? The women and children were sent away in order to avoid such blubbering. I have heard that a man should die in peace, so be quiet and have patience.

He walks about until his legs start to fail. His friends help lay him down on his back. The jailer then looks at his feet and legs and, after a while, presses his foot hard.[6]

JAILER: Do you feel this?

SOCRATES: No.

And so upward and upward the jailer checks: Socrates is growing cold and stiff.[7]

JAILER: When the poison reaches the heart, that will be the end.

Hemlock poisoning can be gruesome, with writhing and convulsions, but Socrates is not suffering these symptoms. He feels the poisoning is going rather well, given what it is, and as a form of thanks, he wants a sacrificial offering to be made to Asclepius, the god of healing and medicine.[8]

SOCRATES: Crito, I think I owe a rooster to Asclepius; will you remember to pay the debt?

CRITO: The debt shall be paid. Is there anything else?

Socrates does not answer.[9]
He goes silent; his breathing ever shallower.
A few minutes pass.
His breathing stops, and his eyes fix still.
Socrates is dead.
Crito gently closes his eyelids.
Phaedo describes his thoughts in this stark moment:

PHAEDO: Such was the end of our friend, whom I may truly call the wisest, most just, and best of all the men I have ever known.[10]

Not far from the jail cell, Callias sits in his magnificent manse watching the last rays of the sun as it has dipped below the horizon. The dying light marks the death of Socrates. Callias nods at the horizon and savors the wine in his silver goblet.
He has won.

44

Aftermath

Socrates had boldly asserted that he would not hold his tongue, so his tongue was forcibly silenced. The law of Persephone "keep the mouth closed" was absolute. Despite Socrates's notion that his own death might protect his followers, they nonetheless feared for their lives and fled Athens.[1] When they had begged him to escape, he may not have realized that they had already planned their own escapes, too. Plato went to Megara and moved on to Cyrene, in present-day Libya, and then to Egypt.[2] Other ancient authors have Plato also going to Sicily and Italy, and even crisscrossing back and forth.[3] This was more than a matter of merely getting out of Athens to escape persecution, but of staying one step ahead of whatever and whoever might be chasing them. Many of Socrates's disciples had been close to Alcibiades, and they knew the reach of the law and the sudden consequences that could befall them.

At some unknown point after the death of Socrates, Athens realizes the monstrosity of its persecution of Socrates and repents, and at least according to one ancient source, it puts Meletus to death and banishes Anytus and Lycon.[4] The rethinking of the charges against Socrates may have coincided with a loss of community standing by Callias. It is reported that he dissipated his wealth and power in the years following the trial of Socrates. There is even an intimation that Callias became a beggar.[5]

> Callias was the master of masses of money, and he lived a life of pleasure . . . However, his voluptuous lifestyle brought him so low, that he was compelled to pass the rest of his life with one barbarian old woman for a servant, and he actually lacked daily necessities, and so he died.[6]

This description seems to indicate that Callias had become such a social pariah that even other members of the aristocracy, the priesthood, and his own family would not take care of him. How he lost access to his resources is unknown.[7] It would be tempting to think that Xanthippe and Socrates had devised a plan to take down Callias before Socrates's death and that Xanthippe had deftly executed the plan, but that is perhaps too far-fetched, and there is no information on this point, but never underestimate the determination of a widow, particularly one as headstrong and brilliant as Xanthippe. In reality, all she had to do was let slip to the wife of the chief priest of Eleusis that it had been Callias himself who had told Socrates about the inner workings of the ritual. The priests of Eleusis, as a group, were the only people in a position to turn Callias into a persona non grata.

The demise of Callias, and the elimination of Socrates's accusers, probably set the stage for Plato's return to Athens around 387 B.C.E. He would not have come back until it was absolutely safe for him to do so. Plato had been on the move for twelve long years, and he had learned many things that he wanted to share. He set up his famed Academy in Athens, the school where Aristotle, among others, would receive training. When Plato finally set out to tell the story of Socrates, he still lived under the same societal restrictions and had to carefully couch his writing in the most inoffensive terms. A new generation of Eleusinian priests was ready to enforce the age-old rules. Plato's version of the trial of Socrates comes across as the story of a man wrongfully put to death for impossibly vague and petty charges. His writings shrewdly leave the nature of Socrates's transgression unclear. Plato worked tirelessly to rehabilitate Socrates's reputation. The legend of Socrates grew in esteem, not least because Plato's writings about Socrates were disseminated far and wide. Eventually, Athens erected a statue of Socrates.[8]

The lingering question is: Why did Socrates do it? What was his motivation in provoking the priests? The closest that Socrates came to answering this question comes from a conversation he had with Callias's brother Hermogenes shortly before the trial. Hermogenes had grown up in Pericles's household along with Callias, Hipparete, and Alcibiades, but somehow ended up being a well-respected, if financially poor, philosopher.[9] Why he was broke while his brother Callias was the richest man in Athens was never adequately explained. Socrates said that Hermogenes had no control over his inheritance but did not elaborate as to why.[10] Perhaps Hermogenes was illegitimate or there may have been intrigues surrounding Hipponicus's estate. While it may have been normal for the eldest son to get the lion's share of the inheritance, it was not normal that a younger son would get nothing. Regardless, Hermogenes, the impoverished but erudite philosopher, is the most "Socrates-like" person of that brood, and a staunch supporter of Socrates.

Hermogenes is aware of the severity of the charges against Socrates—he knows his brother, after all—and is concerned for Socrates's well-being, so he asks Socrates why he's not preparing his defense. Socrates gives a revealing explanation:[11]

> SOCRATES: Do you know that up to this moment, I will not concede to any person to have lived a better life than I have, for what can exceed the pleasure, which has been mine, of knowing that my whole life has been spent justly? . . . And now if my life is to be prolonged, I know that I cannot escape paying the penalty of old age, in increasing dimness of sight and dullness of hearing. I shall find myself slower to learn new lessons, and more likely

to forget the lessons I have already learned. And to the consciousness of failing powers, add the sting of self-reproach,
what prospect have I of any further joy in living? It may be that
God, out of great kindness, is intervening on my behalf to close
my life while I am still healthy and by the gentlest of deaths.
For if a sentence of death is passed upon me, it is plain I shall
be allowed to meet an end which, in the opinion of those who
have studied the matter, is not only the easiest in itself, but one
which will cause the least trouble to one's friends . . . If I were
to effect an acquittal, then I would be but preparing to end my
days wasted by disease and old age . . . No, God knows I shall
display no ardent zeal to win an acquittal. On the contrary, if by
proclaiming all the blessings which I owe to God and men; if,
by blazoning forth the positive opinion which I have of myself, I
will end by wearing out the court, for I will choose death rather
than supplicate in servile to live a little longer merely to gain a
life impoverished by infirmity . . .

Socrates wanted to go out on his own terms, before age and illness
robbed him of his vision, his hearing, and, most importantly, his mental
acuity. Socrates wanted to die with his boots on (to borrow a soldier's
phrase), which is to say, in the glory of battle, but not, in this case, an
infantry clash fought on a muddy field, which he had excelled at in his
younger days, but a philosophical battle fought in the realm of ideas.
When Socrates repurposed the Eleusinian Mysteries in the *Allegory*, he
purposefully provoked the priests, Callias most of all, in an effort to lead
Athenians to philosophical enlightenment. There was, in Socrates's mind,
no higher calling than that. The Eleusinian Mysteries were the perfect
metaphor for philosophical attainment, which can be evidenced by the fact
that the *Allegory of the Cave* is still read the world over to this very day, even
if few realize that it comes from a description of the Mysteries of Eleusis.
The *Allegory of the Cave* has opened the eyes and minds of millions of people
across time, elevating discourse around the world. In short, it might not

be too much to say that Socrates gave his life for the betterment of humanity. Socrates has always been viewed as a kind of hero of the intellect, but now that the true reasons for his trial are revealed, he is even more of a hero, in fact, to my way of thinking, one of the most influential heroes humankind has ever known.

Conclusion

L ight, physical light, is power; the energy that enables life in all its forms. For we humans it also plays a special role in the conceptions within our minds. Throughout time, light has been seen as a conduit to some greater beyond, the concept of divine light issuing throughout human cultures in all their myriad forms. The Mystery religions that dominated the Mediterranean and near-eastern world during antiquity took full advantage of light within their ritual programs where ephemeral visions of floating deities appeared in shafts of light.

Light-borne images enabled belief.

The religious orthodoxy of the time was built, in no small part, on effective displays of light. The new information in this text is how the Eleusinian Mysteries operated and their impact on the philosophical discourse of the time, specifically their role in the life and death of Socrates. The actions of Socrates, Alcibiades, and Callias make sense only when seen through the filter of the "holy vision" of the Eleusinian Mysteries, which is the binding element of their story. Socrates's philosophical perspective was influenced by the Mysteries. Alcibiades was steeped in Socrates's instruction, but he went on to profane the Eleusinian Mysteries, and after turning traitor, joined the Spartans and advised them to cut off Athens's access to Eleusis. Callias, acting under the imprimatur of Eleusis, saw Alcibiades exiled and sentenced to death in absentia. The intervening years would have many absurd twists and turns, including Alcibiades's return to Athens, where he led the sacred procession from Athens to Eleusis. Socrates's *Allegory of the Cave* was a thinly veiled description of the Mysteries of Eleusis, a brazen act of blasphemy, which contributing heavily to his court case and subsequent execution. The words, thoughts, and behaviors of Socrates, Alcibiades, and Callias are direct effects of the Mysteries of Eleusis. Religions can have dramatic influence on the course of daily life and, specifically, individual lives; state religions like Eleusis even more so, because the political and religious structures are intertwined. The Mysteries also played a critical role in the course of the Peloponnesian War; without Callias and the Mysteries driving Alcibiades to the Spartan side, Athens might well have won the war and established an empire that would have precluded the Roman Empire. History turns on moments like these.

The configuration of the personal relationships in this story has been, as stated previously, a triangle, with Socrates, Alcibiades, and Callias each occupying one vertex. The lines that delineate each side—the Socrates/Alcibiades side, the Alcibiades/Callias side, and the Callias/Socrates side—enclose the shape of a triangle. The body of this triangle is the Mysteries of Eleusis, the ever-present whispered-about essence of Athenian religion. In the middle of the triangle is a hole, which was poked by Socrates, and this hole is the *Allegory of the Cave*. Again, it is difficult to fully understand what happened to Socrates without an understanding of the Mysteries of Eleusis, in much the same way you can't really understand what happened to Galileo without understanding the Roman Catholic Church, which is easier to grasp because the Catholic Church still exists and remains, in fact, the biggest religious organization on earth. The goddesses of Eleusis, acting through Callias, eliminated both Alcibiades and Socrates.

The *Allegory of the Cave* is a layered narrative, packed with meaning at almost every turn. The freed prisoner is taken on the philosopher's path to the intelligible world. Would this prisoner at first be painfully dazzled by the fire light and have trouble understanding the real objects? Would he believe that shadows he saw formerly were more real than the actual objects he sees now? It would take time for him to accept that "what he had seen before was all a cheat and an illusion."[1] But if the freed man went back down into the cave to become a prisoner again, he would be, at first, blinded by the darkness, and his fellow prisoners would think him a fool or insane if he told them of their situation and tried to explain to them what he'd discovered. Nevertheless, he would still try to free them.[2]

> SOCRATES: And what about the person who tried to free them and lead them up to the light—if they could grab him would they not kill him?

> GLAUCON: No question they would.

And they did.

The other prisoners—that is, his fellow citizens—killed Socrates, a man who had seen the light but was ever willing to venture back down into the darkness and try to lead them up one by one. The prisoners in the cave were trapped in a world of illusion, just like regular people in the regular world, but life was anything but regular during Socrates's time. The Peloponnesian War—with all its battles, sieges, privations, plagues, and political upheavals—provided the backdrop of the life and mind of Socrates. It might even be said that the mettle of his constitution was forged in the violent and extreme conditions of this long-running war. He was the most rational of men, living in the most irrational of times. When the world had gone mad, Socrates remained steadfast and true, with laser-like focus on the concept of the just. The fog of war understandably clouded the vision of many, but it forced Socrates's vision to become even keener. He learned to "see" with crystalline clarity.

Ultimately, Persephone, the goddess of two worlds, the realm of the dead and the realm of the living, took Socrates away with her. It was what he wanted, after all; it was what he planned. He knew the rules of the society he lived under, as much as you and I know the rules of the societies we live in. When he went after the religious orthodoxy, he knew the price he would have to pay.

The currency of governance is law. The authority to rule was derived in theory, from a Supernatural Realm (the spiritual beyond), as were the laws by which societies conducted themselves. Throughout most of history, priestly and political powers were interconnected. On occasion, the philosopher's Abstract Plane (the domain of pure reason), the seat of one kind of truth, came into conflict with the politico-religious Supernatural Realm, the seat of another kind of truth. The struggle between blind belief and intellectual understanding has played out throughout history, often with severe consequences. Socrates figures in but one round, pivotal as it might have been, of a much-longer-running fight that continues to this day and will likely continue in the future.

Many thousands of people witnessed the light-borne epiphany at Eleusis over the nearly two thousand years that it dominated the religious landscape, and almost all of them came away with the traditional understanding of the event, but Socrates saw something different. It takes a certain mind, a certain genius, to extrapolate the actions of light to greater metaphysical purpose. Socrates was searching for meaning, searching for truth, and he found it in light . . . and shadow.

That is his gift to us.

Bibliography

Ancient Works

Andocides, *Against Alcibiades*
———, *On the Mysteries*
Apuleius, *Metamorphoses*
Aristides, *Orationes*
Aristophanes, *Clouds*
———, *The Frogs*
Aristotle, *Problemata Physica*
———, *Rhetoric*
Athenaeus, The *Deipnosophists*
Cicero, *On the Laws*
———, *On the Nature of the Gods*
Claudius Aelianus, *Historical Miscellany*
Clement, *Protrepticus*
———, *Stromata*
Diodorus Siculus, *Library of History*
Diogenes Laertius, *Lives of Eminent Philosophers*
Isocrates, *Concerning the Team of Horses*
———, *Panegyricus*
Justinus, *Epitome of Pompeius Trogus*
Pausanias, *Description of Greece*
Plato, *Alcibiades I*

————, *Apology*
————, *Cratylus*
————, *Crito*
————, *Euthyphro*
————, *Laches*
————, *Meno*
————, *Phaedo*
————, *Phaedrus*
————, *Protagoras*
————, *Republic*
————, *Symposium*
Plutarch, *Life of Alcibiades*
————, *Life of Nicias*
————, *Life of Pericles*
————, *Life of Themistocles*
————, *Moralia*
————, *On Reading the Poets*
————, *Progress in Virtue*
Proclus, *Commentary on the Plato's* Republic
————, *Platonic Theology*
Sopatros, *Division of Questions*
Stobaeus, *Anthologion*
Tacitus, *Histories*
Themistius, *Orations*
Thucydides, *History of the Peloponnesian War*
Xenophon, *Apology*
————, *Hellenica*
————, *Memorabilia*
————, *Symposium*

Ancient Works with Unattributed or Multiple Authors
Inscriptiones Graecae
Milan Papyrus
Oxyrhynchus Papyrus

Translations of Ancient Works
Babbitt, Frank Cole. *Plutarch: Moralia*. London: William Heinemann, 1927.
Bernardakis, Gregorius N. *Plutarch: Moralia*. Leipzig: Teubner, 1888.
Butterworth, G. W. *Clement of Alexandria*. Cambridge, MA: Harvard University Press, 1919.

Crawley, Richard. *History of the Peloponnesian War.* London: Longmans, Green and Co., 1874.

Dakyns, Henry Graham. *The Works of Xenophon.* London and New York: Macmillan & Co., 1897.

Dindorf, Wilhelm. *Aristides.* Leipzig: Weidmann, 1829.

Erbse, Hartmut. *Scholia Graeca in Homerii Iliadem (Scholia Vetera).* Berlin: Walter de Gruyter et Socios, 1969–1988.

Fowler, Harold N. *Plato in Twelve Volumes.* London: William Heinemann, 1925.

Gaselee, Stephen. *Apuleius. The Golden Ass, Being the Metamorphoses of Lucius Apuleius.* London: William Heinemann; New York: G. P. Putnam's Sons., 1915.

Grenfell, Bernard P., and Arthur S. Hunt. *The Oxyrhynchus Papyri, Part XI.* Oxford: Oxford University Press, 1915.

Hickie, William James. *The Comedies of Aristophanes: A New and Literal Translation*, vol. I. London: Henry G. Bohn, 1853.

Humbel, Achilles. *Ailios Aristeides, Klage über Eleusis (Oratio 22): Lesetext, Übersetzung und Kommentar.* Vienna: Österreichischen Akademie der Wissenschaften, 1994.

Jowett, Benjamin. *The Dialogues of Plato, Translated into English with Analyses and Introductions in Five Volumes*, 3rd ed. Oxford: Oxford University Press, 1892.

———, *The Republic of Plato*, 3rd ed. 1871; Oxford: Clarendon Press, 1888.

———, *Thucydides.* Oxford: Clarendon Press, 1881.

Kroll, Wilhelm. *Proclus: In Platonis Rem publicam commentarii.* Leipzig: Teubner, 1899.

Lloyd-Jones, Hugh. *Sophocles: Fragments.* Loeb Classical Library 483. Cambridge, MA: Harvard University Press, 1996.

Norlin, George. *Isocrates: With an English Translation*, 3 vols. London: William Heinemann, 1928.

Perrin, Bernadotte. *Plutarch's Lives with an English Translation.* Cambridge, MA: Harvard University Press, 1916.

Philomathean Society. *Andocides, On the Mysteries.* Philadelphia: University of Pennsylvania, 1896.

Sandbach, F. H. *Plutarch: Moralia, Volume XV.* Loeb Classical Library 429. Cambridge, MA: Harvard University Press, 2006.

Schuringa, Jacob. *Scholia vetera ad Aristophanes Ranas codicis Ven. Marc. 474.* Groningen, Batavia: J. B. Wolters, 1945.

Shorey, Paul. *Plato: Republic, Books VI–X.* 1935; Cambridge, MA: Harvard University Press, 2000.

Tighe, Mary, and Hudson Gurney. *The Works of Apuleius.* London: H. G. Bohn, 1853.

Wilson, William. *The Writings of Clement of Alexandria.* Edinburgh: T. & T. Clark, 1867.

Yonge, Charles Duke. *Athenaeus, The Deipnosophists.* London. Henry G. Bohn, 1854.

Modern Works

Angus, Samuel. *The Mystery-Religions and Christianity: A Study in the Religious Background of Early Christianity*. New York: Dover, 1975.

Campbell, Joseph, ed. *The Mysteries: Papers from the Eranos Yearbooks*. Bollingen Series XXX, vol. 2. Princeton, NJ: Princeton University Press, 1955.

Clinton, Kevin. "Stages of Initiation in the Eleusinian and Samothracian Mysteries." In Michael B. Cosmopoulos, ed. *Greek Mysteries: The Archaeology and Ritual of Ancient Greek Secret*. London: Routledge, 2003.

Colomo, Daniela. "Herakles and the Eleusinian Mysteries: P. Mil. Vogl. I 20, 18–32 Revisited." *Zeitschrift für Papyrologie und Epigraphik*, Bd. 148 (2004): 87–98.

Cooper, Jacob. "The Eleusinian Mysteries." In *Dickinson's Theological Quarterly*, vol. 3. Edited by W. H. Jellie. London: Dickinson, 1877.

Cosmopoulos, Michael B., ed. *Greek Mysteries: The Archeology and Ritual of Ancient Greek Secret Cults*. London: Routledge, 2003.

Eliade, Mircea. *Rites and Symbols of Initiation: The Mysteries of Birth and Rebirth* [also published as *Birth and Rebirth*]. Translated by Willard R. Trask. New York: Harper & Row, 1965.

———. *The Sacred and the Profane: The Nature of Religion, the Significance of Religious Myth, Symbolism, and Ritual within Life and Culture*. Translated by Willard R. Trask. New York: Harcourt, Brace & World, 1959.

Frisk, Hjalmar. *Griechisches Etymologisches Wörterbuch*. Heidelberg: Carl Winter, 1972–73.

Gatton, Matt. "The Eleusinian Projector: The Hierophant's Optical Method of Conjuring the Goddess." In *The Oxford Handbook of Light in Archaeology*. Edited by Costas Papadopoulos and Holley Moyes. Oxford: Oxford University Press, 2022. 583–603.

Gernsheim, Helmut and Alison. *The History of Photography: From the Camera Obscura to the Beginning of the Modern Era*. New York: McGraw-Hill, 1969.

Gregory, Richard L. *Eye and Brain: The Psychology of Seeing*. New York: McGraw-Hill, 1966.

Hyde, Lewis. *The Gift: Imagination and the Erotic Life of Property*. New York: Vintage, 1983.

Jamieson, Robert, Andrew Robert Fausset, and David Brown. *A Commentary, Critical and Explanatory, on the Old and New Testaments*. Hartford, CT: S. S. Scranton, 1871.

Jung, C. G., and C. Kerényi. *Essays on a Science of Mythology: The Myth of the Divine Child and the Mysteries of Eleusis*. Translated by R. F. C. Hull. Princeton, NJ: Princeton University Press, 1949.

Kingsley, Peter. *In the Dark Places of Wisdom*. Inverness, CA: Golden Sufi Center, 1999.

Lenormant, Charles. "Mémoire sur les spectacles qui avaient lieu dans les Mystères d'Eleusis." *Comptes rendus des séances de l'Académie d'inscriptions et Belles-Lettres* 2, no. 2 (1858): 128-52.

MacGregor, Neil. *A History of the World in 100 Objects*. New York: Viking, 2011.

Marx, Karl, and Friedrich Engels. "The German Ideology." In *Karl Marx: Selected Writings*. Edited by David McLellan. Oxford: Oxford University Press: 1977. 164–76.

Meyer, Marvin W., ed. *The Ancient Mysteries: A Sourcebook, Sacred Texts of the Mystery Religions of the Ancient Mediterranean World*. San Francisco: Harper & Row, 1987.

Mylonas, George. *Eleusis and the Eleusinian Mysteries*. Princeton, NJ: Princeton University Press, 1961.

———. "Eleusis and the Eleusinian Mysteries." *The Classical Journal* 43, no. 3 (December 1947): 130–46.

Parisinou, Eva. *The Light of Gods: The Role of Light in Archaic and Classical Greek Cult*. London: Duckworth, 2000.

Pomeroy, Sarah B. "Optics and the Line in Plato's *Republic*." *The Classical Quarterly* 21, no. 2, (November 1971): 389–92.

Sandridge, Norman. "The Psychopathy of Alcibiades: Applying a Modern Psychological Construct to an Ancient Leader." The Kosmos Society, the Center for Hellenic Studies (November 24, 2016) covering the lecture at Villanova University (September 27, 2016), https://kosmossociety.chs.harvard.edu/the-psychology-of-alcibiades.

Schmitt, Paul. "The Ancient Mysteries in the Society of Their time, Their Transformation and Most Recent Echoes [1944]." In *The Mysteries: Papers from the Eranos Yearbooks*. Edited by Joseph Campbell. Princeton, NJ: Princeton University Press, 1990.

Seaford, Richard. "Mystic Light and Near-Death Experience." In *Light and Darkness in Ancient Greek Myth and Religion*. Edited by Menelaos Christopoulos, Efimia D. Karakantza, and Olga Levaniouk. Lanham, MD: Lexington Books, 2010.

Segal, Alan F. *Life after Death: A History of the Afterlife in Western Religion*. New York: Doubleday, 2004.

Shakespeare, William. *King Henry IV*, Part II.

Sines, G., and Y. Sakellarakis. "Lenses in Antiquity." *American Journal of Archaeology* 91, no. 2 (1987): 191–96.

Taylor, Thomas. *The Eleusinian and Bacchic Mysteries*. 4th ed. New York: J. W. Bouton, 1891.

Temple, Robert. *The Crystal Sun: The Most Secret Science of the Ancient World*. New York: Random House, 2000.

Wasson, R. Gordon, Albert Hofmann, and Carl A. P. Ruck, ed. *The Road to Eleusis: Unveiling the Secret of the Mysteries*. New York: Harcourt Brace Jovanovich, 1978.

Wasson, R. Gordon, Stella Kramrisch, Jonathan Ott, and Carl A. P. Ruck. *Persephone's Quest: Entheogens and the Origins of Religion*. New Haven, CT: Yale University Press, 1992.

Wright, John Henry. "The Origin of Plato's Cave." *Harvard Studies in Classical Philology* 17 (1906): 131–42.

Zajonc, Arthur. *Catching the Light: The Entwined History of Light and Mind*. Oxford: Oxford University Press, 1995.

Acknowledgments

I t has taken more than twenty-years to write this book and along the way there have been plenty of wrong turns, dead ends, stumbles, and outright falls. I spent years hacking through intellectual thickets and I appreciate those whose voices led me back to the path. Many thanks to the brilliant, learned, and profoundly kind Madison Cawein; and the perceptive, strategic, and ever clever Teresa Leger Lucero. You two are the best!

My interest in the Eleusinian Mysteries stems from my former colleague Walter Brock, who holds both undergraduate and graduate degrees from the University of Kentucky where he had long been influenced by noted scholar and classicist Guy Davenport, who inspired Mr. Brock with a fascination for Greek philosophical and religious practice.

I'm grateful to the editors and contributors to the *Oxford Handbook of Light in Archaeology*, particularly Costas Papadopoulos, Holly Moyes, Eva Bosch, and Aaron Watson. They have given the subject of light a well-deserved place in archeological discourse.

Thanks for the instructive insights of Richard Valantasis, Alan F. Segal, Carl A. P. Ruck, Michael Cosmopoulos, and the inimitable E. O. Wilson. They answered key questions that led to the next node on the decision tree.

The estimable classicist Gerald Proietti was ever helpful, as were his colleagues Richard and Angela Dworin. A book like this relies on substantial holdings of classical texts: All hail Tufts University Perseus Library.

My good friend Marjana Tracy, who was there in the early days of reconstruction archeology with Hans-Ole Hansen at Lejre, Denmark, was a steady resource and font of knowledge and technique. My initial experimental foray into the use of physical light in ritual and aesthetic settings sprawled across many time frames and cultures. Lessons learned in one place would sometimes find applicability in others. Sometimes not. I would like to thank the guiding hand of sage archeologists who shaped those early inquiries and experiments, even when they were not specifically about ancient Greece. Light has its own logic. Deep appreciation to Martin Street, Nigel Spivey, Nicolas Barton, Gerhard Bosinski, Jean Clottes, Jean-Michel Geneste, Pierre Cattelain, Claire Bellier, Nicolas Melard, Gillian Morriss-Kay, and John Hale. The aesthetic dimensions of light and image fueled insightful conversations with historians of art Martin Kemp and Matthew Landrus which played a significant role in the outcome of the project. Many thanks also to the wonderful Georgina Leighton. But I should go deeper still, it was my dearly departed professors Donald R. Anderson and Phil Wakeman who instilled in me a love of light. They still shine. I appreciate the help of Ralph Marshall, Luke Johnson, Ron Garrett, Benjamin Studevent-Hickman, Alexandra Thurstone, Shelly Gilles, Michael and Jennifer Ackerman, and Leah Carreon on related lines of inquiry that eventually served as the framework of this topic.

The information in this book stems from independent research, but did involve engagement with several academic institutions. I would like to thank the organizations that allowed me to do presentations or participate in exhibitions and programs: The Archaeology Institute, Oxford University (UK), University of Louisville (US), University of Lisbon (Portugal), Vanderbilt University (US), St. Francis (US), Speed Art Museum (US), Maison de l'Image Basse-Normandie (France), Hugo Obermeier Society, University of Cologne (Germany), STUK

Kunstencentrum (Belgium), Venice International University (Italy), University of Calabria/Museum of Paleontology (Italy), School of Humanities and Journalism (Poland), Slovak University (Slovak Republic), School of Advanced Research (US), and Oberlin College (US). The feedback, good and bad, was helpful in shaping the arguments.

Author Doug Preston was pivotal in getting this book through the pre-publication process. He is a prince. Thanks to him and Marla Grossman, Ed MacKerrow, Nahum Ward-Lev, Edward Borins, Donald Lamm, Ken Cole, Gregory Smith, Lindsay Archuleta, Michael Brown, Leigh Ann Epperson, Joan Blythe, and Wendy Beth Hyman for their astute observations.

Kudos to my literary agent, the ever-feisty Max Sinsheimer, and publishers Claiborne Hancock and Jessica Case for their willingness to bring the story of Socrates to a broad audience, and Maria Fernandez for dotting the 'I's and crossing the 'T's.

Special hugs to Mary, Mickey, Barbie, Vince, Phil, Megan, Gus, Riley, Bela, Eliot, Joe, and Bev. Once we were: together we are.

Notes

Introduction

1   Much of the information in this and the subsequent two paragraphs is based on my work: Matt Gatton, "The Eleusinian Projector: The Hierophant's Optical Method of Conjuring the Goddess," in *The Oxford Handbook of Light in Archaeology*, ed. Costas Papadopoulos and Holley Moyes (Oxford: Oxford University Press, 2022), 583–603.

2   Lewis Hyde, *The Gift: Imagination and the Erotic Life of Property* (New York: Vintage, 1983), 280.

3   Hyde, *The Gift*, 280.

4   George E. Mylonas, "Eleusis and the Eleusinian Mysteries," *The Classical Journal* 43, no. 3 (December 1947): 135. Mylonas notes that the goddess cult at Eleusis appears to extend back to at least the 1400s B.C.E.

5   Cicero, *De Legibus* 2.14.36. Translation by M. Gatton. For the entire passage, see Marvin W. Meyer, ed., *The Ancient Mysteries: A Sourcebook of Sacred Texts* (New York: Harper & Row, 1987), vii.

6   Aristides, *Orationes*, 19.256. Translation by R. Gordon Wasson. See R. Gordon Wasson, "The Wasson Road to Eleusis," in *The Road to Eleusis: Unveiling the Secrets of the Mysteries*, ed. R. Gordon Wasson, Albert Hofmann, and Carl A. P. Ruck (New York: Harcourt Brace Jovanovich, 1978), 17.

7   The scholiast of Aristophanes from *The Frogs*, 158–59. English translation by S. Angus, *The Mystery-Religions and Christianity* (London: John Murray, 1925), 140. For the Greek, see Jacob Schuringa, *Scholia vetera ad Aristophanes Ranas codicis Ven. Marc. 474* (Groningen, Batavia: J. B. Wolters, 1945), 36–37.

8   See Sophocles, *Fragment* 837 in Hugh Lloyd-Jones, ed. and trans., *Sophocles: Fragments*, Loeb Classical Library 483 (Cambridge, MA: Harvard University Press, 1996): 368–69.

9   Isocrates, *Panegyricus* 4.28. English translation by George Norlin. *Isocrates: With an English Translation*, 3 vols. (London: William Heinemann, 1928).

10   Clement of Alexandria, *Stromata* (5.70.7–5.71.1), translated by Kevin Clinton, "Stages of Initiation in the Eleusinian and Samothracian Mysteries," in Michael B. Cosmopoulos, ed., *Greek Mysteries: The Archaeology and Ritual of Ancient Greek Secret Cults* (London: Routledge, 2003), 58.

11   Wasson, "The Wasson Road to Eleusis," 20.

12   Andocides, *On the Mysteries*, 130.

13   This evocation is derived from Plato's *Phaedo* (117a–b) as translated by Benjamin Jowett in *The Dialogues of Plato, Translated into English with Analyses and Introductions in Five Volumes*, vol 2, 3rd ed. (Oxford: Oxford University Press, 1892).

1: Mysteries of Eleusis

1   Much of the information in this chapter and the next two is based on my work: Matt Gatton, "The Eleusinian Projector: The Hierophant's Optical Method of Conjuring the Goddess," in *The Oxford Handbook of Light in Archaeology*, ed. Costas Papadopoulos and Holley Moyes (Oxford: Oxford University Press, 2022), 583–603.

2   George E. Mylonas, "Eleusis and the Eleusinian Mysteries," in *The Classical Journal* 43, no. 3, (December 1947): 135. Mylonas notes that the goddess cult at Eleusis appears to extend back to at least the 1400s B.C.E.

3   Gatton, "The Eleusinian Projector," 584.

4   Apuleius, *Metamorphoses*, XI, 23. English translation from *The Works of Apuleius* (London: H. G. Bohn, 1853), 240, with some minor alterations to improve flow and clarity. For an alternative English translation, see William Adlington (1566), revised by Stephen Gaselee (London: William Heinemann, 1922), 581.

5   Apuleius, *Metamorphoses*, XI, 23. Based on the English translation by Thomas Taylor, *The Eleusinian and Bacchic Mysteries*, 4th ed. (New York: J. W. Bouton, 1891), 101–2, with some minor alterations to improve flow and clarity. For an alternative English translation, see J. Arthur Hanson, ed. and trans., *Apuleius: Metamorphoses, Books 7–11*, Loeb Classical Library 453 (Cambridge, MA: Harvard University Press, 1989).

6   Plutarch, *Moralia* (frag. 178, in Stobaeus, *Anthologion*, IV.52.49, which is also known as *Florilegium* 120, 28, IV). English translation by Jacob Cooper, "The Eleusinian Mysteries," in *Dickinson's Theological Quarterly*, ed. W. H. Jellie, vol. 3 (London: Dickinson, 1877), 16–29. Quote from p. 22.

7   Richard Seaford, "Mystic Light and Near-Death Experience," in *Light and Darkness in Ancient Greek Myth and Religion*, ed. Menelaos Christopoulos, Efimia D. Karakantza, and Olga Levaniouk (Lanham, MD: Lexington Books, 2010), 204.

8   Seaford, "Mystic Light and Near-Death Experience," 202–3.

9   Proclus, *Commentary on the Plato's Republic*, 380. English translation by Thomas Taylor, *The Eleusinian and Bacchic Mysteries*, 108.

10   Gatton, "The Eleusinian Projector," 585.

11   See Paul Schmitt, "The Ancient Mysteries in the Society of Their Time, Their Transformation and Most Recent Echoes [1944]," in *The Mysteries: Papers from the Eranos Yearbooks*, ed. Joseph Campbell (Princeton, NJ: Princeton University Press, 1990), 107. Schmidt cites Tacitus, *Histories*, IV, 81, 84, 85.

12   Pausanias, XIII, 31, 7.

13   Peter Kingsley, *In the Dark Places of Wisdom* (Inverness, CA: Golden Sufi Center, 1999), 80.

14   Kingsley, *In the Dark Places of Wisdom*, 85.

15   Kingsley, *In the Dark Places of Wisdom*, 131.

16   *Oxyrhynchus Papyrus*, 1381, in Bernard P. Grenfell and Arthur S. Hunt, *The Oxyrhynchus Papyri, Part XI* (Oxford: Oxford University Press, 1915), 230.

17   Entheogen expert Carl Ruck made a case that the wheat stalk (symbolized throughout the temple) was used to make a psychotropic LSD derivative, which the initiates drank at the beginning of the rite. See R. Gordon Wasson, Albert Hofmann, and Carl A. P. Ruck, ed., *The Road to Eleusis: Unveiling the Secret of the Mysteries* (New York: Harcourt Brace Jovanovich, 1978). Even if this was so—LSD does act as an amplifier, which could explain the intensity of emotions—it has no power to explain how as many as three thousand people saw the goddess. Without some sort of distinct visual stimulus, everyone's psychedelic experience would have been completely different, and the spell that Eleusis cast over the Mediterranean world would not have worked. Mind-expanding substances were likely a key part of an immersive spiritual experience.

18   Aristides, *Orationes*, 19.256. Translation provided by Richard Dworin of the faculty of the Department of Philosophy at Bellarmine University.

19   Proclus, *Platonic Theology* I, 3. Translation provided by Richard Dworin.

20   Plato, *Phaedrus*, 250c. Based on the English translation by Harold N. Fowler, *Plato in Twelve Volumes*, vol. 9. (London: William Heiniemann, 1925), with some minor alterations to enhance flow and clarity.

21   Heracles as portrayed in the *Milan Papyrus* I, 20, line 31. See Daniela Colomo, "Herakles and the Eleusinian Mysteries: P. Mil. Vogl. I 20, 18–32 Revisited," *Zeitschrift für Papyrologie und Epigraphik*, Bd. 148 (2004): 87–98. Poem on p. 91.

22   Sopatros, *Diairesis Zetematon* (Διαιρεσις Ζητηματων) in *Rhetores Graeci*,
          VIII I 339. The Greek text in this passage is problematic. Charles Lenormant
          amended the words "περι" and "αδελφου" so the passage reads: ἄν δαιδουχίαν
          θεάσωμαι καὶ σχῆμα τι περὶ τοῦ ἀδελφοῦ γιγνόμενον [*une figure qui s'élève
          au-dessus du plancher*," or "the sacred event was an apparition that floated
          above the floor"]. See Charles Lenormant, "Mémoire sur les spectacles
          qui avaient lieu dans les Mystères d'Eleusis," *Comptes rendus des séances de
          l'Académie d'inscriptions et Belles-Lettres* 2, no. 2 (1858): 142.

2: The Temple

1   Plutarch, *Life of Perikles*, 13.5. The exact configuration of this roofhole/
          lantern/chimney (*opaion*) is impossible to discern from the ruins and is thus
          the subject of some scholarly dispute.
2   Matt Gatton, "The Eleusinian Projector: The Hierophant's Optical Method
          of Conjuring the Goddess," in *The Oxford Handbook of Light in Archaeology*,
          ed. Costas Papadopoulos and Holley Moyes (Oxford: Oxford University
          Press, 2022), 595–96.
3   Gatton, "The Eleusinian Projector," 596.
4   Gatton, "The Eleusinian Projector," 596.
5   Plutarch, *Progress in Virtue* (*Quomodu quis suos in Virtute Sentiat Profectus*) 10,
          81e.
6   Heracles as portrayed in the *Milan Papyrus* I.20, lines 18–32.
7   Plutarch, *Life of Themistokles*, 15.1.
8   George Mylonas, "Eleusis and the Eleusinian Mysteries," *The Classical Journal*
          43, no. 3 (December 1947): 135; Michael B. Cosmopoulos, ed., "Mycenaean
          Religion at Eleusis: The Architecture and Stratigraphy of Megaron B,"
          in *Greek Mysteries: The Archaeology and Ritual of Ancient Greek Secret Cults*
          (London: Routledge, 2003), 1–24.
9   Apuleius, *Metamorphoses* XI, 20.
10   Pausanias, V, 12.
11   *Inscriptiones Graecae* I(3) 386. Ox hides are mentioned in lines 24, 34, 112,
          123; stone blocks in lines 70–96; and lumber in lines 96–101.
12   Mylonas, "Eleusis and the Eleusinian Mysteries," 138; Mircea Eliade, *Rites and
          Symbols of Initiation: The Mysteries of Birth and Rebirth* [also published as *Birth
          and Rebirth*], trans. Willard R. Trask (New York: Harper & Row, 1965), 111.

3: Vision of the Goddess

1   Cicero, *De Natura Deorum* I, 42. Translation by Richard Dworin.
2   Clement, *Protreptikos* II. Translation by William Wilson, *The Writings of
          Clement of Alexandria* (Edinburgh: T. & T. Clark, 1867), 27.

3   Clement, *Protreptikos* II. Translation by Wilson, *The Writings of Clement of Alexandria*, 27.

4   For a more general discussion of science and religion see Arthur Zajonc, *Catching the Light: The Entwined History of Light and Mind* (Oxford: Oxford University Press, 1995), 20.

5   Matt Gatton, "The Eleusinian Projector: The Hierophant's Optical Method of Conjuring the Goddess," in *The Oxford Handbook of Light in Archaeology*, ed. Costas Papadopoulos and Holley Moyes (Oxford: Oxford University Press, 2022), 583–603.

6   Gatton, "The Eleusinian Projector," 584.

7   Gatton, "The Eleusinian Projector," 584.

8   Helmut and Alison Gernsheim, *The History of Photography: From the Camera Obscura to the Beginning of the Modern Era* (New York: McGraw-Hill, 1969), 17.

9   Aristotle, *Problematica Physica* XV, (912b). In the fourth century B.C.E., Aristotle made observations on shadows during an eclipse and of light shining through the holes of a sieve. The holes acted as apertures, allowing light to trace through and project the image of the shape of the sun, which is normally a circle, but on an eclipse becomes a crescent. He accurately explained how an image of the sun was formed in a camera obscura by a cone of light with its apex at the hole, creating an inverted cone of light on the inside.

10   Gatton, "The Eleusinian Projector," 591.

11   Proclus, *Commentary on Plato's Republic*, 380. Translation by Thomas Taylor, *The Eleusinian and Bacchic Mysteries*, 4th ed. (New York: J. W. Bouton, 1891), 108.

12   Richard L. Gregory, *Eye and Brain: The Psychology of Seeing* (New York: McGraw-Hill, 1966), 46–49.

13   *Oxyrhynchus Papyrus*, 1381, in Bernard P. Grenfell and Arthur S. Hunt, *The Oxyrhynchus Papyri, Part XI* (Oxford: Oxford University Press, 1915), 230.

14   Robert Temple, *The Crystal Sun: The Most Secret Science of the Ancient World* (New York: Random House, 2000), 190–93; G. Sines and Y. Sakellarakis, "Lenses in Antiquity," *American Journal of Archaeology* 91, no. 2 (1987): 191–96.

15   Gatton, "The Eleusinian Projector," 599.

16   Gatton, "The Eleusinian Projector," 595.

17   Gatton, "The Eleusinian Projector," 595.

18   Gatton, "The Eleusinian Projector," 600.

19   Gatton, "The Eleusinian Projector," 600.

20   Robert Jamieson, Andrew Robert Fausset, and David Brown, *A Commentary, Critical and Explanatory, on the Old and New Testaments* (Hartford, CT: S. S. Scranton, 1871), 575.

21   As quoted by Neil MacGregor, *A History of the World in 100 Objects* (New York: Viking, 2011), 99–100.

4: Socratic Thought

1   For a discussion of Socrates's daily profession, see Diogenes Laertius, *Lives of Eminent Philosophers*, 2.5.19. The vocation and social status of Socrates has been the subject of some scholarly dispute.

2   Plato, *Meno*, 76e.

3   This quote is based on passage 32a of Plato's *Apology* as translated by Benjamin Jowett in *The Dialogues of Plato Translated into English with Analyses and Introductions in Five Volumes*, vol. 2, 3rd ed. (Oxford: Oxford University Press, 1892) and is presented here with some minor alterations to enhance flow and clarity.

4   This exchange is based on 1.328d–e of Plato's *Republic* (Book 1) as translated by Benjamin Jowett in *The Republic of Plato*, 3rd ed. (Oxford: Clarendon Press, 1888) and is presented here with some minor alterations to enhance flow and clarity.

5   Of the many passages that address various aspects of the Theory of Forms (it's discussed in no fewer than eleven of Plato's works), Book 10 of the *Republic* probably best explains the core idea. The following dialogue is based on Plato's *Republic* (Book 10) as translated by Benjamin Jowett in *The Republic of Plato*, 3rd ed., and is presented here with some minor alterations to enhance flow and clarity.

6   Plato, *Republic*, VI.509d–511e.

7   This dialogue is based on Plato's *Republic* as translated by Benjamin Jowett in *The Republic of Plato*, 3rd ed., and is presented here with some minor alterations to enhance flow and clarity.

8   As a side note, the Divided Line has been apprehended as an optical construct. Sarah Pomeroy argues that the Divided Line is a philosophical interpretation of the lens equation of a common magnifying glass, a double convex lens, which was used in antiquity. Given Plato's background in geometry and mathematics, and the use of the camera obscura principle in projecting images at Eleusis, the idea may have some merit. Perhaps the diagram of an object, a lens, and a magnified image suggested the Divided Line of an object, a mind, and an abstract form. Socrates and/or Plato potentially took the framework of a decidedly optical phenomenon and applied it to greater nonmaterial truth. See Sarah B. Pomeroy, "Optics and the Line in Plato's *Republic*," *The Classical Quarterly* 21, no. 2 (November 1971): 391–92.

5: Allegory of the Cave

1   This dialogue of lines 514a–521d of Book VII of Plato's *Republic* was translated by Benjamin Jowett in *The Republic of Plato*, 3rd ed. (Oxford: Clarendon Press, 1888). I have made some minor alterations to enhance flow and clarity.

2   Karl Marx and Friedrich Engels, "The German Ideology," in David
        McLellan, ed., *Karl Marx: Selected Writings* (Oxford: Oxford University Press,
        1977), 164–76.
3   John Henry Wright, "The Origin of Plato's Cave," *Harvard Studies in Classical
        Philology* 17 (1906): 132.
4   Wright, "The Origin of Plato's Cave," 131–42.
5   Wright, "The Origin of Plato's Cave," 140. Wright focused his investigations
        on the grottoes of Syracuse, the Corycian Cave above Delphi, and the Cave of
        Vari in Attica. Wright concluded the Cave of Vari in Attica was most like the
        cave in the *Allegory*, though it was shaped differently.
6   Quote from *Republic* VII (532c), as translated by Paul Shorey, *Plato: The
        Republic, Books VI–X* (Cambridge, MA: Harvard University Press, 2000),
        198. I have made some minor alterations to enhance flow and clarity.

6: Bonds of War

1   The following dialogue and descriptions come from Plato's *Symposium* as
        translated by Benjamin Jowett in *The Dialogues of Plato Translated into English
        with Analyses and Introductions in Five Volumes*, vol. 1, 3rd ed. (Oxford: Oxford
        University Press, 1892) and are presented here with some minor alterations to
        enhance flow and clarity.
2   This dialogue comes from Plato's *Symposium* (220d–220e) as translated by
        Benjamin Jowett in *The Dialogues of Plato Translated into English with Analyses
        and Introductions in Five Volumes* and is presented here with some minor
        alterations to enhance flow and clarity.
3   This quote comes from Plato's *Symposium* (219e–220a) as translated by
        Benjamin Jowett in *The Dialogues of Plato Translated into English with Analyses
        and Introductions in Five Volumes* and is presented here with some minor
        alterations to enhance flow and clarity.
4   This quote comes from Plato's *Symposium* (220b) as translated by Benjamin
        Jowett in *The Dialogues of Plato Translated into English with Analyses and
        Introductions in Five Volumes* and is presented here with some minor alterations
        to enhance flow and clarity.
5   This dialogue comes from Plato's *Symposium* (220c–220d) as translated by
        Benjamin Jowett in *The Dialogues of Plato Translated into English with Analyses
        and Introductions in Five Volumes* and is presented here with some minor
        alterations to enhance flow and clarity.
6   Plato, *Symposium*, 221a.

7: Examination of Alcibiades

1   This dialogue comes from Plato's *Alcibiades I* as translated by Benjamin Jowett
        in *The Dialogues of Plato Translated into English with Analyses and Introductions*

in Five Volumes, vol. 2, 3rd ed. (Oxford: Oxford University Press, 1892) and is presented here with some minor alterations to enhance flow and clarity.

8: The Seduction

1   This dialogue and the descriptions in this chapter come from Plato's *Symposium* as translated by Benjamin Jowett in *The Dialogues of Plato Translated into English with Analyses and Introductions in Five Volumes*, vol. 1, 3rd ed. (Oxford: Oxford University Press, 1892) and are presented here with some minor alterations to enhance flow and clarity.

9: Alcibiades and Callias (The Early Years)

1   Plutarch, *Life of Alcibiades*, 1.1.

2   This famous passage from the speech is based on book 2 of Thucydides's *History of the Peloponnesian War*, as translated by Benjamin Jowett in *Thucydides* (Oxford: Clarendon Press, 1881) and is presented here with some minor alterations to enhance flow and clarity.

3   Pericles's *Funeral Oration* is quite lengthy, about three thousand words, but if you distill its most important themes and key phrases down to fewer than two hundred words, you get much of the third paragraph of Lincoln's Gettysburg Address. Lincoln's address in full:

>   Four score and seven years ago our fathers brought forth on this continent, a new nation, conceived in Liberty, and dedicated to the proposition that all men are created equal.
>
>   Now we are engaged in a great civil war, testing whether that nation, or any nation so conceived and so dedicated, can long endure. We are met on a great battlefield of that war. We have come to dedicate a portion of that field, as a final resting place for those who here gave their lives that that nation might live. It is altogether fitting and proper that we should do this.
>
>   But, in a larger sense, we cannot dedicate—we cannot consecrate—we cannot hallow—this ground. The brave men, living and dead, who struggled here, have consecrated it, far above our poor power to add or detract. The world will little note, nor long remember, what we say here, but it can never forget what they did here. It is for us the living, rather, to be dedicated here to the unfinished work which they who fought here have thus far so nobly advanced. It is rather for us to be here dedicated to the great task remaining before us—that from these honored dead we take increased devotion to that cause for which they gave the last full measure of devotion—that we here highly resolve that these dead shall not have died in vain—that this nation, under God, shall have a new birth of freedom—and that government of the people, by the people, for the people, shall not perish from the earth.

4   The passage is based on Plato's *Protagoras* (319e–320b) as translated by
           Benjamin Jowett in *The Dialogues of Plato Translated into English with Analyses
           and Introductions in Five Volumes*, vol. 1, 3rd ed. (Oxford: Oxford University
           Press, 1892) and is presented here with some minor alterations to enhance
           flow and clarity.

5   Plato, *Meno*, 94b.

6   Andocides, *On the Mysteries*, 130.

7   Andocides, *On the Mysteries*, 130.

8   Plutarch, *Life of Alcibiades*, 2.2, as translated by Bernadotte Perrin in *Plutarch's
           Lives* (Cambridge, MA: Harvard University Press, 1916) and is presented here
           with some minor alterations to enhance flow and clarity.

9   Plutarch, *Life of Alcibiades*, 2.2–2.3.

10   Plutarch, *Life of Alcibiades*, 2.5, as translated by Bernadotte Perrin in *Plutarch's
           Lives* and is presented here with some minor alterations to enhance flow and
           clarity.

11   Plutarch, *Life of Alcibiades*, 2.6.

12   Plutarch, *Life of Alcibiades*, 7.1.

13   Plutarch, *Life of Alcibiades*, 3.1, as translated by Bernadotte Perrin in *Plutarch's
           Lives* and is presented here with some minor alterations to enhance flow and
           clarity.

14   Plutarch, *Life of Alcibiades*, 7.2, as translated by Bernadotte Perrin in
           Plutarch's Lives and is presented here with some minor alterations to
           enhance flow and clarity.

15   This dialogue comes book 1, chapter 2, passages 40–46 of Xenophon's
           Memorabilia as translated by Henry Graham Dakyns in *The Works of
           Xenophon* (London and New York: Macmillan & Co., 1897) and is
           presented here with some minor alterations to enhance flow and
           clarity.

16   Plutarch, *Life of Alcibiades*, 8.1.

17   Plutarch, *Life of Alcibiades*, 8.1–8.2.

10: A Marriage and an Assassination Plot

1   This dialogue comes from chapter 3 of Xenophon's *Symposium* as translated
           by Henry Graham Dakyns in *The Works of Xenophon* (London and New York:
           Macmillan & Co., 1897) and is presented here with some minor alterations to
           enhance flow and clarity.

2   This dialogue comes from chapter 4 of Xenophon's *Symposium* as translated by
           Henry Graham Dakyns in *The Works of Xenophon* and is presented here with
           some minor alterations to enhance flow and clarity.

3   This quote is based on passage 9.1 of Plutarch's *Life of Alcibiades* as translated
           by Bernadotte Perrin, *Plutarch's Lives* (Cambridge, MA: Harvard University

Press, 1916) and is presented here with some minor alterations to enhance flow and clarity.

4   Plutarch, *Life of Alcibiades*, 4.5.

5   Plutarch, *Life of Alcibiades*, 11.1.

6   Plutarch, *Life of Alcibiades*, 11.1; Thucydides, *History of the Peloponnesian War*, 6.16.2.

7   Plutarch, *Life of Alcibiades*, 11.2 as translated by Bernadotte Perrin in *Plutarch's Lives* and presented here with some minor alterations to enhance flow and clarity.

8   Plutarch, *Life of Alcibiades*, 16.3 as translated by Bernadotte Perrin in *Plutarch's Lives* and presented here with some minor alterations to enhance flow and clarity.

9   Andocides, *Against Alcibiades*, 4.17; for corroboration of the false imprisonment, see also Plutarch, *Life of Alcibiades*, 16.4.

10   Andocides, *Against Alcibiades*, 4.15.

11   Plutarch, *Life of Alcibiades*, 8.2.

12   This description is based on passage 8.2 of Plutarch's *Life of Alcibiades* as translated by Bernadotte Perrin in *Plutarch's Lives* and is presented here with some minor alterations to enhance flow and clarity.

13   Andocides, *Against Alcibiades*, 4.14.

14   Plutarch, *Life of Alcibiades*, 8.2.

15   Norman Sandridge, "The Psychopathy of Alcibiades: Applying a Modern Psychological Construct to an Ancient Leader" in *The Kosmos Society*, Harvard Center for Hellenic Studies (November 24, 2016) covering the lecture at Villanova University (September 27, 2016).

11: Breaking the Peace

1   For a translation of the text of the treaty, see book 5 of Thucydides's *History of the Peloponnesian War* as translated by Richard Crawley (London: Longmans, Green and Co., 1874).

2   Plutarch, *Life of Alcibiades*, 14.1.

3   For the full dialogue, see Plato's *Laches*.

4   This line comes from passages 194e and 195a of Plato's *Laches* as translated by Benjamin Jowett in *The Dialogues of Plato Translated into English with Analyses and Introductions in Five Volumes*, vol. 1, 3rd ed. (Oxford: Oxford University Press, 1892) and is presented here with some minor alterations to enhance flow and clarity.

5   This description is based on passage 14.2 of Plutarch's *Life of Alcibiades* as translated by Bernadotte Perrin in *Plutarch's Lives* (Cambridge, MA: Harvard University Press, 1916) and is presented here with some minor alterations to enhance flow and clarity.

6   Plutarch, *Life of Alcibiades*, 14.2.

7   Plutarch, *Life of Alcibiades*, 14.4.

8   This description is based on passage 14.6 of Plutarch's *Life of Alcibiades* as translated by Bernadotte Perrin in *Plutarch's Lives* and is presented here with some minor alterations to enhance flow and clarity.

9   This quote is based on passage 14.7 of Plutarch's *Life of Alcibiades* as translated by Bernadotte Perrin in *Plutarch's Lives* and is presented here with some minor alterations to enhance flow and clarity.

10   Plutarch, *Life of Alcibiades*, 14.8.

11   Plutarch, *Life of Alcibiades*, 14.8.

12   This description is based on passage 14.9 of Plutarch's *Life of Alcibiades* as translated by Bernadotte Perrin in *Plutarch's Lives* and is presented here with some minor alterations to enhance flow and clarity.

13   Plutarch, *Life of Alcibiades*, 15.1.

12: The Golden Horse Takes the Cake

1   This quote is based on passage 2.10 of Xenophon's *Symposium* as translated by Henry Graham Dakyns in *The Works of Xenophon* (London and New York: Macmillan & Co., 1897) and is presented here with some minor alterations to enhance flow and clarity.

2   Claudius Aelianus, *Historical Miscellany*, XI.12.

3   Thucydides, *History of the Peloponnesian War*, 5.84–5.116.

4   Plutarch, *Life of Alcibiades*, 16.4.

13: Run-up to War

1   Thucydides, *History of the Peloponnesian War*, 6.6.2.

2   Thucydides, *History of the Peloponnesian War*, 6.6.3.

3   Thucydides, *History of the Peloponnesian War*, 6.8.3.

4   The speeches of Nicias and Alcibiades are based on book 6, chapters 9–23 of Thucydides's *History of the Peloponnesian War* as translated by Richard Crawley (London: Longmans, Green and Co., 1874) and are presented here with some minor alterations to enhance flow and clarity.

5   Thucydides, *History of the Peloponnesian War*, 6.24.1.

6   Thucydides, *History of the Peloponnesian War*, 6.24.2.

7   Thucydides, *History of the Peloponnesian War*, 6.24.4.

8   Thucydides, *History of the Peloponnesian War*, 6.25.2.

9   Thucydides, *History of the Peloponnesian War*, 6.26.1.

10   Plutarch, *Life of Alcibiades*, 17.4.

11   This quote comes from 13.6 of Plutarch's *Life of Nicias* as translated by Bernadotte Perrin in *Plutarch's Lives* (Cambridge, MA: Harvard University

Press, 1916). The source text gives Socrates's opinion of the Sicilian expedition as a description, but I chose to present it as dialogue.

14: Desecration of the Mysteries of Eleusis

1   Plutarch, *Life of Alcibiades*, 18.4.

2   Plutarch, *Life of Alcibiades*, 19.1.

3   This speech is based on section 1.11 of Andocides, *On the Mysteries*, as translated by the Philomathean Society of the University of Pennsylvania (1896) and is presented here with some minor alterations to enhance flow and clarity.

4   Andocides, *On the Mysteries*, 1.12.

5   Andocides, *On the Mysteries*, 1.12.

6   Plutarch, *Life of Alcibiades*, 19.1.

7   This quote comes from 20.2 of Plutarch's *Life of Alcibiades* as translated by Bernadotte Perrin in *Plutarch's Lives* (Cambridge, MA: Harvard University Press, 1916) and is presented here with some minor alterations to enhance flow and clarity.

8   I have cobbled this dialogue together from Plutarch, *Life of Alcibiades*, 19.5 (Bernadotte Perrin translation), and Thucydides, *History of the Peloponnesian War*, 6.29.1 and 6.29.2 (Richard Crawley translation), who both wrote it from an observer-neutral perspective. I just felt that it was more assertive as a dialogue, even though the source texts do not present it this way.

9   Plutarch, *Life of Alcibiades*, 19.3.

10   This speech comes from 19.4 of Plutarch's *Life of Alcibiades* as translated by Bernadotte Perrin in *Plutarch's Lives*. Plutarch presents this information partially from an observer-neutral perspective and partially as a dialogue. I chose to present it all as a dialogue in an effort to make it uniform and the delivery more active.

15: The Expedition to Sicily

1   Thucydides, *History of the Peloponnesian War*, 6.30.1.

2   Thucydides, *History of the Peloponnesian War*, 6.30.1–6.30.2.

3   Thucydides, *History of the Peloponnesian War*, 6.31.6.

4   Thucydides, *History of the Peloponnesian War*, 6.32.1–6.32.2.

5   Thucydides, *History of the Peloponnesian War*, 6.32.2.

6   This speech is based on 6.33.1-4 of Thucydides's *History of the Peloponnesian War* as translated by Benjamin Jowett in *Thucydides* and is presented here with some minor alterations to enhance flow and clarity.

7   This speech is based on 6.37.1 of Thucydides's *History of the Peloponnesian War* as translated by Benjamin Jowett in *Thucydides* (Oxford: Clarendon Press, 1881) and is presented here with some minor alterations to enhance flow and clarity.

8   This speech is based on 6.41.2-4 of Thucydides's *History of the Peloponnesian War* as translated by Benjamin Jowett in *Thucydides* and is presented here with some minor alterations to enhance flow and clarity.

9   Thucydides, *History of the Peloponnesian War*, 6.42.1.

10   Thucydides, *History of the Peloponnesian War*, 6.44.4.

11   Thucydides, *History of the Peloponnesian War*, 6.47.1.

12   Thucydides, *History of the Peloponnesian War*, 6.48.1.

13   This text is based on 19.5 of Plutarch's *Life of Alcibiades* as translated by Bernadotte Perrin in *Plutarch's Lives* (Cambridge, MA: Harvard University Press, 1916) and is presented here with some minor alterations to enhance flow and clarity.

14   Thucydides, *History of the Peloponnesian War*, 6.50.1.

16: Prosecution, Prison, Torture, and Death

1   Plutarch, *Life of Alcibiades*, 20.5.

2   Andocides, *On the Mysteries*, 1.43.

3   Andocides, *On the Mysteries*, 1.43.

4   The following dialogue is based on section 1.48 of Andocides, *On the Mysteries*, as translated by the Philomathean Society of the University of Pennsylvania (1896) and is presented here with some minor alterations to enhance flow and clarity.

5   The following dialogue is based on section 1.49–1.50 of Andocides, *On the Mysteries*, as translated by the Philomathean Society of the University of Pennsylvania (1896) and is presented here with some minor alterations to enhance flow and clarity.

6   The following dialogue is based on section 1.51 of Andocides, *On the Mysteries*, as translated by the Philomathean Society of the University of Pennsylvania (1896) and is presented here with some minor alterations to enhance flow and clarity.

7   The following dialogue is based on section 1.52–1.53 of Andocides, *On the Mysteries*, as translated by the Philomathean Society of the University of Pennsylvania (1896) and is presented here with some minor alterations to enhance flow and clarity.

8   Plutarch, *Life of Alcibiades*, 21.4.

9   Andocides, *On the Mysteries*, 1.28.

10   Thucydides, *History of the Peloponnesian War*, 6.61.1.

17: Trouble in Sicily

1   Thucydides, *History of the Peloponnesian War*, 6.50.3.

2   Thucydides, *History of the Peloponnesian War*, 6.52.2.

3   Thucydides, *History of the Peloponnesian War*, 6.61.6. See also Plutarch, *Life of Alcibiades*, 22.1.

4   Thucydides, *History of the Peloponnesian War*, 6.61.6.

5   Thucydides, *History of the Peloponnesian War*, 6.61.7.

6   Thucydides, *History of the Peloponnesian War*, 6.62.1.

7   Thucydides, *History of the Peloponnesian War*, 6.62.2.

8   Thucydides, *History of the Peloponnesian War* 6.62.4.

9   This quote comes from book 6, chapter 63, section 3 of Thucydides's *History of the Peloponnesian War* as translated by Benjamin Jowett in *Thucydides* (Oxford: Clarendon Press, 1881) and is presented here with some minor alterations to enhance flow and clarity.

10   The charges come from 22.3 of Plutarch's *Life of Alcibiades* as translated by Bernadotte Perrin in *Plutarch's Lives* (Cambridge, MA: Harvard University Press, 1916) and is presented here with some minor alterations to enhance flow and clarity.

11   This text comes from 22.4 of Plutarch's *Life of Alcibiades* as translated by Bernadotte Perrin in *Plutarch's Lives* and is presented here with some minor alterations to enhance flow and clarity.

12   This quote comes from 22.2 of Plutarch's *Life of Alcibiades* as translated by Bernadotte Perrin in *Plutarch's Lives* and is presented here with some minor alterations to enhance flow and clarity.

18: Ruse in Syracuse

1   Thucydides, *History of the Peloponnesian War*, 6.64.1.

2   Thucydides, *History of the Peloponnesian War*, 6.66.1.

3   Thucydides, *History of the Peloponnesian War*, 6.64.1.

4   Thucydides, *History of the Peloponnesian War*, 6.64.1.

5   Plutarch, *Life of Nicias*, 16.2.

6   Thucydides, *History of the Peloponnesian War*, 6.64.2.

7   Thucydides, *History of the Peloponnesian War*, 6.64.3.

8   Thucydides, *History of the Peloponnesian War*, 6.65.1.

9   Thucydides, *History of the Peloponnesian War*, 6.65.2.

10   Thucydides, *History of the Peloponnesian War*, 6.65.3.

11   Thucydides, *History of the Peloponnesian War*, 6.66.1–6.66.2.

12   Thucydides, *History of the Peloponnesian War*, 6.65.3.

13   This speech from book 6, chapter 68 of Thucydides's *History of the Peloponnesian War* was translated by Benjamin Jowett in *Thucydides* (Oxford: Clarendon Press, 1881) and is presented here with some minor alterations to enhance flow and clarity.

14   Thucydides, *History of the Peloponnesian War*, 6.69.1.

15   This text comes from 6.69.3 of Thucydides's *History of the Peloponnesian War* as translated by Benjamin Jowett in *Thucydides* (Oxford: Clarendon Press, 1881) and is presented here with some minor alterations to enhance flow and clarity.

16   Thucydides, *History of the Peloponnesian War*, 6.70.1.

17   Thucydides, *History of the Peloponnesian War*, 6.70.3–6.70.4.

19: Turning Traitor

1   Plutarch, *Life of Alcibiades*, 23.1.

2   Plutarch, *Life of Alcibiades*, 23.2.

3   Plutarch, *Life of Alcibiades*, 23.3.

4   This description comes from passage 23.5 of Plutarch's *Life of Alcibiades* as translated by Bernadotte Perrin in *Plutarch's Lives* (Cambridge, MA: Harvard University Press, 1916) and is presented here with some minor alterations to enhance flow and clarity.

5   Plutarch, *Life of Alcibiades*, 23.4. As a side note, chameleonlike abilities are considered a characteristic of antisocial personality disorder, or ASPD, which is commonly referred to as psychopathy.

6   Plutarch, *Life of Alcibiades*, 23.3.

20: Boa Constrictor

1   Thucydides, *History of the Peloponnesian War*, 6.71.1.

2   Thucydides, *History of the Peloponnesian War*, 6.71.2.

3   Thucydides, *History of the Peloponnesian War*, 6.72.4 through 6.73.1

4   The full speech of the Syracusan envoy appears in book 6, chapters 76–80 of Thucydides's *History of the Peloponnesian War* as translated by Benjamin Jowett in *Thucydides* (Oxford: Clarendon Press, 1881) and is excerpted here with some minor alterations to enhance flow and clarity.

5   The full speech of the Athenian envoy appears in book 6, chapters 82–87 of Thucydides's *History of the Peloponnesian War* as translated by Benjamin Jowett in *Thucydides* and is excerpted here with some minor alterations to enhance flow and clarity.

6   Thucydides, *History of the Peloponnesian War*, 6.88.2.

7   Thucydides, *History of the Peloponnesian War*, 6.88.3.

8   Plutarch, *Life of Nicias*, 17.2.

9   Plutarch, *Life of Nicias*, 18.1.

10   Plutarch, *Life of Nicias*, 17.3, 18.1.

11   Plutarch, *Life of Nicias*, 18.2.

12   Plutarch, *Life of Nicias*, 18.2.

13   Plutarch, *Life of Nicias*, 18.2.

14   Plutarch, *Life of Nicias*, 18.4.

15   Plutarch, *Life of Nicias*, 18.4.
16   Plutarch, *Life of Nicias*, 18.6.

21: Treachery

1   This portion of Alcibiades's speech appears in book 6, chapters 89–91 of
        Thucydides's *History of the Peloponnesian War* as translated by Benjamin Jowett
        in *Thucydides* (Oxford: Clarendon Press, 1881) and is presented here with
        some minor alterations to enhance flow and clarity.
2   Plutarch, *Life of Alcibiades*, 23.2.
3   This portion of Alcibiades's speech appears in book 6, chapter 92 of
        Thucydides's *History of the Peloponnesian War* as translated by Benjamin Jowett
        in *Thucydides* and is presented here with some minor alterations to enhance
        flow and clarity.
4   Plutarch, *Life of Nicias*, 18.6.

22: The Tide Turns

1   Plutarch, *Life of Nicias*, 18.7.
2   Plutarch, *Life of Nicias*, 19.1.
3   Plutarch, *Life of Nicias*, 19.2.
4   Plutarch, *Life of Nicias*, 19.5.
5   Plutarch, *Life of Nicias*, 19.7.
6   Plutarch, *Life of Nicias*, 20.1.
7   Plutarch, *Life of Nicias*, 20.2.
8   Plutarch, *Life of Nicias*, 20.5.
9   Plutarch, *Life of Nicias*, 21.1.
10   Plutarch, *Life of Nicias*, 21.5.
11   Plutarch, *Life of Nicias*, 21.6.
12   Plutarch, *Life of Nicias*, 21.9.
13   Plutarch, *Life of Nicias*, 21.9.
14   Plutarch, *Life of Nicias*, 22.4.
15   Plutarch, *Life of Nicias*, 24.4.
16   Plutarch, *Life of Nicias*, 25.3.
17   Plutarch, *Life of Nicias*, 26.3.
18   Plutarch, *Life of Nicias*, 26.4.
19   Plutarch, *Life of Nicias*, 25.3.
20   Plutarch, *Life of Nicias*, 27.1.
21   Plutarch, *Life of Nicias*, 26.6.
22   Plutarch, *Life of Nicias*, 27.2.
23   This quote comes from 27.4 of Plutarch's *Life of Nicias* as translated by
        Bernadotte Perrin in *Plutarch's Lives* (Cambridge, MA: Harvard University

Press, 1916) and is presented here with some minor alterations to enhance
flow and clarity.

24   Plutarch, *Life of Nicias*, 27.5.

25   Plutarch, *Life of Nicias*, 27.5.

26   Plutarch, *Life of Nicias*, 28.4.

27   Plutarch, *Life of Nicias*, 29.1.

23: Double Betrayal

1   This portion of Alcibiades's speech appears in 6.91.6-7 of Thucydides's
        History of the Peloponnesian War as translated by Benjamin Jowett in *Thucydides*
        (Oxford: Clarendon Press, 1881) and is presented here with some minor
        alterations to enhance flow and clarity.

2   Plutarch, *Life of Alcibiades*, 34.3.

3   Thucydides, *History of the Peloponnesian War*, 7.27.4.

4   Thucydides, *History of the Peloponnesian War*, 7.27.4.

5   Thucydides, *History of the Peloponnesian War*, 7.28.2.

6   This dialogue is based on section 18 of Xenophon's *Apology* as translated by
        Henry Graham Dakyns in *The Works of Xenophon* (London and New York:
        Macmillan & Co., 1897) and is presented here with some minor alterations to
        enhance flow and clarity.

7   Plutarch, *Life of Alcibiades*, 23.7.

8   Thucydides, *History of the Peloponnesian War*, 8.45.1.

9   Plutarch, *Life of Alcibiades*, 24.2.

24: Persian Power

1   Thucydides, *History of the Peloponnesian War*, 8.45.1.

2   Plutarch, *Life of Alcibiades*, 23.5.

3   Plutarch, *Life of Alcibiades*, 24.5.

4   Thucydides, *History of the Peloponnesian War*, 8.45.1.

5   Plutarch, *Life of Alcibiades*, 24.5.

6   This dialogue is based on book 8, chapters 45 and 46 of Thucydides's *History
        of the Peloponnesian War* as translated by Benjamin Jowett in *Thucydides*
        (Oxford: Clarendon Press, 1881) and Plutarch's *Life of Alcibiades* as translated
        by Bernadotte Perrin in *Plutarch's Lives* (Cambridge, MA: Harvard University
        Press, 1916). Both Thucydides and Plutarch cover this information but
        present it from an observer-neutral perspective, but I chose to present it as
        a dialogue to make the delivery more active, even though the source texts
        do not present it this way. The text has also been streamlined from the two
        accounts, which are fairly convoluted, for flow and clarity.

7   Thucydides, *History of the Peloponnesian War*, 8.46.5.

8   Thucydides, *History of the Peloponnesian War*, 8.46.5.
9   Thucydides, *History of the Peloponnesian War*, 8.46.5.

25: The Offer

1   Thucydides, *History of the Peloponnesian War*, 8.48.1.
2   Thucydides, *History of the Peloponnesian War*, 8.47.2.
3   Thucydides, *History of the Peloponnesian War*, 8.48.3.
4   Thucydides, *History of the Peloponnesian War*, 8.48.3.
5   This text appears in 8.48.4-7 of Thucydides's *History of the Peloponnesian War* as translated by Benjamin Jowett in *Thucydides* (Oxford: Clarendon Press, 1881). Thucydides presents it from an observer-neutral perspective, but I chose to present it as a dialogue to make the delivery more active, even though the source text does not present it this way. I have made some minor alterations to enhance flow and clarity.
6   Thucydides, *History of the Peloponnesian War*, 8.49.1.
7   Thucydides, *History of the Peloponnesian War*, 8.53.1.
8   Thucydides, *History of the Peloponnesian War*, 8.53.2.
9   This text appears in book 8.53.2 of Thucydides's *History of the Peloponnesian War* as translated by Benjamin Jowett in *Thucydides* and is presented here with some minor alterations to enhance flow and clarity.
10   This text appears in 8.53.3 of Thucydides's *History of the Peloponnesian War* as translated by Benjamin Jowett in *Thucydides*. I have made some minor alterations to enhance flow and clarity.
11   Thucydides, *History of the Peloponnesian War*, 8.54.1.
12   Thucydides, *History of the Peloponnesian War*, 8.54.2.
13   Thucydides, *History of the Peloponnesian War*, 8.56.1.
14   Thucydides, *History of the Peloponnesian War*, 8.56.4.
15   Thucydides, *History of the Peloponnesian War*, 8.56.4.
16   Thucydides, *History of the Peloponnesian War*, 8.56.4.
17   Thucydides, *History of the Peloponnesian War*, 8.56.3.

26: Trapped

1   Plutarch, *Life of Alcibiades*, 23.7. The timeline of events surrounding Timaea's pregnancy and delivery are ordered differently by ancient authors.
2   Plutarch, *Life of Alcibiades*, 23.7.
3   This quote is based on passage 23.7 of Plutarch's *Life of Alcibiades* as translated by Bernadotte Perrin in *Plutarch's Lives* (Cambridge, MA: Harvard University Press, 1916) and is presented here with some minor alterations to enhance flow and clarity.
4   Plutarch, *Life of Alcibiades*, 23.8.
5   Plutarch, *Life of Alcibiades*, 26.5.

6   This quote is based on section 551d of Book 8 of Plato's *Republic* as translated
           by Benjamin Jowett in *The Republic of Plato*, 3rd ed. (Oxford: Clarendon
           Press, 1888) and is presented here with some minor alterations to enhance
           flow and clarity.

7   This dialogue is based on section 551c of Book 8 of Plato's *Republic* as
           translated by Benjamin Jowett in *The Republic of Plato*, 3rd ed. and is
           presented here with some minor alterations to enhance flow and clarity.

8   Plutarch, *Life of Alcibiades*, 26.3.

9   Plutarch, *Life of Alcibiades*, 26.4.

10   Plutarch, *Life of Alcibiades*, 26.3.

11   Plutarch, *Life of Alcibiades*, 27.2.

12   Plutarch, *Life of Alcibiades*, 27.2.

13   Plutarch, *Life of Alcibiades*, 27.3.

14   Plutarch, *Life of Alcibiades*, 27.3.

15   Plutarch, *Life of Alcibiades*, 27.3.

16   Plutarch, *Life of Alcibiades*, 27.4.

17   Plutarch, *Life of Alcibiades*, 27.5.

27: Vengeance at Sea

1   Xenophon, *Hellenica*, 1.1.10; Plutarch, *Life of Alcibiades*, 28.1.

2   Plutarch, *Life of Alcibiades*, 28.1.

3   This passage is based on 28.2 of Plutarch's *Life of Alcibiades* as translated by
           Bernadotte Perrin, in *Plutarch's Lives* (Cambridge, MA: Harvard University
           Press, 1916) and presented here with some minor alterations to enhance flow
           and clarity. I chose to present the information as a dialogue to make the
           delivery more active, even though the source text does not present it this way.

4   Compare with Winston Churchill's June 4, 1940, speech: ". . . We shall fight
           on the beaches, we shall fight on the landing grounds, we shall fight in the
           fields and in the streets, we shall fight in the hills; we shall never surrender . . ."

5   Plutarch, *Life of Alcibiades*, 28.2.

6   Plutarch, *Life of Alcibiades*, 28.3.

7   Plutarch, *Life of Alcibiades*, 28.4.

8   Plutarch, *Life of Alcibiades*, 29.1.

9   Plutarch, *Life of Alcibiades*, 28.6.

10   Plutarch, *Life of Alcibiades*, 29.2.

11   Plutarch, *Life of Alcibiades*, 29.3.

12   Plutarch, *Life of Alcibiades*, 30.1.

13   Plutarch, *Life of Alcibiades*, 30.5.

14   Plutarch, *Life of Alcibiades*, 31.1.

15   Aristophanes, *Frogs*, 1425; Plutarch, *Life of Alcibiades*, 16.2. This famous
           quote is based on passage 16.2 of Plutarch's *Life of Alcibiades* as translated by

Bernadotte Perrin in *Plutarch's Lives* (Cambridge, MA: Harvard University Press, 1916) and is presented here with some minor alterations to enhance flow and clarity.

28: Return Home

1   Plutarch, *Life of Alcibiades*, 32.1.

2   Plutarch, *Life of Alcibiades*, 32.3.

3   Plutarch, *Life of Alcibiades*, 32.4.

4   Plutarch, *Life of Alcibiades*, 32.4.

5   This dialogue is cobbled together from two sources: Plutarch's *Life of Alcibiades* (32.4–5 and 33.2) and Xenophon's *Hellenica* (1.4.13–16 and 20), both of which describe what Alcibiades talked about in general terms and what other people said about it, but do not present the specific text of the speech. I chose to reconstruct the speech and present it as a dialogue to make the delivery more active, even though the source texts do not present it this way.

6   Plutarch, *Life of Alcibiades*, 33.2.

7   Plutarch, *Life of Alcibiades*, 33.3.

8   This quote is based on passage 33.3 of Plutarch's *Life of Alcibiades* as translated by Bernadotte Perrin in *Plutarch's Lives* (Cambridge, MA: Harvard University Press, 1916) and is presented here with some minor alterations to enhance flow and clarity.

9   Plutarch, *Life of Alcibiades*, 34.1.

10   Plutarch, *Life of Alcibiades*, 34.2.

11   This dialogue is based on book 2, chapter 2 of Xenophon's *Memorabilia* as translated by Henry Graham Dakyns in *The Works of Xenophon* (London and New York: Macmillan & Co., 1897) and is presented here with some minor alterations to enhance flow and clarity.

12   This quote is based on passage 2.2.5 of Xenophon's *Memorabilia* as translated by Henry Graham Dakyns in *The Works of Xenophon* and is presented here with some minor alterations to enhance flow and clarity.

13   This quote is based on passage 2.2.5 of Xenophon's *Memorabilia* as translated by Henry Graham Dakyns in *The Works of Xenophon* and is presented here with some minor alterations to enhance flow and clarity.

14   This quote is based on passage 2.2.6 of Xenophon's *Memorabilia* as translated by Henry Graham Dakyns in *The Works of Xenophon* and is presented here with some minor alterations to enhance flow and clarity.

29: Road to Eleusis

1   Plutarch, *Life of Alcibiades*, 34.5.

2   Plutarch, *Life of Alcibiades*, 34.5.

3   Plutarch, *Life of Alcibiades*, 34.6.

4   Plutarch, *Life of Alcibiades*, 34.6.
5   From Aristophanes, *Frogs*, lines 1431 and 1432. This text is based on
           section 16.2 of Plutarch's *Life of Alcibiades* as translated by Bernadotte
           Perrin in *Plutarch's Lives* (Cambridge, MA: Harvard University Press,
           1916) and is presented here with some minor alterations to enhance flow
           and clarity.

30: Stripped
1   Plutarch, *Life of Alcibiades*, 35.1.
2   Plato, *Republic*, VIII.564a.
3   Plato, *Republic*, VIII.565d.
4   Plato, *Republic*, VIII.565e.
5   This passage is based on section 565e of book VIII of Plato's *Republic* as
           translated by Benjamin Jowett in *The Republic of Plato*, 3rd ed. (1871; Oxford:
           Clarendon Press, 1888) and is presented here with some minor alterations to
           enhance flow and clarity.
6   This passage is based on section 567d of book VIII of Plato's *Republic*
           as translated by Benjamin Jowett in *The Republic of Plato*, 3rd ed. and is
           presented here with some minor alterations to enhance flow and clarity.
7   Plutarch, *Life of Alcibiades*, 35.1.
8   See William Shakespeare, *King Henry IV*, Part II, act III, scene i.
9   Plutarch, *Life of Alcibiades*, 35.1.
10   Plutarch, *Life of Alcibiades*, 35.1.
11   Plutarch, *Life of Alcibiades*, 35.1.
12   This description is based on passage 35.2–3 of Plutarch's *Life of Alcibiades* as
           translated by Bernadotte Perrin in *Plutarch's Lives* (Cambridge, MA: Harvard
           University Press, 1916) and is presented here with some minor alterations to
           enhance flow and clarity.
13   Plutarch, *Life of Alcibiades*, 35.3.
14   Plutarch, *Life of Alcibiades*, 35.4.
15   Plutarch, *Life of Alcibiades*, 35.6.
16   Plutarch, *Life of Alcibiades*, 35.6.
17   Plutarch, *Life of Alcibiades*, 36.2.
18   Plutarch, *Life of Alcibiades*, 36.3.

31: Clash at Aegospotami
1   Xenophon, *Hellenica*, 2.1.11–2.1.12.
2   Xenophon, *Hellenica*, 2.1.12.
3   Xenophon, *Hellenica*, 2.1.14.
4   Plutarch, *Life of Alcibiades*, 36.4.
5   Plutarch, *Life of Alcibiades*, 36.5.

6   This dialogue is cobbled together from two sources and four passages:
        Plutarch's *Life of Alcibiades*, 36.5 and 37.1, as translated by Bernadotte Perrin
        in *Plutarch's Lives* (Cambridge, MA: Harvard University Press, 1916); and
        Xenophon's *Hellenica*, 2.1.25 and 2.1.26, as translated by Henry Graham
        Dakyns (London and New York: Macmillan & Co., 1897). The source texts
        have a combination of dialogue and narrative description. I chose to present
        the information entirely as a dialogue to make the delivery more uniform,
        even though the source texts only partially present it this way.
7   Xenophon, *Hellenica*, 2.1.28.
8   Xenophon, *Hellenica*, 2.1.28.
9   Xenophon, *Hellenica*, 2.1.32.
10   Xenophon, *Hellenica*, 2.2.2.
11   Xenophon, *Hellenica*, 2.2.9.
12   Xenophon, *Hellenica*, 2.2.11.
13   Xenophon, *Hellenica*, 2.2.16.
14   Xenophon, *Hellenica*, 2.2.20.
15   Xenophon, *Hellenica*, 2.3.11.

32: The Thirty Tyrants

1   Xenophon, *Hellenica*, 2.3.12–2.3.15.
2   This dialogue is based on passage 1.2.32 of Xenophon's *Memorabilia* as
        translated by Henry Graham Dakyns in *The Works of Xenophon* (London and
        New York: Macmillan & Co., 1897) and is presented here with some minor
        alterations to enhance flow and clarity.
3   This dialogue is based on passages 2.3.15–56 of Xenophon's *Hellenica* as
        translated by Henry Graham Dakyns in *The Works of Xenophon* and is
        presented here with some minor alterations to enhance flow and clarity. In
        the source text most of the speeches are given as dialogue, with some portions
        being presented as narrative description about what was said. I chose to make
        this presentation uniformly dialogue.
4   Xenophon, *Hellenica*, 2.3.17.
5   This dialogue is based on section 1.2.33–37 of Xenophon's *Memorabilia* by
        Henry Graham Dakyns in *The Works of Xenophon* and is presented here with
        some minor alterations to enhance flow and clarity.
6   Plutarch, *Life of Alcibiades*, 38.3.
7   Plutarch, *Life of Alcibiades*, 38.4.

33: Ambush

1   Plutarch, *Life of Alcibiades*, 37.4.
2   Plutarch, *Life of Alcibiades*, 39.2.
3   Plutarch, *Life of Alcibiades*, 39.3.

4   Plutarch, *Life of Alcibiades*, 39.3.

5   Plutarch, *Life of Alcibiades*, 39.4.

6   See Justinus, *Epitome of Pompeius Trogus*, V.8.12f; Isocrates, *Concerning the Team of Horses*, 16.40; Diodorus Siculus, *Bibliotheca Historica*, 14.II.I; Plutarch, *Life of Alcibiades*, 39.1 and 39.5.

7   Plato, *Apology*, 32c.

8   Plato, *Apology*, 32d.

9   Plato, *Apology*, 32d.

34: Civil War

1   Xenophon, *Hellenica*, 2.4.2.

2   Xenophon, *Hellenica*, 2.4.6.

3   Xenophon, *Hellenica*, 2.4.8.

4   This dialogue is based on passages 2.4.13–17 of Xenophon's *Hellenica* as translated by Henry Graham Dakyns in *The Works of Xenophon* (London and New York: Macmillan & Co., 1897) and is presented here with some minor alterations to enhance flow and clarity.

5   Xenophon, *Hellenica*, 2.4.28.

6   Xenophon, *Hellenica*, 2.4.38.

7   Xenophon, *Hellenica*, 3.1.1.

35: The Charges and the *Clouds*

1   Plato, *Apology*, 19c.

2   The following dialogues are based on Aristophanes's *Clouds* as translated by William James Hickie in *The Comedies of Aristophanes: A New and Literal Translation*, vol. I (London: Henry G. Bohn, 1853) and are presented here with some minor alterations to enhance flow and clarity.

36: Trial of Andocides

1   This speech is based on sections 111–116 of Andocides, *On the Mysteries*, as translated by the Philomathean Society of the University of Pennsylvania (1896) and is presented here with some minor alterations to enhance flow and clarity. Andocides's speech includes embedded quotes and descriptions, which I have chosen to break out into freestanding dialogue.

2   Andocides, *On the Mysteries*, 116.

3   This speech is based on sections 117–123 of Andocides, *On the Mysteries*, as translated by the Philomathean Society of the University of Pennsylvania (1896) and is presented here with some minor alterations to enhance flow and clarity.

4   This speech is based on sections 124–129 of Andocides, *On the Mysteries*, as translated by the Philomathean Society of the University of Pennsylvania

(1896) and is presented here with some minor alterations to enhance flow and clarity.

5   Andocides, *On the Mysteries*, 150.

37: Socrates's Accusers

1   Plutarch, *Life of Alcibiades*, 4.5.

2   Xenophon, *Apology*, 30.

3   Xenophon, *Apology*, 31.

4   The following dialogue is based on 94c–95a of Plato's *Meno* as translated by Benjamin Jowett in *The Dialogues of Plato Translated into English with Analyses and Introductions in Five Volumes*, vol. 2, 3rd ed. (Oxford: Oxford University Press, 1892) and is presented here with some minor alterations to enhance flow and clarity.

5   The following dialogue is based on 99e–100c of Plato's *Meno* as translated by Benjamin Jowett in *The Dialogues of Plato Translated into English with Analyses and Introductions in Five Volumes*, vol. 2, 3rd ed., and is presented here with some minor alterations to enhance flow and clarity.

6   Diodorus Siculus, *Library*, 14.5.7.

7   Plato, *Euthyphro*, 2b.

8   Andocides, *On the Mysteries*, 1.94. There has been some scholarly debate as to whether the Meletus who charged Socrates and the Meletus who charged Andocides were the same person. Most agree that he's the same person.

9   Diodorus Siculus, *Library*, 13.64.6.

38: The Big "Why"

1   See Aristophanes, *Clouds*.

39: Trial of Socrates

1   The dialogue and descriptions in this chapter are based on Plato's *Apology* as translated by Benjamin Jowett in *The Dialogues of Plato Translated into English with Analyses and Introductions in Five Volumes*, vol. 2, 3rd ed. (Oxford: Oxford University Press, 1892) and are presented here with some minor alterations to enhance flow and clarity.

40: Sentencing

1   The dialogue and descriptions in this chapter are based on Plato's *Apology* as translated by Benjamin Jowett in *The Dialogues of Plato Translated into English with Analyses and Introductions in Five Volumes*, vol. 2, 3rd ed. (Oxford: Oxford University Press, 1892) and are presented here with some minor alterations to enhance flow and clarity.

41: Closing Remarks

1   The dialogue and descriptions in this chapter are based on Plato's *Apology* as translated by Benjamin Jowett in *The Dialogues of Plato Translated into English with Analyses and Introductions in Five Volumes*, vol. 2, 3rd ed. (Oxford: Oxford University Press, 1892) and are presented here with some minor alterations to enhance flow and clarity.

2   The following lines come from section 28 of Xenophon's *Apology*, as translated by Henry Graham Dakyns, in *The Works of Xenophon* (London and New York: Macmillan & Co., 1897) and are presented here with some minor alterations to enhance flow and clarity.

42: The Wait

1   Plato, *Phaedo*, 58b.

2   Plato, *Phaedo*, 58b–c.

3   The following dialogue and descriptions are based on Plato's *Crito* as translated by Benjamin Jowett in *The Dialogues of Plato Translated into English with Analyses and Introductions in Five Volumes*, vol. 2, 3rd ed. (Oxford: Oxford University Press, 1892) and are presented here with some minor alterations to enhance flow and clarity.

4   Xenophon, *Apology*, 23.

43: Execution

1   The following dialogue and descriptions are based on Plato's *Phaedo* as translated by Benjamin Jowett in *The Dialogues of Plato Translated into English with Analyses and Introductions in Five Volumes*, vol. 2, 3rd ed. (Oxford: Oxford University Press, 1892) and are presented here with some minor alterations to enhance flow and clarity.

2   Plato, *Phaedo*, 116b.

3   Plato, *Phaedo*, 117b–c.

4   Plato, *Phaedo*, 117c.

5   Plato, *Phaedo*, 117c–d.

6   Plato, *Phaedo*, 117e.

7   Plato, *Phaedo*, 118a.

8   The dialogue comes from section 118a of Plato's *Phaedo* as translated by Benjamin Jowett in *The Dialogues of Plato Translated into English with Analyses and Introductions in Five Volumes*, vol. 2, 3rd ed. and is presented here with some minor alterations to enhance flow and clarity.

9   This description of the final moments of Socrates is based on section 118a of Plato's *Phaedo* as translated by Benjamin Jowett in *The Dialogues of Plato Translated into English with Analyses and Introductions in Five Volumes*, vol. 2, 3rd ed.

10   The dialogue comes from section 118a of Plato's *Phaedo* as translated by
          Benjamin Jowett in *The Dialogues of Plato Translated into English with Analyses
          and Introductions in Five Volumes*, vol. 2, 3rd ed. and is presented here with
          some minor alterations to enhance flow and clarity.

44: Aftermath

1   Diogenes Laertius, *Lives of Eminent Philosophers*, 2.10.106.
2   Diogenes Laertius, *Lives of Eminent Philosophers*, 3.1.6.
3   Other perspectives on the wanderings of Plato are recorded by Cicero,
          Appuleius, Quintilian, and Valerius Maximus, among others.
4   Diogenes Laertius, *Lives of Eminent Philosophers*, 2.5.43.
5   Aristotle, *Rhetoric*, 3.2.10.
6   Athenaeus, *Deipnosophists*, 12.52, as translated by Charles Duke Yonge in
          Athenaeus, The Deipnosophists (London: Henry G. Bohn, 1854). I have made
          some minor alterations to enhance flow and clarity.
7   A complicating factor of this description of Callias's downward slide is that a
          "Callias, son of Hipponicus" is recorded by other authors as being a military
          general and political leader at around the same time as he was said to be a
          destitute beggar, which is impossible. The issue of incompatible information
          is one of the struggles of ancient studies. Invariably, some ancient authors
          wrote down dates incorrectly or got certain details wrong, which muddies
          the picture. All we can say is that both chronicles can't be right, unless the
          descriptions are of two different people.
8   Diogenes Laertius, *Lives of Eminent Philosophers*, 2.5.43.
9   Xenophon, *Memorabilia*, 2.10.2–2.10.6.
10   Plato, *Cratylus*, 391c.
11   The following dialogue come from sections 5–9 of Xenophon's *Apology*, as
          translated by Henry Graham Dakyns, in *The Works of Xenophon* (London and
          New York: Macmillan & Co., 1897) and is presented here with some minor
          alterations to enhance flow and clarity.

Conclusion

1   Plato, *Republic*, VII.515d. As translated by Paul Shorey, *Plato: The Republic,
          Books VI–X* (1935; Cambridge, MA: Harvard University Press, 2000 edition),
          122. For complete text, see volumes 5 and 6 of Paul Shorey, *Plato in Twelve
          Volumes* (Cambridge, MA: Harvard University Press, 1969).
2   This dialogue of 517a of Plato's *Republic* is based on the translation by
          Benjamin Jowett in *The Republic of Plato*, 3rd ed. (1871; Oxford: Clarendon
          Press, 1888) with some minor alterations to enhance flow and clarity. Also
          consulted was Shorey, *Plato: The Republic, Books VI–X*, 129.

Index

priests
    Callias as, 107, 156, 159, 178, 195
    chief, 64
    methods of, 14–15, 33–34
    temple positioning of, 7, 8
    procession to Eleusis, 129, 155–158, 161
    profanation, 90–92, 97–98, 99–100, 185,
        191–196
    psychopathy, 73
    purpose, 19

R
reality
    Divided Line, 19, 23–26
    Theory of Forms, 19, 20–23
religious rites, 3, 5–6, 8, 15, 16, 157,
    265n17
Republic (Plato), 18, 19–20, 26, 27
Rhegium, 96–97
Ruck, Carl, 265n17
Rumsfeld, Donald, 48–49

S
Sacks, Jonathan, 15
Samos, 136, 141, 145, 164
Sanctuary of the Great Goddesses, 4
Sandridge, Norman, 73
Sappho, xvi
sensory archeology, 11
sexual practices, xv–xvi
Sicilian Expedition, 81–88, 94–98, 103–
    107, 114, 120–122, 126–127, 185
Silenus, 97, 106
social contract, 231–232
Socrates
    accusers of, 197–201
    and Alcibiades, xvii, 35–38, 50–55, 250
    atheism accusations, 212–215
    Battle of Delium, 38
    Battle of Potidaea, 35–38
    birth of Lamprocles, 80

    blamed for actions of Alcibiades, 122,
        127, 131
    and Callias, xvii–xviii, 69, 209, 225, 250
    at Callias's dinner party, 64–69
    character traits, xii, 51, 130–131
    corruption of youth charges, xvi, 35,
        185, 190, 203–204, 212–213, 216
    criticism of Pericles, 57–58
    and Crito, 226–233
    execution of, xiii, xviii, 234–243
    as father of western philosophy, 17
    guilty verdict, 217
    indictment, 184, 202–203
    influence of, xi
    "inner voice," 204–205
    marriage to Xanthippe, 78–80
    Mysteries of Eleusis initiation, 2–3
    physical appearance, 17, 51
    sentencing proposal, 218–220
    sexual relationships, xv
    on the Sicilian Expedition, 88
    on siege of Athens, 130
    trial of, xi–xii, 32, 57, 65, 183, 185,
        200–201, 206–217, 218–220,
        221–225, 246–247
    writings on, 17–18
    See also philosophical dialogues
Socratic method, 19, 45–46, 49
sophists, 209–210
Sparta
    Aegospotami victory, 164–167
    aid to Syracuse, 122–127
    black soup, 113
    brokers amnesty agreement between
        Athens and the Thirty, 182–183
    Callias as proxenus to, 74, 178
    defection of Alcibiades to, 112–113,
        119–122
    occupation of Decelea, 128–131
    occupation of road to Eleusis, 155–158
    peace agreement with Athens, 74–77